CW01494858

WOMEN WHO KILL

WOMEN WHO KILL

A HISTORY OF BRITAIN'S MOST DANGEROUS WOMEN

ERIN FETTERLY

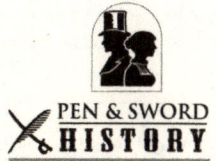

First published in Great Britain in 2024 by
Pen & Sword History
An imprint of
Pen & Sword Books Ltd
Yorkshire – Philadelphia
Copyright © Erin Fetterly 2024
ISBN 9781399047708

The right of Erin Fetterly to be identified as Author of this work has
been asserted by her in accordance with the Copyright, Designs and
Patents Act 1988.

A CIP catalogue record for this book is
available from the British Library.

All rights reserved. No part of this book may be reproduced or
transmitted in any form or by any means, electronic or mechanical
including photocopying, recording or by any information storage and
retrieval system, without permission from the Publisher in writing.

Set in Aldine 401 13/16.75
Printed in the UK on paper from a sustainable source by CPI Group
(UK) Ltd, Croydon, CR0 4YY

Pen & Sword Books Limited incorporates the imprints of After the
Battle, Archaeology, Atlas, Aviation, Battleground, Discovery, Family
History, History, Maritime, Military, Politics, Select, Transport,
True Crime, Fiction, Frontline Books, Leo Cooper, Praetorian Press,
Seaforth Publishing, Wharncliffe and White Owl.

For a complete list of Pen & Sword titles please contact
PEN & SWORD BOOKS LIMITED
George House, Beevor Street, Off Pontefract Road, Hoyle Mill,
Barnsley, South Yorkshire, England, S71 1HN
E-mail: enquiries@pen-and-sword.co.uk
Website: www.pen-and-sword.co.uk
Or
PEN AND SWORD BOOKS
1950 Lawrence Rd, Havertown, PA 19083, USA
E-mail: Uspen-and-sword@casematepublishers.com
Website: www.penandswordbooks.com

For my family,
without whose infinite love and support this
would not have been possible.

TABLE OF CONTENTS

INTRODUCTION

It's a chilly winter day in England in the year 1688. Mary Aubry awaits her punishment after receiving a guilty verdict for her crime just days before. Mary's reality is not unlike other women throughout British history, including Sarah Malcolm in 1733 or Margaret Shuttleworth in 1821. Their stories may differ slightly based on their situation, age, social standing, marital status, and the era in which they lived, but they all share a common trait; they have all committed murder.

Throughout British history, it has been assumed that women are far less likely, and less capable, than men to commit felonies of all types, especially murder. Statistics clearly show that women's involvement in crime over the past 700 years has been significantly lower than men's, this does not imply that they were any less capable or that it did not occur.

This book will unveil the stories of women who committed some form of murder in England, Scotland, and Wales over the past 700 years.

Throughout British history, most female crimes were considered less threatening than those perpetrated by men. This viewpoint was partially due to the generalization that men were believed to be more aggressive and because female crimes did not occur as frequently. However, there certainly were women who committed murder and they were almost always harshly punished.

During the period of examination, murderers received considerable attention from society, some even becoming spectacles. Female killers were seen as an unnatural phenomenon. By committing violent acts, particularly murder, they defied gender and societal norms, questioning and confronting female stereotypes. Not only did they commit felonies, but they deviated from the expected qualities and life women were expected to lead. Women were not expected to be courageous, violent, hot-tempered, selfish, or even intelligent enough to commit a murder.

These were traits men were assumed to possess. Women were expected to be ruled by their emotions and act more passive, pious, modest, chaste, lusty, lazy, and passionate. They were expected to fulfil roles centred around motherhood and the home. If they strayed from societal norms, they were often expected to commit crimes more closely related to sex and emotions, like infanticide and prostitution. When women deviated from these expected norms and adopted behaviours more like men, it was considered shocking and unusual. Many people feared such conduct might disrupt the accepted societal norms and therefore have a wider impact on society. Though there was some overlap of male and female activities and expectations, certain behaviours and traits were still defined as expected and unexpected for women.

Some murder trials attracted considerable attention, both as in-person spectacles and in print. They were particularly popular when they featured female killers, and the crimes that captured the public's attention reflected the cultural and societal beliefs about violence and murder during that period. Throughout British history, women who committed murder have been a fascination, often more so than men. A man's act of murder, while acknowledged, had to be exceptionally brutal to generate as much sensation as any murder committed by a female.

It would have been incredibly intimidating for a woman to be on trial. Until relatively recently, the entire staff of a courtroom would have consisted of men. There may have been female witnesses, experts, or a jury of matrons called in, but the people questioning the accused woman and deciding her fate would have all been men. There were even instances where juries were more hesitant to believe women's evidence and testimonies compared to those of men. An ongoing debate among historians revolves around whether women's treatment within court proceedings was equivalent to that of men, and it is challenging to reach a definitive verdict.

Overall, historians agree that women were treated similarly to men in court proceedings, but there is no denying the presence of gender bias. This bias occasionally worked to a woman's advantage, particularly in later centuries, but more often than not, it worked against her. When laws were established to maintain social order throughout the country, they had to consider the factors that structured accepted social order, like gender, class, and age hierarchies. This desire for order resulted in biased legislation and procedures.

Murder, manslaughter, homicide, petty treason, and infanticide are all terms describing different types of homicide used during the period under examination. The term homicide served as a broad category including any act of killing, whereas the others were more situation-specific. 'Murder' referred to the deliberate and premeditated act of killing someone whereas 'manslaughter' denoted a reckless act that resulted in a person's death, possibly occurring in the heat of an argument. However, the term 'murder' was not officially used to denote an act of premeditation until 1390, and there was no distinction between 'murder' and 'manslaughter' in records until the sixteenth century. Some contemporaries believed that when angry, men often let it burst out quickly, resulting in fights and many unintentional manslaughter incidents. By contrast, women were more likely to keep their anger to themselves, allowing it to fester within, so when it was released, it resulted in more malicious and murderous crimes. For women to be deemed relatively acceptable when displaying violence and anger, it was expected to be for defensive measures rather than offensive ones.

Petty treason was a crime defined in the Treason Act of 1351, which included scenarios such as a wife killing her husband, a servant killing their master or mistress, or a priest killing his superior. In essence, it applied when a subordinate killed their authority figure, reflecting the expected relationship dynamics of the medieval and early modern periods, particularly between wives and their husbands. The act of petty treason ceased to be separate from murder in 1828.

During the pre-modern era, a certain level of violence was fairly common within society, especially as a form of discipline, such as when a master beat his disobedient servant or a husband his wife. Killing was deemed unnecessary when the violence exceeded the accepted norms for the situation, and the punishment was often influenced by the degree of unnecessary violence involved.

Appalling, disgusting, desperate and frustrating, are all adequate words to describe the act of murdering an infant or child. The term 'infanticide' was widely used throughout the early modern period to refer to the killing of a child under one year old. Another term, 'neonaticide', was used to refer to the murder of a newborn within twenty-four hours of its birth. However, in many records, 'infanticide' is used to indicate both.

Some historians debate about which term to use and when, but for the purposes of this book, the term 'infanticide' will be used to describe the killing of newborns and infants under one year old, while the killing of a child over one year will be considered murder.

Unfortunately, British history, like most other histories, contains a startling amount of infanticide cases. This offence is closely linked to the history of women's crime because it predominantly applies to women. In many legal definitions, the term itself implies the act of a woman murdering a newborn or infant. Interestingly, records of men committing this offence are rarely seen in British crime records. Men were occasionally involved as accomplices, but infanticide was primarily a female-centred crime. The word infanticide was not used to denote a specific crime in the criminal justice system of the medieval era and only gained popularity after a 1624 statute. Equally unfortunate and distressing are the historical rates of child murder. These unimaginable acts were often the result of the mother's mental health struggles, desperation, or panic-stricken choices, but occasionally, they arose from sheer cruelty. Infanticide was frequently connected to women's limited social and economic opportunities. Throughout this book, there are stories resembling each of these situations, shedding light on one of the darkest aspects of female crime.

Until the nineteenth century, the most common punishment for convicted female murderers was hanging. Any prisoner to be hanged, living in or near London, would likely face execution at Tyburn. Located at the site of the present-day Marble Arch, the Tyburn Tree, wooden gallows, stood for centuries as London's primary execution site. The first recorded hanging there dates back to 1196, and even though the Tyburn Tree was removed in 1759, new gallows were erected, and remained in use until 1783. After that, prisoners in and near London were typically hanged at Newgate prison. Executions were typically public events until the nineteenth century, and often drew in spectators from all around town.

Close in notoriety to hanging was the agonizing death by burning, reserved primarily for women convicted of petty treason or witchcraft. This form of punishment was prevalent during the medieval and early modern periods but ceased to be used in the late eighteenth century, with Mary Bailey being the last woman to be burned for petty treason in 1784. Interestingly, the last time this punishment was used on a man was more than one hundred years prior. If a woman convicted of murder was deemed 'mad' by the jury in court, she would have likely been pardoned or, have been kept in prison 'at His/Her Majesty's Pleasure.' This effectively meant that she would remain incarcerated until the reigning monarch decided to grant her a pardon or release.

From 1624 onwards, the punishment for infanticide was death, unless the mother was declared mentally unfit. This practice continued until 1922 when the death penalty was replaced with imprisonment. If a woman pleaded pregnancy or pleaded 'the belly' she would be examined by a jury of matrons. If found to be with child, she would be excused, typically sent to prison to await the birth of her child. After giving birth, she would face her sentence once again. If found not to be pregnant, her sentence would proceed as planned. In later centuries, judges and juries tended to show more leniency towards pregnant women, often reducing their sentences or granting pardons. Starting in the nineteenth century, hangings for murder became less frequent, with more people being imprisoned instead. However, it wasn't until the twentieth century that the practice of hanging for murder was completely abolished. Susan Newell was the last woman executed in Scotland in 1923, and Ruth Ellis Neilson was the last woman hanged for murder in all Great Britain in 1955.

As time passed, record-keeping systems for crimes and criminals developed, and improved. During the medieval period, they lacked the level of detailed and organized records related to criminals that are available today or even those that were gathered during the nineteenth century. Nevertheless, they had their own systems, including the Court of King's Bench, coroners' rolls, eyres and the assize courts. The records of these systems provide valuable insight into the workings of their justice, as well as information on crimes, criminals, and proceedings of that era. Starting in the twelfth century, England was divided into six regions for the assize court circuits. Judges from London would travel to these regions and preside over court procedures in various towns. The records from these courts are valuable, but most are brief and offer more detail about the justice system rather than the criminals themselves. Records from the sixteenth century onward became increasingly accessible and thorough, especially due to the shift from writing records in Latin to producing them in the vernacular. The advent of printed crime literature in the 1500s, and the development of the Old Bailey Courthouse with its record-keeping practices in the 1600s further contributed to the accessibility, variety, and thoroughness of criminal and judicial records.

From medieval Britain through to the twentieth century, many women found themselves facing murder convictions. The criminal justice system and criminal culture in Britain underwent significant changes over these centuries, and women were as much a part of this transformation as men. Women's involvement in crime, their treatment, and their punishments all evolved during this time, providing these criminal women with varying, though sometimes similar experiences. Some of these women were victims of their specific circumstances and the societal standards of their era, others received guilty verdicts for committing ruthless acts of murder. Dive into Britain's criminal justice world and explore the fascinating stories of these women to understand what, unfortunately, pushed them to the point of no return…and its aftermath.

Chapter One

THE LATER MEDIEVAL PERIOD (1300–1500)

The later medieval period, 1300-1500CE, was an era when crime was comparatively rampant, and some modicum of violence was an accepted aspect of society. Although historical records indicate that instances of female crime and homicide were not as frequent as those involving males, Garay's article 'Women and Crime in Later Medieval England: 1388–1409' challenges traditional notions. According to Garay, women of this era did not shy away from brutality and violence, dispelling the perception that medieval women were passive and submissive. Contrary to conventional beliefs, medieval women were often comparable to their husbands in terms of strength, toughness, and tenacity, shaped by the challenges of their lives. Garay suggests that they were 'more fit to be the mothers of brigands than to rear gentle daughters or honest sons'. In medieval Scotland, women also defied gender stereotypes, displaying assertiveness and a willingness to resort to violence or forcefully expressing themselves. Interestingly, it was not uncommon for English or Scottish men to openly speak out against the women who attacked or harmed them in court during this period. This trait, however, did not persist into the following centuries, as men became increasingly reluctant to show their weakness/vulnerability in the presence of women.

From 1388–1399, a total of 211 females were indicted for various crimes in England, with thirty-three of them being homicides, accounting for about sixteen per cent. 'Indicted' was a commonly used term during the early modern and Victorian periods and continues to be in use today. Although this eleven-year period represents a small sample of female crime in medieval England, it offers insight into the prevalence of female perpetrated homicides relative to overall female crime. This becomes particularly noteworthy when juxtaposed with the percentage of all homicides encompassing both male and female crimes, which also stands at around sixteen per cent. These statistics illustrate that, despite the lower number of crimes committed by women, their likelihood of committing murder was nearly equal to that of men.

Examining the victims of female killers during the later medieval period reveals that when women committed murders within their family, which was likely given their predominant role at home, their husbands were the most common targets. On occasion, the killing of children, along with others, was accompanied by a plea of insanity, also known as madness or frenzy. However, this specific plea is infrequently used in the gaol delivery records of the later medieval period when compared to subsequent centuries. As for methods of killing during this period, women often employed knives, hatchets, or axes for their nefarious deeds. Although poison was available, it was not used much. However, it gained popularity during the eighteenth and nineteenth centuries as a notable method of murder for female felons.

To some extent, violence was accepted as a method of discipline in England, Scotland and Wales. However, for women, it would only be condoned within her household, such as with children or servants. During the medieval period, the seriousness of certain murders was often debated by the Justices of the Peace, influencing the corresponding punishment. This process was based on how well they could justify the murder, and the decisions made reflected the prevailing morals and societal ideas surrounding violence at that time.

Crime rates were generally higher in cities and densely populated towns compared to rural areas, a trend that persisted over several centuries. As expected, instances of female crime were also more prevalent in cities than in rural towns. One contributing factor was the limited opportunities for mischief available to women in rural England. Their responsibilities centred around the homestead, children, and pets, keeping them close to home and away from activities that might lead to criminal behaviour. Women in rural areas typically didn't handle tools, frequent alehouses, or engage in brawls. In contrast, women in cities had more independence, often lived away from family and friends, and were on a more equal footing, especially economically, with men. It has been suggested that women in such urban environments were more likely to participate in criminal acts.

One of the significant changes to the criminal justice system of medieval England was the introduction of the Treason Act of 1351. As mentioned in the introduction, petty treason was defined as an act in which a subordinate killed their authority figure. Examples included a wife killing her husband, a servant killing their master or mistress, or a priest killing his superior within the church. This disproportionately affected medieval women, with wives being specifically targeted as offenders. Throughout the medieval and early modern periods, hundreds of women were burned at the stake for petty treason.

There was no official national police force until the nineteenth century, but in later medieval towns and cities certain groups and procedures existed to maintain order, such as decennaries, and those who patrolled neighbourhoods. Policing was the responsibility of local authorities and community efforts. Medieval governments and local authorities put significant effort into controlling and punishing crime and criminals. A procedure called the hue and cry played a crucial role in the justice system during the medieval period and continued into the early modern era. When someone discovered a body, witnessed a murder, or faced a threatening situation, they would raise the hue and cry. This involved a local shout that summoned community members to join together and assist the caller. Subsequently, community members would collaborate to apprehend the criminal, contact the appropriate authorities, such as the coroner if needed, and potentially assist in unravelling the events.

The coroner was an integral member of the governments of towns and cities during the later medieval, and most of the early modern, period. He was summoned to investigate any unexpected, unexplained, or violent death. Upon arrival, he would carefully inspect the body for wounds, bruises, and any clues regarding the cause of death. Additionally, he documented the time, place, and date of the incident, and recorded his findings in the coroner's rolls. The coroner's duties extended to arranging the arrest of any suspects and collecting their belongings for transfer to the local prison. The coroner conducted these investigations in the presence of the coroners' jury, composed of men from the local community. These individuals played a crucial role in the judicial process by assisting in identifying the body, determining the circumstances surrounding the death, and engaging in discussions about possible suspects.

Frequently, the calling of the hue and cry was a prerequisite for prosecution and punishment, as its initiation indicated that a crime had occurred. This process was designed to maintain peace within the towns and cities and was one of the ways communities upheld their local justice and policing systems. Historians like Teresa Phipps in 'Medieval Women and Urban Justice: Commerce, Crime and Community in England, 1300-1500' (2020) and Janka Rodziewicz in 'Women and the Hue and Cry in Late Fourteenth-Century Great Yarmouth' (2013), emphasise how the hue and cry was an accessible and inclusive aspect of the typically gender-biased and repressive medieval justice system. It provided a means for women to be involved and contribute, as they were just as capable of raising the hue and cry as men and were equally, if not sometimes more, listened to.

As mentioned, women did not wield the same influence in the later medieval justice system as men did. However, aside from raising the hue and cry, they found involvement through various means. The most prominent and influential role was that of matrons, responsible for examining both women and men in court to determine aspects such as pregnancy and virility. Occasionally, women were called upon as the closest neighbours to a homicide and, in at least one recorded instance, a woman acted as sheriff in a medieval town. Upon examining records from medieval England, it becomes evident that women did not appear before medieval courts as frequently as men did. Some postulate this discrepancy may be attributed to the notion that women were adept at deception and concealment when committing crimes, making them more challenging to apprehend and indict. This perspective suggests that women committed crimes almost as frequently as men did but were more skilful at concealing their actions. While the veracity of this claim is challenging to ascertain, it holds some validity, especially considering that one of the most prevalent women's crimes, infanticide, was typically conducted in private, making it relatively easy to conceal.

In addition to being gender-biased, the criminal justice system of the medieval period was also marked by class bias. The higher echelons of medieval society were not subjected to the same scrutiny by the assizes or gaol delivery courts as frequently as the lower orders did. The majority of individuals indicted and tried in medieval courts hailed from the lower classes of society. The focus of the courts was typically on the lay people of later medieval England, Scotland, and Wales, possibly because the nobility surrounding the royal court had their own justice systems. The upper classes with their greater wealth, power and connections, often had the means to extricate themselves from legal entanglements. In some instances, the courts of justice didn't bother with crimes committed by members of the upper classes. An analysis of 9,000 indictments during the medieval period revealed that only eleven defendants belonged to the nobility or gentry. Furthermore, among those eleven members of high society, only one was a woman.

Scotland, much like England and Wales, was a place where women did not enjoy the same rights and opportunities as men, particularly within the criminal justice system. Both primary and secondary records about women and crime in medieval Wales are scarce but become more available as we progress into the sixteenth century. One significant aspect of women and Welsh law during the medieval period is the concept of coverture. This law governed a husband's authority over his wife, stating once a woman married, her property, possessions and person belonged to and were the responsibility of her husband, emphasising the wife's subordination. This concept was generally followed in England and Scotland, though Scotland's laws differed slightly and were much less stringent. In Scotland, during court cases, husbands were often responsible for ensuring their wives showed up for their trials. Alternatively, if husbands were unavailable, a male member of their family or a neighbour could fulfil this duty. Husbands were also permitted to pay fees on behalf of their wives or even take their punishments.

A study conducted by Lizabeth Johnson on the town of Dyffryn Clwyd in Wales reveals an interesting pattern regarding coverture in medieval Wales. Johnson's research illustrates that married women were subjected to the rules of coverture when dealing with the courts, except when they were arraigned for, or accused someone, of assault (including homicide) or defamation. In cases of these serious felonies, even married women were responsible for the costs incurred and for defending themselves. Importantly, they were allowed to come forward as victims of these crimes without the oversight of their husbands, which could prove beneficial if their husband was the perpetrator. For these specific offences, married women had as many rights and responsibilities as single women and men. In England the coverture laws were relatively comparable. If a wife committed a crime other than murder or treason, she fell under the responsibility of her husband and was consequently not held liable for her actions.

Considering the low literacy rate during this period, the impressive quantity of court and crime records that were kept and survived to the present day becomes evident. Later medieval society had various systems in place to manage crime, contributing to the abundance of records available.

To prosecute homicide throughout later medieval England, the assize courts played a crucial role, operating on a six-circuit schedule around the country. Justices from London would travel to hold court within six different geographical areas, a process that typically occurred twice a year. Although the records related to these circuits are not near as detailed or numerous as those from later centuries, a wealth of information is available in records related to coroner's rolls, gaol delivery courts, assize courts, eyres, the Court of King's Bench, and others. Medieval Wales adhered to its own legal systems until the Statute of Rhuddlan in 1284 introduced English law into Wales, while still permitting some Welsh laws to persist. This legal structure changed in 1536 with the Act of Union, when Wales became part of England and English law was imposed throughout the country.

By examining the records of these courts and rolls, historians can glean valuable insights into crime, the workings of the courts, and the intricate layers and participants of the later medieval justice system in England, Scotland and Wales. However, these records do not offer much detail about the accused's life or their journey from crime to sentence. Typically, the accounts include a combination of the date, crime, accused, victim, any witnesses, the sentence and any goods or chattels (personal possessions and money) they possessed. It is not until a little later that more background information or thorough descriptions about the defendant and their crime emerge. This shift becomes particularly noticeable with the widespread dissemination of newspapers and broadsides (posters conveying news and information), coinciding with the Old Bailey, Central Criminal Court, gradually overtaking the London criminal justice system.

The term 'infanticide' was not commonly used in the later medieval period to denote the killing of a young child. This specific term was not regularly used until the seventeenth century. Instead, terms such as 'homicide', 'formyrthrian', 'bearnmyrdhran,' and 'overlaying' were employed. Some records did not use a specific term but simply relayed that a woman had murdered her infant son or daughter. While the frequency of infanticide cases in the records is low, it does not imply such incidents did not occur. There could be various reasons for this, but it's likely this crime was easy to cover up. Sandidge, in her article, *Changing Contexts of Infanticide in Medieval English Texts* (2017), suggests that despite scarce records, infanticide did occur, citing frequent mentions of it in medieval literature.

In *The Female Felon in Fourteenth-Century England* (1974), Barbara Hanawalt examines a survey of 2,933 homicide cases within fourteenth-century gaol delivery and coroner's rolls. Out of these cases, only one instance of infanticide is reported, indicating the infrequency of reporting and recording such incidents. Hanawalt agrees that this is likely due to the concealment of these murders by the mothers. Some historians, like the controversial Philippe Ariès, take the stance that medieval parents had a more relaxed attitude toward infant and child mortality then we do today. Sandidge disagrees, citing her readings in medieval literature and supports the idea that parents were just as concerned with their children's wellbeing as they are in the modern day. It is possible, due to the unfortunate commonality of infant mortality, parents were less shocked by it than parents would be today, though this doesn't imply they cared less. The overall consensus during the medieval period, from both people and the law, was disdain for infanticide, especially from the medieval church.

The most common form of punishment for a guilty homicide verdict in later medieval England, Scotland and Wales was hanging, which applied to both men and women. Burning alive was another punishment inflicted on both sexes. After the Treason Act of 1351, if a wife killed her husband, she committed petty treason and would be sentenced to burn, a sentence not applicable to men, who were hanged for killing their wives. If someone was deemed insane during their trial, they were likely to be acquitted. Prisons were somewhat scarce in medieval communities due to limited funds. Any prisons they did have were small, dirty, and patrolled by guards tasked with preventing escapes. Prisoners often had to pay for their own food, relying on charity or dying of starvation. The act of being hung, drawn and quartered was also a punishment used during this period, primarily on men for crimes like high treason, murder or counterfeiting.

Other punishments, such as being pulled on the rack, being pressed by a weight, or having your limbs broken on the breaking wheel, were also practised, often resulting in death. In Scotland, one punishment for violent or disobedient women was the iron collar – a hinged metal collar attached to a chain, which forced the prisoner to stand in pain and humiliation. The pillory and the stocks, designed for pain and shame, were also examples following this model.

The pleading of pregnancy was often used in the later medieval period by convicted women trying to escape, or at least, delay their punishment. If a woman was found to be pregnant by a jury of matrons, her punishment would be postponed until after she gave birth but was almost always carried out afterward. Due to the limited knowledge during this time, matrons and medical professionals likely missed instances where women were actually pregnant. Magistrates would occasionally give women the benefit of the doubt if they pleaded pregnancy but were too early for it to be proven. This demonstrates that medieval women were sometimes shown some leniency, but this was not always the case. Before 1348, records show that matrons were only looking at a woman's pregnant state and not the size or development of the child, to define her as with child. Matrons before 1348 conducted examinations that included probing the abdomen and breasts, examining their urine, distinguishing weight gain and having a private conversation with the woman about her last menstrual cycle.

After 1348 the term 'quickened,' or 'quickening' began to be used in court for pregnancy determinations, referring to when the baby could be felt moving or kicking. This ability was mistakenly believed to indicate a fully formed foetus with a soul. Foetal movement usually occurs in the fourth or fifth month of pregnancy, so if a woman was not that far along, her child would be without a soul and not a hindrance to her punishment. If a woman who was 'quick with child' was executed, it was believed that two souls had been killed. In 1348, a coroner's roll first mentions the quickening of a child in relation to justice. Even for decades after, only a handful of the records regarding pleas of pregnancy refer to a 'live' child rather than just conception.

It wasn't until the sixteenth century, that the concept of being pregnant only when a woman had a child who had quickened became commonplace. One might have conceived, but they were not pregnant with a living child until it had a soul. The matron's examination of a woman quick with child would have been much easier, as the mother would have been a lot further along in her pregnancy, and therefore would likely have a larger stomach, swollen breasts, and could feel the baby kick and move.

Some historians have discussed that the ability to plead pregnancy, and possibly change your fate within the criminal courts provided women with a somewhat equalising advantage within the system, to counter the ability of men receiving benefit of the clergy. In cases where male convicts were convicted of certain felonies, they might be able to get a reduced sentence or punishment if they could prove they were literate by reading passages from the Bible. This please could however not be used in cases of murder. Women, whether they could read or not, were not allowed to plead benefit of the clergy until a few centuries later. Even with the advantage of pleading the belly, women were still deprived of equality within the justice system, as ninety per cent of the roles were filled by men. Married women were considered dependants of their husbands, with little or no control over their own legal processes.

The question of whether medieval women received more leniency from the courts than men is a topic of debate. While they sometimes did, particularly concerning the prospect of pregnancy, their conviction rates were quite similar. Gender during legal proceedings was not as crucial as other factors, such as social standing. Overall, women were treated fairly similar to men in the medieval court. However, when examining specific cases like petty treason, a gender bias becomes apparent, coupled with the sexist gender roles and expectations prevailing in medieval society.

Medieval Wales shared many of the same punishments as England and Scotland, but Welsh law had a unique practice involving specific fines after a homicide, known as 'galanas' and 'sarhad'. Galanas represented the compensation paid for the person killed, while sarhad assessed the worth of the man's honour, typically applied in cases of premeditated homicide. These fines were negotiated between the families of the murderer and victim and had to be paid. This medieval tradition began to fade after 1284, as Wales started falling under English rule. Subsequently, most Welsh laws became English, and by the time of the Act of Union in 1536, this medieval process, along with many other Welsh legal practices, had either been forgotten or ceased to exist.

In cases where women were defendants in homicide cases, it was more common for them to be accomplices or partners in crime rather than solo perpetrators. A notable instance is the case of Agnes Ferthing. On 3 December 1379, Agnes, along with her husband's servant, John, killed her husband Robert, in the middle of the night, in the parish of St. Clement Danes, Middlesex. The court records do not provide details about why they decided to commit this felony. Perhaps they were lovers seeking Robert's disappearance, or maybe they both disliked him and chose to eliminate him. When brought before the king and the jury,

John pleaded guilty, while Agnes pleaded not guilty. It is possible that Agnes was not as involved in the crime as John, or at all. Even if she committed the murder she seemed to be attempting to avoid a guilty verdict. After the jury deliberated, they found Agnes guilty, and she was sentenced to be burned for petty treason. Whether Agnes was actually guilty or not remains unknown, and if she truly was not involved, her fate is unfortunate and represents the unjust suffering experienced by some medieval women.

Many homicide cases in the court records involve women, but they were not always the main assailants. In these instances, many still faced punishment for aiding and abetting, even though they had not physically committed the crime. Some cases involve women giving permission for other men to kill their husbands, supplying the killers with the necessary weapons, encouraging assailants to commit specific crimes or actively participating in planning ambushes or attacks.

One example of this features Elizabeth Walton, a woman from Hampshire whose husband was killed by their two servants in 1387. When they were caught, it was discovered that Elizabeth gave permission to and assisted them in the killing. She was indicted, pleaded not guilty, and claimed she had nothing to do with the murder. All three were found guilty, and Elizabeth was sentenced to be burned. Later, she pleaded pregnancy, which was confirmed. Her execution was postponed until after she gave birth and was carried out in 1388. The records do not provide any indication of the evidence that incriminated Elizabeth; she was nonetheless found guilty. While she may have been involved, she could also have been a victim of the intense societal feelings toward petty treason. This crime was taken very seriously and treated harshly; it was considered to be an act against the natural order of things.

Alice de Ellefeld and Alice le Barber were involved in a murder in 1325 where Nicholas atte Mulle was killed by Adam de Cheddesleye and John Burel. They attacked him with two knives supposedly provided by Alice and Alice, and the two women were apparently present at the scene of the felony. They were supposed to be indicted for the murder, but both women fled before a trial could take place. A similar example is of Cristina Galeye, who orchestrated the murder of John de Saxtone in 1324. William Campion and Robert de Baldok struck John on the side of the head with a sword, creating a large wound from which he died a few days later. Christina aided in the killing, and they were all indicted. Just as the Alices' had fled, so did Cristina, William and Robert. Their whereabouts were unknown, preventing any trials for punishments from taking place.

Violence was a more accepted aspect of life in later medieval England than it is today. This included disciplining children, and unfortunately there were instances where accidental deaths occurred. In 1324, Emma le Latthere accidently killed the son of William de Burgh after hitting him under his left ear with her fists. She continued to discipline him, as he had attempted to steal wool from her house, and he later died from his wounds. It was determined that she was responsible, but it was not considered a felony as it had been an accident. Emma fled but later returned and surrendered herself to Newgate prison. A similar incident took place in Northamptonshire when a woman whipped her ten-year-old son too hard during a fit of anger, and he died from his wounds. Often, if an accidental death could be proved, the perpetrator would be pardoned or given a reduced sentence. Today and in later centuries, these unfortunate incidents would be referred to as manslaughter or second-degree murder, depending on the situation.

What we now call mental health but was declared insanity or madness in the later medieval period was sometimes seen in the courts as the cause of homicide. Margery Marten of Norfolk was said to have killed her husband in a fit of insanity around 1342 and didn't realise what she had done until fifteen days later. Also, Agnes Moyses from Yorkshire was apparently prone to bouts of insanity, or 'amentia' as it was described, and killed her son Adam in 1342 during one of her fits. There were also instances where women committed homicide while defending themselves or someone else. Between 1307 and 1317, there were at least two cases in Norwich where this occurred. In one instance, a woman was attacked by a man who dragged her around by her hair until she managed to overtake him and kill him. In another case, a woman killed a burglar who was attacking her husband in their house. In these instances, it is hard to imagine the women getting punished for defending themselves, but sometimes they did. They had to prove that their motive was self-defence and had to convince the jury and the justices they had no other choice but to kill. If the jury agreed, the perpetrator was pardoned. However, there would have been instances where the jury was not easily convinced, especially if it was their husband whom they had killed in self-defence. Women were not given the same respect or validity as men were in the later medieval period or in centuries to come; they were seen as inferior, so getting the judicial authorities to believe them came with its difficulties.

As previously mentioned, most of the later medieval homicide records did not provide detailed information about the defendant, victim, or the crime itself, but gave more of a summary of what occurred throughout the proceedings. The following three cases exemplify this. The three women featured here had brief summaries of their misdeeds in coroners' rolls, gaol delivery rolls, and records from the Court of King's Bench.

EMMA LE BERE (–1316)

Emma le Bere lived during the late thirteenth century and early fourteenth century and was from a village in north Bedfordshire called Yelden. She was married to John le Bere and had at least five children: Nicholas, John, Helen, Felise, and Maud. On 15 June 1316, something went horribly wrong. Emma was lying down due to what was described in the *13th-14th Century Bedfordshire Coroner's Rolls* as a 'frenesye'. She got out of bed, grabbed a large axe, and killed four of her children by cutting their throats. Interestingly, it says in the records that she killed the children of John le Bere; it does not mention that they were her children. It can be assumed the children were hers as she shared his last name, and it mentions that she had a husband. This wording in the records reflects the position of women in later medieval England. Even in her own home, her husband was the head, she and her children belonged to him.

After committing the dreadful act, Emma sadly took two cords of hemp and hung herself in her home. She and her children were eventually discovered by another one of their children, Nicholas. Nicholas raised the hue and cry and received assistance from his father, John le Bere, and another local man named Nicholas le Murye. There was no court or trial, as the defendant had killed herself, but there was an inquest in which this record was written down by the coroner, who would have been called after Nicholas raised the hue and cry. Her goods and chattels were assessed, and it was found that she owned none because she was married, so all of her goods belonged to her husband.

It is difficult to speculate what happened with Emma, but it was more than likely to be a mental health issue that would have been treated very differently had she lived in modern-day England. There were no records discussing Emma's past or specifically, her medical history, so it cannot be said whether or not she had previous health issues related to what happened that day. One would hope that if Emma had been alive today, she would have received the medical care she needed, and this awful offence would have been prevented.

MARGARET DE STANTON (UNKNOWN)

Margaret de Stanton was from a village in the south of Cambridgeshire and lived in the early fourteenth century. Her story is similar to Emma's, though with a slightly less permanent ending for Margaret. She was the daughter of Robert de Stanton and had a daughter named Alice. On Saturday 1 February 1332, around 6pm she took a knife, in what was deemed a fit of madness, and killed Alice. Margaret was arrested on 3 February and escorted by the sheriff to the local prison. When asked how she pleaded, she said not guilty due to madness and 'put herself on the country'. This was what happened in medieval England when someone pleaded not guilty and proceeded to ask for a trial by jury. This developed into the typical procedure of using a jury to determine guilt used in our justice systems today but was a process that only began shortly before Margaret was tried.

The jury determined that from 29 January to 4 February 1332 Margaret was overcome by madness and in that state, she murdered her daughter. The homicide did not occur because of malice or premeditation, but madness, so Margaret did not receive a death sentence. She was returned to the prison and waited for a pardon from the king. There is no record that a pardon occurred, but she more than likely received one.

Similar to Emma, it is hard to determine in modern terms what was ailing Margaret when she was in her mad state. We don't know how she felt or acted during this period, or what her life was like before or after her crime. Was the jury too lenient with Margaret, or was it the right decision? It is hard to know, but if madness could be proven, then most people were not condemned, as they were deemed not responsible for their actions.

AGNES CRAN (–C.1400)

The last later medieval woman to be discussed is Agnes Cran, who lived in the late fourteenth century until the year 1400. She was from a village southeast of London called Bexley, which is considered part of Greater London today. Agnes was married to a man named John Cran who was a shipman for a living. No records were found about their life or marriage, but it is likely there was some unhappiness because on the night of 31 March 1400, Agnes took an axe and hit her husband over the head with it while he was sleeping, killing him instantly.

After she was indicted, she was brought before the king at Westminster (sometimes the king wanted certain cases to come to him to be determined). She claimed that she was not guilty and like Margaret 'put herself on the country,' as she desired her case to be examined by a jury and trial. Unlike Margaret, however, when the jury deliberated before Agnes and the king, they found her guilty of the newly defined crime 'petty treason', and she was sentenced to be burned. She was determined to have no goods, chattels, lands, or houses, because it was all in her husband's name. There were no records found about the burning, but it more than likely occurred because being convicted of petty treason was almost always a death sentence.

It is hard to know what the Crans' situation was and whether Agnes was actually guilty or not. If she was guilty, was it because she was at her wits end due to abuse and took matters into her own hands, or was Agnes the aggressor who took things too far? Nonetheless, this case illustrates that by 1400, the new charge of petty treason was in full effect, and the sentence was no joke. Whether women pleaded guilty or not guilty, it took the lives of many women over the next 500 years.

The later medieval period underwent significant developments in its criminal justice system that had substantial impacts on female crime. The introduction of the Treason Act in 1351 resulted in several more women being sentenced to burn over the next four centuries. The establishment of a child quickening in the womb as the assuring sign of pregnancy, resulted in more women in their first few months of pregnancy being burned or hanged. Women were deemed secondary members of medieval society, an unfortunate fact that would only slowly correct itself over the following 650 years. As for Emma, Margaret, and Agnes, they, along with many other later medieval women, due to circumstances we can't be certain of, ended up at the stake or at the end of a noose. If these women were living today, their situations may have been very different. The sixteenth century held more developments for women's crime, though they remained disadvantaged in many ways. Let's continue our journey through British history and meet the criminal women of the 1500s who, through bad situations and less than friendly actions, landed similar fates to Emma, Margaret, and Agnes.

Chapter Two

THE SIXTEENTH CENTURY

The beginning of the sixteenth century in England was reminiscent of the later medieval period in terms of the criminal justice system. However, as the century progressed, there were advancements and changes that continued to shape the legislation and procedures of the judicial system. Despite these developments, women's rights were still overlooked or at least considered secondary to men's, and the entire system remained notably gendered, a characteristic that persisted for centuries. In sixteenth-century Scotland, Wales and England, women continued to be more involved in violent assaults than is typically assumed. They didn't shy away from expressing themselves through verbal or physical actions. It was still a rather violent society, with some level of violence accepted in everyday life. An important aspect of crime and a motive for murder, was the concept of honour. People took this very seriously, and if one felt their honour or person had been insulted, whether man or woman, it could lead to violence and/or homicide.

Wales seems to have had minimal guilty verdicts for murderous women during the sixteenth century. For example, a study conducted by Elizabeth Anne Howard for her PhD thesis *Women and Crime in Sixteenth-Century Wales* (2020), examines records from Montgomeryshire and Flintshire from 1542-1590, revealing only three cases of wives murdering their husbands. Records from Scotland indicate that, similar to England, magistrates treated women as less intimidating, less dangerous, and less problematic than male criminals when going through the court processes. However, if these women committed a crime believed to drastically threaten societal order, such as when a wife killed her husband, they would then be dealt with very seriously. Even though, at this time, there wasn't specific legislation regarding the act of petty treason, it would still have produced societal anxiety and would have been addressed by high court officials.

By the middle of the sixteenth century, judges during court proceedings began distinguishing between manslaughter and murder, even though they had both been separately defined since 1390. This distinction more than likely saved many people from the harsh punishments associated with premeditated murder, often leading to death. Alongside these legislative changes, there were stricter modifications for handling murder cases in court. There was a heightened awareness of the brutality and unacceptability of murder, leading to harsher punishments and eventually the discontinuation of any benefit of the clergy, the ability to seek sanctuary with the church, or the option to abjure the realm and never return. The latter part of the sixteenth century witnessed a general increase in homicide cases that persisted until the early eighteenth century. Multiple factors could account for this rise, such as changes in regulations and opinions that made certain crimes more visible, like infanticide, or developments in medical knowledge and techniques that contributed to the same.

A survey completed by K.J. Kesselring in her article *Murder's Crimson Badge: Homicide in the Age of Shakespeare* (2016), examined records from the Elizabethan period, highlighting 1,235 individuals indicted as killers. Not all of these defendants were deemed guilty, but the numbers still provide a sense of the gender ratio during this time. Out of these 'supposed' killers, thirty-one per cent were women, and sixty-eight per cent were men (the rest being unknown). So, women, though fewer in number than men, still played a significant role in Elizabethan murders.

Poisoning was a relatively common form of murder, though not as popular as stabbing or strangling. When looking at incidents of poisoning, women were the majority of perpetrators. An examination of the survey above reveals women were also the prime perpetrators when it came to killing servants and infants, as well as using witchcraft to kill. The sixteenth and seventeenth centuries were filled with accusations of witchcraft; a craze that didn't relent until the eighteenth century.

In the mid sixteenth century, a new act came into effect in England under Henry VIII. It began a slew of legislation against supposed witches. The Witchcraft Act of 1542 was the first in England to establish that the practice of witchcraft was a crime and could possibly be punishable by death. This Act was replaced by a new, more influential and serious Witchcraft Act in 1562/3, which was officially called 'Act agaynst Conjuracons Inchantments and Witchecraftes'. This Act announced that anyone who used witchcraft to kill or destroy another would be punished by death. Wales was officially incorporated into England under English law with Henry VIII's Act of Union in 1536, so these witchcraft laws would have applied in Wales too. However, the instance of witchcraft sentencing and punishment in early modern Wales is very minimal. A similar Witchcraft Act was introduced in Scotland in 1563 which made the practice of witchcraft punishable by death. Both of these acts resulted in the deaths of thousands of people (the majority of which were women), over the next 150 years. So, if a woman was accused of murder and the murder looked at all like witchcraft, she could be sentenced to death because of it, even though she may have been innocent of both.

As mentioned, Henry VIII's Act of Union in 1536 brought Wales under English law. There was a second Act of Union in 1543 that continued to produce legislation regarding Welsh law. This new act created the Court of Great Sessions in order to continue the assimilation of English procedures into Welsh law. It provided a Welsh-run, but English-monitored, centre for criminal justice. This court divided Wales into four three-county circuits and met twice a year to hear pleas from across Wales.

As the printing press was invented less than a century before, new forms of literature were being produced, including a new type of crime literature called murder pamphlets. These pamphlets, sometimes referred to as street literature, were extremely popular in the sixteenth and seventeenth centuries. These pamphlets were early modern journalistic endeavours that told tales about recent murders around the country. They were often padded with local gossip, so they cannot be taken as complete truth. However, they do provide a fascinating way to learn about homicides and the players involved, before there were in-depth records about murder cases or media like newspaper articles that would tell a more in-depth story. Another form of popular street literature was broadsides. They started to be seen in the sixteenth century and were single sheet pages announcing royal proclamations, news, public notices, speeches, and ballads that could be read as poetry or sung as songs. During the seventeenth century, they became very popular and were increasingly used as expressive tabloids about crimes and criminals. They continued as a key form of print literature until the end of the nineteenth century.

An analysis of the survey completed by Kesselring shows only nineteen per cent of the killers and victims examined were considered participants in domestic killings. Furthermore, only ten women of the thirty-one per cent were indicted for petty treason, and five of whom were deemed guilty. This number does not reflect the increasing number of murder pamphlets, broadsides, and ballads revolving around domestic murder, especially husband killers, during the sixteenth and seventeenth centuries. The inaccuracy points to the idea that many pamphlets and ballads written about domestic homicides were overly publicised and dramatized for people's interest, while other types of murder were not. This popularity and interest might be due to the fact that, not only were they breaking the law, but female murderesses were doing something that disrupted the societal expectations and stereotypes of sixteenth-century women.

In the court records of sixteenth-century Scotland, there aren't many instances of women being charged by the High Court of the Justiciary or executed for their crimes. This scarcity may be attributed to the tendency to handle less serious crimes committed by women through local justice systems and kinspeople. However, when women did appear in the records, it was usually for serious felonies, particularly murder. While the records for female convicts in medieval and sixteenth century Wales are somewhat scarce, a few do survive, indicating murderous women were prevalent across Britain.

There are more records of infanticide occurring in the sixteenth century than in the later medieval period, although the word 'infanticide' was not widely used. In England, the incidence was relatively low but slowly increased over the century, and continued into the seventeenth century, possibly influenced by the 1624 Infanticide Act. The rate of infanticide cases did not decrease significantly until the eighteenth century, although throughout the entire early modern period, the occurrence of such a heinous act was relatively common. Even before the 1624 Infanticide Act came into effect, if a woman was found guilty of infanticide, she likely faced the noose. In Wales, cases of women killing children are limited. For the counties of Flintshire and Montgomeryshire (now Powys), there are only two cases of this occurring over much of the sixteenth century.

On 6 June 1589, Mary Mowser, a spinster residing in Southover, Sussex gave birth to a female child. Details about Mary's life before this event are unknown. For reasons we cannot ascertain, she decided to take drastic measures as she did not want to, or could not, care for her child. Tragically, with the assistance of her mother Agnes, Mary disemboweled the child with a knife. Both were apprehended and sent to the local gaol to await the next assizes. They both pleaded not guilty. However, the jury found Mary guilty, and in response she quickly claimed to be pregnant. A jury of matrons examined her and found, to their knowledge, that she was not pregnant. Consequently, her sentence was carried out, and she was hanged. Surprisingly, Agnes was acquitted and released.

In another case of infanticide in Tudor England, we encounter the tragic story of Elizabeth Gery. On 13 August 1575 she gave birth to a baby boy. The original inquest merely mentioned she murdered him, but upon reaching the assizes, it was discovered to be inaccurate. A new indictment, providing much more detail about the incident, was issued. Following childbirth, Elizabeth swiftly took a piece of a nettle (a stinging or prickly plant), inserted it into the boy's mouth, and then threw the child into a gutter, where he soon perished. Although she pleaded not guilty to the jury, they found her culpable and sentenced her to be hanged. Much like Mary, Elizabeth claimed pregnancy in an attempt to avoid execution, but a jury examination determined she was not with child. While the record does not definitively state she was hanged, it is likely the execution proceeded.

Hanging, burning, being hung, drawn, and quartered, beheading, the rack, death by pressure, boiling, imprisonment and outlawing were among the punishments administered during the sixteenth century. For women who were convicted of murder and sentenced to death, the punishments were hanging or burning, depending on whether they committed petty treason or not. While the conviction rate for women was lower than it was for men, some studies suggest once a woman was found guilty, she had a higher chance of being hanged than a man did.

Similar to the later medieval period, sixteenth-century female convicts used the pleading of pregnancy to attempt an escape from their sentence and punishment. The rules were relatively consistent with those of the later medieval period. If a sentenced felon was found to be pregnant by a jury of matrons, she would be sent to prison to await the birth of her child, after which her punishment would resume. It wasn't until later centuries that judges became more lenient towards new mothers, making it increasingly likely for convicts to be pardoned or have their sentences reduced after giving birth.

The act of poisoning became increasingly feared among the population, and in 1531, it was declared that the punishment for poisoning (now considered high treason) was death by boiling. This harsh penalty was enforced in the case of one of Henry VIII's unfortunate cooks. Although this severe punishment was later repealed by Edward VI, the fear and reputation of poisoning persisted strongly among the people. Poison was sometimes the weapon of choice for sixteenth century murderesses, but it wasn't until the eighteenth and nineteenth centuries that it became one of the most frequently employed methods of murder by female killers.

The ducking stool, cucking stool and scold's bridle were punishments primarily applied to women for less serious crimes. The ducking stool, resembling a chair on the end of a lever, would be repeatedly dunked in water, posing a risk of drowning or shock. The cucking stool was a special seat that people would carry on their shoulders. The offender would sit on it and be paraded around town. This was typically used as a punishment for scolding, talking back, or not obeying one's husband. Lastly, the scold's bridle was a headpiece with a built-in muzzle worn by women. It featured a large iron stake poking into the mouth that often caused bleeding. Women would have to wear this for a period of time as they were paraded around town, again often for scolding. All these punishments aimed at causing humiliation and deterring others from similar behaviour. The fact that the majority of people sentenced to these punishments were women, with no equivalent punishments for men scolding others, underscores the gender inequality embedded in the early modern criminal justice system.

People convicted of serious crimes, involving high treason, were sometimes sentenced to death by beheading, using either an axe, sword, or occasionally the famed guillotine. Unfortunate women like Anne Boleyn, Katherine Howard, Margaret Pole, and Mary, Queen of

Scots met their end by axe or sword. Although the guillotine gained popularity in France during the eighteenth century, its use dates back to the sixteenth century in England and Scotland. Two forms of the guillotine were employed across Britain. One of them, known as The Maiden, was built in Edinburgh in 1564. It executed 150 individuals over 145 years, including prisoners from all over Scotland. Notably, it was used on Jean Kincaid, Lady Warriston, whose story is explored in the upcoming chapter on the seventeenth century. Today, The Maiden is on display at the National Museum of Scotland.

The second guillotine in use was known as the Halifax gibbet. Although the exact date of its establishment is unknown, it was erected in the sixteenth century. Its installation was prompted by the need to regulate the wool trade, which was vital to Halifax's and England's economies. The blade of the gibbet was axe-shape but never sharpened, relying on its weight and speed of descent to tear the head off rather than slice it. The gibbet remained in use until 1650, and today, a modern replica stands in its place. Interestingly, these two guillotines were often employed for commoners rather than nobility. Swords and axes were considered more reliable, despite their occasional accuracy issues, and were reserved for the upper levels of society.

Many murders involving women of the sixteenth century entail a woman assisting in the killing, either directly or by getting or hiring someone to commit the deed – often to kill their husband. In 1583 Worcestershire, a woman named Mistress Beast was indicted and sentenced to burn after she begged, pressured, and finally convinced her husband's servant, Christopher Tomson, to kill her husband, Thomas Beast. Mistress Beast and Christopher were lovers, and she wanted her husband out of the picture, especially after neighbours alerted Thomas to her affair, and he told Christopher to leave. Thomas is described as well reputed, godly, and honest, while Mistress Beast is described using stereotypical early modern women weaknesses, such as lust and desire.

Women's sexuality was perceived as fundamentally dangerous and capable of leading to trouble and disobedience. Christopher was so infatuated with Mistress Beast that despite his initial protests, he eventually gave in and struck Thomas Beast in the back with a tool similar to a halberd but used for agriculture. Christopher was hanged and then hung in chains, while Mistress Beast was burned. Although she did not physically commit the crime, Mistress Beast played an instrumental role in her husband's demise and paid the price. There are not too many examples of women acting alone, except when it comes to infanticide, where they often, but not always acted independently.

A similar situation took place in 1591, in Plymouth when a woman named Mistress Page plotted to kill her husband with her lover, George Strangewidge. George and Mistress Page had wanted to marry, but her father desired her to marry Master Page instead, and she was forced to comply and marry him. She was never pleased to be with him and over their short marriage, tried to poison him many times but never succeeded. She and George had been planning her husband's demise from early on in her marraige, and they decided to hire two people to assist them in the dirty deed. Mistress Page acquired the help of one of her servants, Robert Priddis whom she paid with gold and silver, and George hired a man named Tom Stone, whom he promised would receive a hearty payment afterward. On 12 February 1591, Priddis and Stone went into Master Page's room while he was lying awake, jumped on him, tackled him, and strangled him with his headscarf, all while Master Page was trying to fight back. After they succeeded in killing him, they broke his neck to make sure he was dead and then laid him back on the bed as if he were sleeping.

After a while, Priddis called for Mistress Page to check on her husband. She did so and very convincingly acted worried and called for some relatives to come. No one suspected any foul play until Master Page's sister noticed scratch marks on him where he was trying to get the scarf off his neck. She immediately asked for an investigation. They discovered his broken neck and that it had likely been murder. They questioned Priddis, who folded under the pressure and gave up Stone too. The murder unfolded, and Mistress Page and George were implicated. All three were indicted, and at the following assizes, were found guilty and were executed on 20 February 1591. So, even though Mistress Page did not commit the dreadful act herself, she was still sentenced to death due to her organisation and planning of the vicious murder. This murderous tale is taken from a murder pamphlet, which tended to dramatize their stories to really grab the public's attention, so all the details must be read with this in mind. The overall tale is likely to be true, but it is hard to tell if all the specific details are accurate or there to add panache (not that a daring tale of murder should need more panache).

In Wales, Anne Bromlow was indicted for assisting in the murder of her husband, Thomas, in 1554. The records state Thomas was killed with three wounds to the head, so violent they hit his brain. The person who gave Thomas these wounds was Richard ap Mathew, but both he and Anne were charged with the murder, as Anne had supposedly hired Richard to commit the dastardly deed. They were both sentenced to hang. Now, Anne was charged with murder, not petty treason. It is not exactly clear why, but Elizabeth Anne Howard believes it may be because the category and sentencing for petty treason had not been integrated into the Welsh legal system yet. So, Anne was saved from being burned at the stake but was still hanged for assisting in her husband's demise.

The story of Joan Wolffe is an example of a woman and a man working together to commit murder. In 1547, Joan and her husband, Edward Wolffe Jr., murdered Edward's servant, Joan Symond, in their house in Ashington, West Sussex. They wounded the back of her head and somehow crushed her neck, which quickly killed her. There is not much detail as to what happened afterwards, but they were indicted and later pardoned. There is not much detail as to why they were pardoned, but this happened quite often in homicide cases. In 1510, Joan Murry's sentence was waived, while her accomplice Robert was outlawed after they supposedly killed Robert's son, Thomas, by mistreating him and breaking his neck in 1507.

Phyllis Phanthazious and Joan Pryggmaryon allegedly assaulted and killed an unknown woman in Radcliffe on Trent in 1555. They fled and were eventually pardoned. In Sussex, Alice Warner was indicted for killing an eight-year-old girl in 1559 by giving her a nasty head wound, which led to her death days later. Alice pleaded not guilty and was acquitted. It's difficult to know whether the jury actually believed she was not guilty or if she was released for some other lenient reason. It could have had something to do with the fact that the girl did not die right away from the wound, so the killing may have been classified as manslaughter, which usually carried a lighter punishment.

The story of Margery Peat of Poole, Wales, is a little different from the ones above. First, because she acted all on her own, and second, because she was more fortunate than most of them, managing to gain an acquittal, although it is not clear why. Margery was indicted for poisoning and killing her husband, Edward ap William, in August 1570. She used 'ratten bane' or arsenic, which caused him to fall very ill but only killed him after twenty-four days. She was indicted on the charge of petty treason, but for some reason was shortly acquitted. This could be from lack of evidence or because the court could not be sure Edward didn't die from something else, as it was a further twenty-four days after he had been poisoned that he passed. Regardless, Margery was extremely lucky to have been acquitted and saved the fate of being burned at the stake.

In Scotland, there was no lack of homicide cases involving women either. In 1532, Edinburgh, Janet Pyott killed George Lindsay and mutilated Patrick Lindsay. She was indicted, and Alexander Scrimgeour was deemed responsible for making sure she appeared for her court case.

However, she did not appear and ended up fleeing. As a result, Alexander was charged with a fee of £66, meant for Janet, her goods were seized, she was declared a fugitive, and she was 'put to the horn'. This was an old Scottish process where the news of her being an outlaw was declared to the town, as a large horn was sounded off three times at the Cross of Edinburgh. Janet was one of many women who found themselves on the wrong side of Scottish law during the sixteenth century.

ALICE NEATE (–1577)

On the chilly evening of 24 January 1577, Alice Neate sneaked into where her sister-in-law was sleeping and brutally slit her throat, instantly killing her. Alice, originally from Colchester, was married with children. One suggested motive for Alice's heinous act was her belief that her sister-in-law (also named Alice Neate), had been responsible for the deaths of two of her children. While unproven, it was known Alice did not get along with her husband's sister. After the murder, Alice wrapped up the body in a red blanket and dragged it out into the yard. The next morning, the victim's body was discovered, prompting authorities to immediately search for the culprit. After eliminating all the people who were with the victim or around their house the previous night, the investigation turned to Alice.

Unfortunately for Alice, it was the comments and testimony of her family members that sealed her fate, especially those of her young daughter's. Her husband strongly believed she had committed the crime and explicitly expressed it by shouting, "God save [my] wife!" However, the most damaging testimony came from her daughter Abigail. When Abigail was taken aside and questioned, she initially insisted on her mother's innocence. Yet, under continued questioning and pressure, she eventually revealed how her mother had asked Abigail to keep Alice's involvement a secret. Abigail, who shared a room with her aunt, had witnessed the entire murder. She saw her mother come in, slit her aunt's throat, and dispose of the body. One can't imagine the stress Abigail had to deal with, especially having to disclose such a traumatic experience and implicate her own mother in the process.

After these admissions, Alice was indicted, confined, and during the subsequent gaol delivery session, she was found guilty and sentenced to hang. Although there is no clear evidence of the hanging taking place, it is likely it did happen, as there is a note in the records indicating either it had taken place or needed to. The shadow of suspicion got the best of Alice, and regardless of whether she was right or wrong, she suffered the consequences of her actions.

JOAN FARNECOMBE (–1578)

Joan Farnecombe was a spinster who lived in Catsfield, Sussex, during the middle of the sixteenth century. It's worth noting that it was not until the seventeenth century that the term 'spinster' began to mean an unmarried woman; here it likely refers to the job of spinner. We don't know much about her family situation, but based on what happened next, it can be assumed there was some unhappiness. On 13 March 1578, things took a dark turn when Joan went to a local pond with ten-year-old Leonard Farnecombe. It is likely Leonard was her son, given they shared the same last name, but the record does not specify. For unknown reasons, Joan then pushed young Leonard into the pond. Unfortunately, the ability to swim was not common in children of the Tudor period, including young Leonard, and he quickly drowned.

Joan was discovered, although the method of how is not specified, and subsequently indicted. On 7 July, at the East Grinstead assizes in Sussex, Joan was asked how she wished to plead, and she said, 'not guilty'. Following the jury's deliberation, they concluded she was guilty. The verdict resulted in her being sentenced to hang, and it was determined she had no goods to her name, indicating her low financial status. While there is no record of the hanging, it is probable it occurred shortly after sentencing. Was it a wicked impulse? A perfected plan or a brief lapse in judgement? Why Joan committed this heinous deed, we cannot know.

Anne Welles (–1592)

Anne Welles was a young woman who lived in Elizabethan London. Admired by many, she was known for being a proper lady. Described in a sixteenth century murder pamphlet written by Thomas Kyd as possessing 'good behaviour and other commendable qualities'. Anne had two admirers: John Brewen and John Parker, both goldsmiths revered for their skills. Anne seemed to prefer John Parker over John Brewen; the author of the pamphlet depicted Parker as undeserving and Brewen as plain and true. Whether these descriptions actually portrayed them before the murder occurred is unclear. The author may have provided these descriptions based on hindsight.

Brewen tried to win Anne's heart by presenting her with jewels and gold, gifts she accepted, endearing him to her friends and family. However, Anne only had eyes for Parker, so she sent Brewen away. Eventually, Brewen grew weary of trying to win Anne's affections and realised she did not want to be with him. He demanded she return the gifts he had given her, and when she refused, he had her detained until she returned them. Anne, hurt and surprised by these actions, for some reason told Brewen if he released her and stopped demanding the jewels, she would marry him. Perhaps it was out of fear of imprisonment, or maybe she wanted to keep the jewels? We don't know, but Brewen was overjoyed at this prospect, and their wedding preparations began.

When John Parker learned of this arrangement, he was hurt and outraged. The pamphlet describes him as having 'interest in the possession of her person,' illustrating how Elizabethan society placed and viewed men and women within relationships; it was normal for men to treat women like possessions. Parker confronted Anne about her decision until Anne told him she regretted the arrangement, explaining there was nothing she could do to stop the marriage. Parker's outrage, combined with Anne's remorse, fuelled her growing resentment toward her upcoming nuptials. Despite Parker lacking the means to marry her at the time, even though she was pregnant, he persistently urged her to eliminate Brewen. Although Anne initially resisted, she eventually agreed to a plan to poison Brewen, with the assertion Parker would marry her soon after the deed was done.

Brewen apparently showed great tenderness towards her, but Anne harboured intense loathing for him and their arrangement. On the night of their marriage, she refused to sleep in his bed with him and never spent another night there again. Her rationale for doing so was that until he could provide her with a better house, she would not live with him. She insisted on being called Anne Welles, refusing to take his name. When not at Brewen's residence, she lived at her own home close to Parker, giving them ample time to concoct their murderous plan. Anne, eager to proceed swiftly, implemented their plan only three days after her marriage to Brewen. Parker had procured the poison, although the records do not specify the type.

On that cold Wednesday morning, Anne took the poison when she visited Brewen's house, greeting him with a pleasant disposition. She offered to make him some 'suger soppes,' a dish made with bread soaked in ale and mixed with sugar and spices, known as 'alebery'. According to Anne's account, Brewen expressed gratitude for having married such a wonderful woman. She responded that if she could not fulfil this small task for him, particularly so soon after their marriage, he might think ill of her. According to Anne's account, she prepared the 'suger soppes' but accidentally spilled the first batch. She then asked Brewen to fetch some red herring, claiming a craving for it, providing her with more time and privacy to prepare his poisoned food. She made three portions, one for Brewen, one for herself and one for a boy she had brought along with her (the records do not specify who he was), but only Brewen's was poisoned.

When he returned, they had their meal. Shortly after, Brewen began experiencing severe stomach pains, vomiting profusely. He asked Anne to take him to bed, and when he asked Anne to stay, she refused and left. The pamphlet discusses how Brewen endured a night of considerable pain. Upon Anne's return in the morning, Brewen was still alive and upset that she had not stayed. She reminded him of the conditions she had set for staying there. He expressed the feeling of impending death and asked her to stay with him. She portrayed sadness for him and remained with him. He died that day and was buried the next, with neither him nor anyone around suspecting a thing.

No one believed anything to be amiss, as Anne was known to be an honest woman. However, it was collectively agreed she could have treated John Brewen better. People attributed her behaviour to her youth and therefore, ignorance. While all of this was happening, Anne was pregnant with Parker's baby. Unfortunately, the infant died shortly after birth. This cannot have been an easy thing for Anne to handle after the stress of what she had recently done.

For two years Anne and Parker continued their tryst, spending most of their time at Anne's house. Over time, Parker became abusive, possessive, and demanding. She wanted to please him but more than likely feared him. It was relayed that if she refused any demand, errand, or task he asked of her, he would threaten to stab her with his dagger. Anne had become pregnant again but was self-conscious and cautious because Parker had still not married her, despite his promise to do so. Anne hid the pregnancy for as long as she could and eventually stopped venturing outdoors to avoid scorn and shame from her neighbours.

She begged Parker to marry her, and he responded with a brazen comment, telling her that she should not dictate when he must marry her. He continued with an accusation of her being a strumpet (whore), and she said that she had been with no one else but him and it was, of course, his baby. She was bewildered and furious when he said that if he married her, she would likely poison him like she did to Brewen, so he was avoiding getting too close to her. He said he would be a fool to trust her. Obviously, she was deeply offended by this. She called him a beast, and said that everything she had done she did for him, and that he had made her poison Brewen, instructing her with what to do. She finished by saying she regretted doing such a thing for him.

Unfortunately for the unhappy couple, this yelling match was overheard by the neighbours, and they alerted the magistrates. When brought in for questioning, both Anne and Parker claimed they were not guilty. Eventually, Anne was tricked into spilling the entire story (which was written into the pamphlet) when they told her Parker had betrayed her. They were put in Newgate prison in the interim, and when Anne was due to have her baby, she was brought to the countryside. After she had given birth, Anne was returned to the prison where both offenders were charged and sentenced. Both were found guilty, and Anne was sentenced to burn for petty treason, while Parker was sentenced to hang while in view of Anne. They were both executed on 28 June 1592, two and a half years after they committed their deadly deed.

What Anne did to Brewen was despicable, but one cannot help but feel sorry for the young woman who was distracted by love, manipulated into killing, and then abused afterwards. There is no doubt she made horrible choices and treated Brewen with less respect than was probably deserved, but she was not treated in the way she should have been either. It is understandable that Parker was mad at the prospect of his lover marrying another, but his response was extreme. There is no mention of what happened to her child, but one would hope she had relatives to look after it. Unfortunately, it is likely that the child went into an orphanage of some sort. Parker is referred to in the pamphlet as 'the villain', and based on what happens throughout this tale, one cannot blame the author for using this term. The fact that this tale was retrieved from a murder pamphlet sold in London makes it highly probable that some details may have been embellished to provide a more tantalising story for its readers. Regardless, this printed pamphlet provides details of a sneaky sixteenth century murder, that we would otherwise have very little information about. A love triangle, a lovelorn and unwise woman, and a manipulative and angry lover, make this murderous tale intriguing and harrowing and show that love could be a dangerous game in Elizabethan London.

There weren't an excessive number of people executed for murder during the Elizabethan period; many individuals were sentenced but later had their crimes pardoned or sentences reduced. Anne Welles was not one of them, and it is likely that neither were Joan and Alice. Alice was one of only two people sentenced to be hanged in Colchester between 1575 and 1577.

Though the criminal justice system of the sixteenth century was slowly moving towards early modern ideas and practices, it still had many similarities to the later medieval period. Between the 1590s and 1630s the number of women accused of murder remained relatively stagnant at around fourteen per cent. Women were still disadvantaged in the justice system and as subordinates to their husbands. Nevertheless, they continued to express themselves and act against the societal expectations of female behaviour, through words, actions, and at times murder. The sixteenth century served as a bridge connecting the developments and new ideas of the early modern period with the systems and classic thinking of the medieval period. As the seventeenth century began, new legislation came into effect, and more extensive records and better methods of record keeping were designed. Therefore, more records are available for historians to analyse.

Chapter Three

THE SEVENTEENTH CENTURY

During the seventeenth century, there was continued development of the justice system, especially with the frequency and thoroughness of record keeping. It makes sense that as society developed and made advancements, so too did the courts and their procedures. One of those improvements was that testimonies relating to health and medicine now had to be supported by sufficient medical expertise. This knowledge, however, was not quite like the expertise we have today, as medicine and science were still developing. Those considered 'experts' were not necessarily always certified, formally educated professionals. Medical and science-based evidence was strong but didn't always take precedence over all other evidence.

In the latter part of the 1600s, moving into the 1700s, there was a spike in women's violence in and around London. With that surge came new trends in female perpetrated murder. Specifically, from the years 1674–1713, Caroline A. Conley (2020) found that women were more likely to kill outside of the family, which is the opposite of the statistics from the rest of the early modern period. Moreover, women killed twice as many males who weren't their husbands as they did 200 years later. These statistics and facts illustrate that early modern women could, in fact, be very 'aggressive and assertive,' as noted by Jenine Hurl-Eamon (2009).

Gender roles were intrinsically defined and acknowledged during the early modern period. Women were perceived in a specific way, and if they strayed from the idyllic image of a proper woman and wife, they were considered unnatural and a threat to the societal order, particularly if they were violent or committed homicide. Petty treason remained a common indictment, as women were still seen as subordinates to their husbands. Court and trial processes were evolving, and some historians have observed that the use of provocation for a woman's defence concerning petty treason became increasingly common and somewhat understood. However, this was not always the case, as the tale of Mary Aubry will clearly show.

Societies continued to exhibit a certain level of accepted, everyday violence, and some historians of Wales have postulated that early modern Wales may have been more violent than England. They suggest Welsh citizens had a fondness and longing for the old Welsh laws, which the Act of Union engulfed in 1536. Part of these laws included a higher tolerance for murder, leading to Welsh residents being more comfortable with commonplace violence. That being said, homicide rates in Wales during the mid to late seventeenth century were very similar to much of England. There was a general decline in homicide rates in England and Wales from the late seventeenth century to the nineteenth century, though certain areas in both countries had staggered fluctuations. It is interesting to note that at the peak of Welsh homicide rates between 1686 and 1690, (perhaps related to the different crises and upheavals occurring during that time), the number of women accused of murder doubled from previous years. Some historians postulate it could have been due to the upheavals, which led to people being nosier and more cautious.

Women of seventeenth century England did have specific functions within the justice system. They were permitted certain roles and were often called upon during cases and trials to assist, being far more involved than they were during the medieval period. Some women took on roles as matrons and were called upon as jurors in trials involving female defendants. Midwives, along with women referred to as 'practitioners' and 'surgeons,' were also involved in trials. It's important to note that these terms did not have the same meanings as they do today. Women wouldn't have been professionally trained or educated doctors; rather, they would have engaged in more everyday medical assisting, such as dressing wounds. While not considered equal to male practitioners, they were known for their extensive knowledge in certain areas and were called upon to assist with crimes, evidence, and criminal procedures, particularly in infanticide trials or cases involving pregnant women.

Some women even acted in a policing or forensic capacity, such as a female practitioner from Yorkshire who, in 1667, ran to help when she heard a man had been stabbed. Upon arrival, finding the man already dead, she decided to investigate the cause of death. She examined the wound and inserted her finger into the injury to discern what had been severed. At times, female surgeons and practitioners were called to incidents to assist with wounds and were later relied upon during trials to provide their expertise. In 1646, a woman from Pontefract informed a court that a head wound she had cleaned and dressed on a man had more than likely caused his death, as it had been exposed to the outside air and was not attended to promptly. In another case in 1654, a female surgeon was summoned to aid a man with a head wound at an ale house and stated the person responsible needed to be found as the man was going to die. While the accuracy of these verdicts may be debated, they highlight how women contributed their expertise during criminal investigations.

Sometimes, women were even given the task of unwrapping bodies during exhumations. It was also typically women who prepared bodies before they were buried. This practice dates back to early religious acts and served as a means to hopefully expose an unnatural death. The overseer might discover hidden bruises or cuts that could lead to an alternate cause of death. Examining the body could also save someone from the noose if they could disprove certain actions by looking for wounds that were not there. This process is reminiscent of early forensic work.

Over the sixteenth and seventeenth centuries, definitions of and criminal procedures relating to murder became more specific and organised. In the seventeenth century, distinctions developed between different types of murder and related felonies, along with their seriousness. This was similar to the introduction of the distinction between manslaughter and murder in the sixteenth century but was much more specific. In 1660, a jury made a list of the five most serious felonies. This list is beneficial because it provides a glimpse into what the courts and society deemed the most morally unacceptable. The five felonies were poisoning, suicide, infanticide, stabbing and the killing of law officers. Poisoning is included due to its criminalisation as high treason during the sixteenth century and subsequent fear, as well as its inherent secretiveness. People in Wales, England, and Scotland collectively believed that poisoning was a despicable and terrifying method of murder. It was used more often by women than men, but in all three countries, women were still more likely to use a weapon of some sort to hit, strike, or stab their victims. Suicide and infanticide were against specific religious teachings, and infanticide was an act preformed in secret that contradicted the natural, expected behaviour of women and mothers. For stabbing, it may have been considered an especially violent way to murder, and to kill a law officer was likely akin to treason and seen as especially unacceptable, given the authority vested in such individuals.

Juries during the early modern period used the evidence brought forward to help form their opinions, much like juries today. Unfortunately, they would also consider the social order of the convict, as well as popular opinion and rumours when making their judgements. This undoubtedly worked against people who may have been innocent but had low social standing or were simply disliked. Examples of this influencing decision making can be seen during some seventeenth century witch trials.

The Old Bailey Courthouse, or the Central Criminal Court located about two hundred yards northwest of St. Paul's Cathedral, is and was an integral part of England's criminal justice history, especially concerning the records kept during the proceedings. These thousands of records are usually very detailed and often provide more than just the crime, trial, and verdict information about the defendants. They often paint a brief picture of their lives leading up to the crime, allowing historians and researchers to contextualise the crimes. The Old Bailey records offer detailed reports of the trials that took place, including witness statements and medical results, allowing for a more detailed understanding of what people thought of the defendant and what occurred leading up to, during, and after the crime.

The Old Bailey was named for the street it was built on and was originally a medieval courthouse. This courthouse burnt down during the great fire of London in 1666 but was rebuilt as a three storey, Italian-style building. The records now available online begin in 1674, shortly after it was rebuilt, and continue up until 1913.

The popularity of broadsides exploded in the seventeenth century. They discussed the latest news, gossip, and public announcements. They were posted on walls throughout town or read aloud in the streets. Murder pamphlets continued with their popularity as well, with both providing narratives of tantalising crimes throughout Britain. In Scotland, broadsides became widespread during the seventeenth century and provided informative and entertaining news for the public. Murder ballads were sung around town, and news and gossip spread quickly. Some of the information about the ladies in this chapter is taken from broadsides and murder pamphlets. Again, the information they provide, though likely true, may have some embellishments or events tweaked to entice the public. One can also clearly hear opinionated tones while reading these sources, as they were written as seventeenth century journalistic pieces. They were a way to spread sensational news to the public as a form of printed entertainment. All of this century's featured ladies have at least one broadside, pamphlet or poem/ballad written about their crimes, showing the popularity of print media. It also means their stories caught the public's attention as scandalous and intriguing in one way or another.

Some of these ballads, broadsides, and pamphlets, were written narratively about the crime, but a few are written using the words of the condemned women. Those pieces present a portrait of the criminal that may be sneakily written to coincide with idyllic ideas of who these ladies were supposed to be. The writers often express that they try to be accurate and report the words and events exactly as it was told to them, but they would have had the opportunity to tweak their words to represent the ladies how they wanted. They may have made the women seem more repentant than they were, more begrudging, more afraid or calmer, to paint the picture that was desired. This literature was often dramatized and narrativized to entice more people and make it more approachable to the public. It was also sometimes used to perpetuate the popular religious values of the time and written to show God's grace and the value of penitence and prayer.

The seventeenth and eighteenth centuries were the heydays for broadside ballads and murder pamphlets. Printers produced this contemporary media based on changing public interests. Broadsides usually cost around a penny, making them relatively accessible for all levels of society. Murder ballads also tended to point fingers at certain levels of society, covertly 'warning' them and others to be careful of what could happen. These targeted groups were usually the merchant and working classes. Kane, in his article 'Wives with Knives: Early Modern Murder Ballads and the Transgressive Commodity' (1996), expresses this idea when he discusses his belief that broadside ballads acted as a veiled guide for the labouring classes of the seventeenth century of what not to do, and therefore helped to regulate crime in lower society.

Like the later medieval period and the sixteenth century, hanging was the most common punishment used for convicted murderers in the seventeenth century. This was true for both male and female convicts unless the woman committed petty treason, in which case the punishment would be burning at the stake. The burning of women for petty treason was widely practised during the 1600s, accompanied by murderous witch crazes all across England, Scotland and Wales that sent hundreds of women to the stake for supposedly practising witchcraft. There was an increase in instances of burning at the stake that began in the 1500s due to the growing intensity of witch hunting. The seventeenth century had very similar punishments to the sixteenth century, especially for women. These included the cucking and ducking stools and the scold's bridle. The guillotine, as discussed in the sixteenth century chapter, was still used throughout the 1600s and into the 1700s, gaining popularity in France as its popularity in Britain began to falter. The last beheading in Britain was in 1747. Swords and axes were also still used for beheading too as King Charles I's execution illustrates. There are not many instances of women getting beheaded as punishment in the seventeenth century, as it was more frequently used on men, though not exclusively.

Benefit of the clergy, which was previously only accessible to men, was available for women to use starting in 1623 when they were accused of petty larceny. The full privilege was granted to women in the 1690s for crimes including manslaughter, but never for murder or rape. The pleading of pregnancy was widely used during the 1600s, and the courts were beginning to show more leniency towards pregnant felons; a sympathy that accelerated during the following two centuries. If a guilty woman was found to be pregnant, she would be sent away until her child was born. Afterwards, her sentence would be continued, but occasionally the courts would end up pardoning the woman or would reduce her death sentence to transportation. It was less likely, however, that a woman who was convicted of murder would be pardoned.

In and around London, the patrolling of crime was often left to citizens. There was an obligation for people to assist in catching the perpetrator of a crime if they witnessed it. They then had to alert a constable or bring the culprit to a constable or a justice of the peace to be arrested. Constables were unpaid patrollers who monitored crime on a daily basis. Night watchmen were similarly employed to keep the peace. The act of locals being responsible for catching criminals slowly began to fade over the eighteenth century and were replaced with salaried constables or men called thief-takers.

In Scotland, there were no local constables during the early years of the early modern period, as there were in England. So, when the crowns united in 1603, the King's Privy Council of Scotland wanted to implement some sort of control over the streets of Edinburgh. Thus in 1611, the High Constables of Edinburgh was established. It was a group of appointed men who had various duties around the city, similar to English constables, who were mostly focused on petty crime. They could be seen as one of the first police forces, as they were more organised and professionalised than typical constables.

The term infanticide was popularised during the seventeenth century. In 1624, the Act to 'Prevent the Destroying and Murdering of Bastard Children' was passed. It brought considerable changes to the prosecution of women for infanticide in England and Wales. Originally, the court had to find a way to prove that a woman was guilty, but this legislation made that difficulty vanish. Now, women had to prove they were innocent to be let off the charge. As the title suggests, this applies to bastard children and therefore to unmarried women. It could also refer to children born outside of one's marriage, but it was more often than not, single women who were indicted.

A woman could prove her innocence by showing she had prepared for the arrival of her baby by purchasing or making clothes, making arrangements for when the baby came, or providing at least one witness that could testify the baby had not been born alive. This new rule more than likely sent a few innocent women to the noose because they could not provide convincing evidence, though the courts were known to be somewhat sympathetic towards mothers depending on the situation. In Scotland, a similar act called the 'Act Anent Child Murder in Scotland' was passed in 1690, which made infanticide a capital crime resulting in the death penalty. This too was a harsh law against infanticidal mothers as it presumed their guilt and often resulted in convictions based on little evidence. If they concealed their pregnancy and did not ask for help during the birth, they would more than likely be deemed guilty.

It was less probable that married women would be charged with infanticide than single women because, if a woman could show she was married to a good man who could provide for her and the baby, she would be less suspected of killing the newborn; the court would see little reason for her to do so. If a woman had concealed her pregnancy, though, it was much more suspicious. There are also many cases of women, both single and married, found not guilty because they were believed to have not been of sound mind during the incident. There were many mental health issues these women may have suffered from – or it is entirely plausible some women in these types of situations were driven mad by their circumstances, stress, or anxiety. If a married woman committed infanticide, she was more likely to be labelled as insane, as it was assumed to be less of an act of desperation than when committed by single women on their illegitimate children.

There was some knowledge among society and the courts of certain mental health issues that could result in a woman committing infanticide, but it was nowhere near the knowledge needed to really assist her. Despite what the courts thought, there were reasons why a sane married woman might have felt the urge to commit infanticide. She might have been extremely poor and couldn't afford to feed or clothe her child, possibly because she already had numerous children or, she may have wanted to get revenge on her husband for something by depriving him of his children. Neither of these reasons justify the act, but they can provide context as to why some married women went so far as to commit this deed.

Anne Philmore is a rare example of a married woman not presumed insane when she should have been, as she showed signs of being mentally unstable before and after the murder. Instead, she was found guilty. Anne killed her nine-week-old child by drowning it. She had four other children, and her husband was a shoemaker. She did laundry to supplement their income, and she was known as an honest woman and caring mother. Originally, the pamphlets that came out about the case said that Anne did it because she was greedy and did not want to spend more money on another child. What she actually said was that the child was taking too much time away from her work and costing her money. She was still deemed simply greedy, even though her mental health should have played a part. She was nine weeks postpartum, more than likely suffering from depression. The night before the murder she had been up all night with a raging fever. This could have caused her delirium, which is supported by the fact she said she felt 'distracted'. After the murder, she wandered aimlessly around seeming confused. Nonetheless, at her trial she was deemed covetous and guilty and was executed.

The act of infanticide cannot be taken lightly, but for many of the accused women, it was an act of desperation and fear due to unimaginable social and economic situations and repercussions. They had no money or would have no job if found to be pregnant; they would be shamed, their reputation ruined, and would likely be a societal outcast. Some of these women saw no way out. It makes sense that many of these accused women were single and often servants in noble households. It was also likely that many of these women's pregnancies were the result of their master's seducing or taking advantage of them. Many of these women, though they made a horrible and drastic decision, more than likely felt they had no choice.

A uniquely Welsh custom may have made the prospect of an unmarried pregnancy, not as socially damaging as in other places. This custom called 'courting on the bed' accepted sexual relations while courting as well as pre-marital sex to make sure 'everything was working' for fertility purposes. This process was apparently acknowledged by parents and employers, so it is understandable to wonder if this may have had a positive effect on the attitudes towards illegitimate pregnancies and therefore the rate of infanticide cases. Despite this custom, there were still cases of infanticide throughout Wales during the seventeenth century.

When it came to investigating infanticide, women and their knowledge were incredibly valuable. Gaskill in his book '*Crime and Mentalities in Early Modern England*' (2000), writes about their importance and how 'magistrates relied upon women to get to the heart of an investigation in a way men could not.' Female investigators were able to provide more intimate examinations of fellow women and crime scenes involving women, like a living woman lying in bed covered in blood, for example. A male examiner might take a quick look at the woman but would likely not look under the bed sheets at specific areas of a woman's body, especially if she was alive. A woman could take a closer look and determine what was ailing her.

In 1680 in Yorkshire, after a dead infant was found outside, constables were directed to assemble a jury of matrons to find all possible women around town who could have recently had a child. In 1653 a group of women from a community in Yorkshire (who may not have even had specific titles of expertise) believed a local woman had given birth and gotten rid of her baby. They informed a constable, who managed to coax the woman into confessing, but she chose to disclose the location of the body exclusively to a midwife. The assigned midwife found the baby and brought it back to the group of local women to be examined. To examine the bodies of infants was common practice for female practitioners of all sorts and during the early modern period, when examining the bodies of babies who had passed, special attention would be paid to the development at the time of death. This would let the courts know if it might have been murder, if the baby was fully grown, if the baby was too underdeveloped to live, or if a miscarriage had occurred. One of the tests administered on the infants would be to examine the growth of certain body parts, like fingernails or hair, which would help determine the age of the baby.

Throughout England, Scotland, and Wales, unfortunately, numerous accounts of infanticide occurred during the seventeenth century. Elizabeth Taylor from Camberwell threw her child into a bushy hedge, causing the child's death. Found guilty, she was sentenced to hang in 1605. A similar story unfolded with Joan Hooke in 1610 from Croydon, who strangled her newborn boy and faced a hanging sentence. Anne Millawaie from Newington met the same fate for strangling her newborn girl and discarding her in an outhouse. Marion Burt from Southwark gave birth to a female child in 1613 and proceeded to strangle her, leading to her execution by hanging. Agnes and Alice Crockford from Stoke, a mother and daughter, committed the dreadful crime together. In 1618 Agnes gave birth to a boy, and immediately after, Alice fatally struck him on the head with a rock. Scottish-born Bessie Brebuer from Fife had a similar tragic tale in 1663. After giving birth to a baby girl, she suffocated her by stuffing sand into her mouth.

The reasons behind these women's crimes are unclear and could stem from a range of situations. Some might not have been able to afford basic necessities for themselves, let alone a baby. Others may have faced the threat of losing their livelihoods due to a job that depended on their childlessness. The fear of stigma and hardships associated with being a single, unwed mother could have motivated some. Others might have been overwhelmed with numerous children or simply cruel and unwilling to care for a child. Mental health struggles would likely have played a role in some cases too. Bessie's situation involved an extramarital affair, leading her to attempt to avoid the shame and stigma associated with her actions.

In seventeenth century England, Scotland, and Wales, while slowly transitioning to more modern practices, society remained relatively violent. As in previous centuries, certain levels of violence were deemed acceptable and expected, particularly in matters of discipline, whether in child rearing or dealing with insubordinate servants, apprentices, or wives. Unfortunately, there were instances where women, such as Elizabeth Wigenton (d.1681), Elizabeth Crosman (d.1682), and Elizabeth Deacon (d.1690), exceeded these allowances and, whether accidentally or through cruelty, caused the deaths of their servants or apprentices.

The first case involves Elizabeth Wigenton, a coat maker in London (although some accounts label her as a 'School-Mistris, or Sempstris), who had a thirteen-year-old girl as an apprentice. One day, Elizabeth assigned her a task, and when the girl completed it, it was not to Elizabeth's liking or standards. Enraged, Elizabeth, with the assistance of one of her lodgers, John Sadler, subjected the young girl to a brutal beating. They stripped her, tied her up, and whipped and beat her so severely that, 'the blood ran down like rain.' They even rubbed salt in her wounds while Elizabeth covered her mouth to stifle any cries. Overwhelmed by pain, the girl fainted, and a few days later succumbed to her injuries. During the trial, Elizabeth claimed she did not mean to kill her. However, some neighbours testified that she had been harsh and cruel on other occasions. Both Elizabeth and John Sadler were charged with murder and hanged.

Next is the case of Elizabeth Crosman from St. Martin in the Fields, who fatally stabbed her male apprentice following a drunken misunderstanding. Returning home after drinking at her local ale house, a slightly intoxicated Elizabeth found her male apprentice John Bret, playing with her young son. Mistakenly thinking that he was harming her son, she grabbed a stick and began beating him. Although he managed to wrestle the stick away, Elizabeth quickly seized a carving tool and stabbed him in the left side of his chest. As he attempted to escape, she threw another tool at him. He managed to make it to the downstairs neighbours but soon died. Despite her claim that he had provoked her into beating him, Elizabeth could not prove it during the trial. The jury still believed her to be guilty and she was sentenced to hang. This case illustrates that some women engaged in activities traditionally associated with men, such as drinking at the local pub, and in some instances, it negatively influenced them to commit felonies, mirroring patterns observed in male-instigated homicides.

The third Elizabeth accused of killing her subordinate, is Elizabeth Deacon. Elizabeth had a servant maid named Mary Cox, approximately seventeen years old, whom she suspected of stealing and engaging in nefarious activities. According to two apprentices employed by Elizabeth and her husband Francis, when Elizabeth found a shilling on Mary's person, she demanded an explanation of its origin. Dissatisfied and doubtful of her response, Elizabeth tied her to the bedpost and subjected her to brutal whipping. A few days later, she repeated the inquiry, and when Mary refused to confess, Elizabeth resumed the beatings until the girl cried out 'murder!' Elizabeth covered her mouth to stifle the cries. The beatings persisted, and on the next occasion, Elizabeth escalated the brutality. She tied Mary's neck and heels and fastened her to the bedposts. She proceeded to burn her on her neck, shoulders, and back with a fire poker, and shockingly, used a hammer to deliver a severe blow to her head. Following this, Mary confessed to conspiring with thieves to rob the Deacon house during Francis's absence. Worried about this and nothing else, Elizabeth took Mary to stand before the justices and confess her guilt. Mary, admitted to providing copies of the house key to the thieves, stealing goods, and participating in other robberies in neighbouring houses.

There is no record of Mary receiving a sentence for these crimes, but it appears she returned home with Elizabeth. Severely ill from the beatings and exacerbated by overeating, Mary received no care or comfort from Elizabeth, who continued to advocate for her hanging. Mary died shortly after, and Elizabeth was indicted for her murder. Elizabeth claimed Mary was a poor employee and very obstinate. Unlike the other two Elizabeth's, this one pleaded pregnancy and was found to be pregnant by a jury of matrons, resulting in the respite of her punishment. A year later, she sought a pardon from the courts, which she received.

Another Elizabeth, distinct from the previously mentioned Elizabeths, deviates from the pattern and, like many of the women featured in this chapter, killed her husband, leading to her execution by burning. Elizabeth Lillyman (d.1675) was accused of stabbing her husband William in the heart with a cobbler's knife. Elizabeth and William lived near Goodman's Fields, where Elizabeth, a former nurse, and William, a cooper at a brewery, had been married for just over a year. He was Elizabeth's sixth husband, and the primary motive behind the assault was believed to be jealousy. Elizabeth was more than twenty years older than William, who was described as handsome, hard-working, and honest. Despite neighbours advising her against jealousy, it remained an issue for her. One afternoon, William returned home and finding Elizabeth at the local alehouse, took his shoes to the cobbler next door and then joined her for supper at the alehouse. He borrowed a long, sharp knife from the cobbler to cut his mutton and mackerel.

Inside the alehouse, he sent for his wife to come and eat with him. Unfortunately, on the way in to meet her husband, a maid jokingly said something to Elizabeth about being with her husband, and it sent Elizabeth into a jealous rage. Her fury was not helped by her already drunken state. She was known to have outbursts of jealousy where she would threaten William, but this was far more than that. Elizabeth yelled at him, grabbed the cobbler's knife, and thrust it into the left side of William's chest. When the maid returned to the alehouse, William called to her to fetch the cobbler, as his wife had just stabbed him. Before the maid returned, William had staggered up, walked over to where they were coming in from and said that his wife had stabbed him with the knife he had borrowed. Elizabeth watched as all this happened. When hearing him accuse her, she acted falsely sweet and impudent and said, 'why would I stab you? I have not touched you'. She pretended to kiss him, which William fended off. He fainted and was brought into the alehouse. Awakening, he said over and over that his wife had killed him. Eventually, he passed out again and died.

Elizabeth tried to leave, but her neighbours stopped her, and she was detained. At both her examination and trial, she denied killing William. She acted very strangely, being silly and detached at first, and then after her indictment was read as petty treason, she began to rave madly that she must see her husband and wanted him there. Though this could have been part of a mental breakdown that would have been examined further in present day, the court believed she was trying to feign innocence and deflect the blame from herself. They deemed her guilty. She did not say anything in her defence except that she didn't kill her husband but wanted to hurt the maid like he had been. While she was waiting for her execution, she seemed rather detached until the Sunday before when she recognised the reality of her situation. She told her friends she was a sinner and deserved what was ahead, but still denied killing William. Eventually, after talking to many ministers, she finally admitted that she had killed him and seemed very remorseful. She made a final speech before her execution on Tower Hill and told people to see her as an example and not repeat her actions. She recited some touching prayers and was burned until dead.

Some women during the seventeenth century, like in the sixteenth, were sentenced to hang or burn because they assisted in murders, despite not carrying out the act of killing themselves. One example of this occurring is the case of a Scottish woman, Jean Kincaid, or Lady Warriston, as she was also referred. This was a relatively high-profile case for the time as it involved someone of the Scottish nobility instead of a commoner. In England, Scotland, and Wales during the early modern period, it was far less likely for someone of the upper order of society to be indicted, sentenced, and especially punished unless it was a crime relating to the monarch like high treason or religious reform. For crimes like murder and theft, the lower orders of society were the majority of people tried and punished. This prejudiced system was due to a variety of reasons, including social connections, influence, and money.

Jean Kincaid was born in 1579 to John Livingston, Laird of Dunpice, and hailed from a family with considerable wealth and influence, earning the respect of James VI of Scotland (I of England). In her youth, she was wedded to John Kincaid of Warriston, residing north of Edinburgh. Unhappiness marred her marital life, possibly stemming from mistreatment and abuse inflicted by her husband, as historical records note instances of him biting her arm and subjecting her to repeated physical harm. Dissatisfied with her marriage, Jean expressed her desire to end it. In collaboration with her nurse, Janet Murdo, Jean devised a plan to kill her husband, opting to enlist someone else to do the deed. They selected a family servant, Robert Weir, to carry out the act. On the night of 1 July 1600, John Kincaid, was persuaded or compelled to consume an excessive amount of wine, and retired to bed in an inebriated state. Taking advantage of the situation, Weir entered John's room, attacked him, and subsequently strangled him. Jean and Janet, feigning ignorance, approached the scene when they heard a commotion, although they were well aware of the sinister plot. Weir emerged and declared that John was dead, the deed was complete.

News of John's mysterious death reached Edinburgh, prompting the arrest of Jean, Janet and two other women who worked at the castle. The main perpetrator, Robert Weir, managed to evade capture and remained at large for 4 years before being found. Despite her family's wealth and influence, Jean faced indifference from them during her trial. Sentenced to hanging and subsequent burning alongside her maid, Jean showed an initial lack of remorse. However, as her execution drew closer, she relented, becoming penitent and resigning herself to her fate. She prayed, made her will, and faced her execution on 5 July 1600.

Her punishment was altered to beheading by a guillotine called The Maiden, more than likely due to her status and/or her family's desire for a less public spectacle. Jean Kincaid's family planned to carry out the execution early in the morning to avoid spectators. To shift the focus, they arranged a double feature - as Jean was secretly beheaded, they made sure Janet, the maid, was getting publicly burned. Executed on the Girth Cross at Canongate, Jean's brother kissed and forgave her and her relatively cheerful demeanour persisted until the end. Weir was found and tried in 1604, and sentenced to be taken to Edinburgh and broken on the wheel. This punishment was not typical in Scotland at the time, adding to the interest surrounding their decision to employ it. Over the years ballads and poems have been written about Jean and her dreadful deed, illustrating the sensation the case and trial produced throughout Scotland.

Similar to previous centuries, women also committed murders in pairs or groups. Two examples of this are presented in a pamphlet titled *Murther upon Murther: Or A True and Faithful Relation, of Six Horrid and Bloody Cruelties, And Barbarous and Unheard of Murthers, And Tragical Villanies, Lately Committed in Several Counties of England*. Printed in 1684, the cases detailed in the pamphlet occurred around that time. This murder pamphlet was one of many produced throughout the early modern period. It contains two different tales that involve a woman as part of a murderous team. In one case, a woman took matters into her own hands when her male counterparts hesitated, illustrating that women could be as violent as men were believed to be. This pamphlet also discusses one of the cases featured later in this chapter involving Sarah Elston. As mentioned in the 1500s, these murder pamphlets were created as popular press, and even though they depict real events, they are likely dramatized by the writers to engage the most people possible. These resources provide fascinating and detailed narratives, but when reading them, one must realise/acknowledge there may be some enhanced aspects.

The first tale is about a man and a woman who pretended to be husband and wife; they killed the elderly woman who was letting them lodge in her house. Eighty-year-old Widow Fewers lived in Middlesex and owned a tidy little house with many rooms that she sometimes rented out. One day, two strangers, a man and woman, rented a room from her. In the evening, they invited the old woman up to their room to share a meal with them. She, being unaware of their plan, accepted the invitation and went upstairs. When she entered the room they attacked her, stuffed a dirty towel in her mouth and strangled her with a napkin. Once she was dead, they stole her keys and proceeded to rifle through her belongings. They stole her money and many other items that could be carried easily. It is not known when the male murderer left, but the female went downstairs shortly after and said to the other tenant she was going out for cheese. When she didn't return, and the landlady had not come back downstairs, the other tenant and a neighbour went upstairs to check on her. They found her body on the floor and no sign of the murderers. At the time this story was printed, the murderers were still on the run and had not been apprehended.

In the second tale of villainy, the woman takes centre stage as the main culprit. In a Yorkshire village, Anthony Wilson, a respected farmer lived with his wife, two daughters and their servants. Although they were known to be wealthy, the farmer had recently settled his half-yearly rent, leaving them with a lesser sum than usual in the house. During the night, a gang of six men and one woman broke into the house and went to the room where the family slept. They bound and gagged Anthony, his wife and his two daughters and then did the same to the servants. Pointing a pistol at Anthony, they demanded he tell them where their money was kept. Anthony told them it was in his trunk and gave them the key.

When they opened it, they found only six pounds in it. They knew he was wealthy, and believed he was hiding more. They demanded he tell them where the rest was hidden and tortured him for information by burning his finger down to the bone with a match. He told them there was no more, which was the truth, but they didn't believe him. They went to the wife next and burnt her too while they asked her where the money was. She repeated what Anthony had said. Frustrated, the thieves tied them up, took linens, clothes, and a silver bowl. They were leaving when the female thief, who the author described as 'most cruel' and 'instigated by the devil', suggested they kill the entire family. The men who were slightly less vicious refused, but the woman took a knife she was carrying, thrust it into poor Anthony, and then left with the rest of her malicious gang. The family was found the next morning, still tied up. Anthony had died from his wound, but everyone else survived, though they were traumatized and devastated. The town was alerted, and an immediate search began for this violent gang.

To introduce a new weapon of choice, two Welsh women from Wrexham used poison to murder family members in 1686. Interestingly, their fates were very different. Jane Foulkes and Lettice Lloyd collectively used poison to kill their husband and son-in-law, respectively. The difference, however, is that Jane received a not guilty verdict, but Lettice did not. The reason? Jane's story incriminated Lettice while exonerating herself of any malefic intent and made her murder seem like an accident. Whether this was true or not, she was set free. Lettice was not so fortunate. With testimonies from Jane, Lettice's daughter, and neighbours, combined with Lettice's decision to remain silent in court, her act was seen as premeditated, and she was deemed guilty. Once the distinction between manslaughter and murder was defined, the idea of intent was extremely important in homicide cases and could be the difference between a light punishment and death.

There was no shortage of murderous women throughout the seventeenth century. Agnes Johnston from Scotland killed her grandniece in 1674, and Esther Ives from Hampshire, murdered her husband with her lover, by planning and then letting her lover strangle him in 1686. Similarly, Ann Hampton from London supposedly killed her husband in 1641 by putting antimony in his wine, and Margaret Osgood from Southwark, slayed her husband in 1680 by hitting him on the head with a sharp weapon, cutting off his ears and wounding him in several other places. Husband murder was a common offence for criminal women, whether they were mistreated by them and desired revenge and freedom, or simply wanted to be rid of them.

The following four women have very different stories about how their lives unfortunately turned upside down. Though most of their victims are very similar, all of their situations are extremely different. Let's explore these tantalising tales featuring four of Britain's most sensational seventeenth century murderesses.

MARGARET FERNESEEDE (C.1560–1608)

Margaret Ferneseede (Fernesede or Ferneseed) was a former prostitute, and later a feisty brothel keeper, or bawd, as they were known in the early modern period. She lived in London during the later part of the sixteenth century and the early seventeenth century. Her house, which doubled as a brothel, was close to the Iron-gate of the Tower of London. Margaret had a reputation due to her salacious profession, past, and proclivities and was called many things, including wretched and unchaste. She was criticised even more harshly because she was not only a prostitute, but she brought young women into the trade and taught them her profession. In the murder pamphlet about her misdeed, the author describes her as someone who 'was gi(u)en to all the loosenesse & lewdnesse of life, which either (v)nlawfull lust, or abominable prostitution could violently cast (v)ppon her with the greatest infamie'. At some point in her illustrious career, Margaret married Anthony Ferneseede. Anthony was a tailor who lived on Duck Lane. He was known to be friendly with his neighbours, polite and a good conversationalist.

It's fair to assume Margaret and Anthony did not have a harmonious relationship and Anthony was less than comfortable with Margaret's situation. There was one instance where Margaret attempted to poison Anthony's broth by slipping some sort of powder into it (arsenic maybe?), clearly illustrating a rather unhappy circumstance. Their marriage was turned upside down when Anthony was found dead in Peckham Field near Lambeth in either late 1607 or early 1608; the records do not specify. His throat had been cut, and he was holding a knife in one of his hands, because the killer wanted the scene to look like a suicide. This placement of the body did not play into the killer's favour, because it was steadily decomposing, with maggots and worms around and within the wounds. This shows any investigator he had been dead for some time. This didn't quite make sense, as there had been nobody in the field the previous day. If he had committed suicide, either there wouldn't be any maggots within the body, or someone would have spotted the body earlier.

When authorities finally identified the body, they went to Duck Lane to inform Margaret. She was apparently very unperturbed when she heard the news, and carried herself with an air of nonchalance, as if the news were of no particular significance. She also asked whether his throat had been cut by someone or if he had done it himself. This was before the authorities mentioned how he died, which would have seemed suspicious. She then went to see the body and brought their servant boy too. On her way, she met two of her husband's acquaintances who expressed their sympathies towards her. Similarly, to earlier, she responded with rather unemotional and casual remarks, hardly appropriate of a grieving wife. When asked why she was not crying she complained her eyes were already weak, so she was saving them to make clothes instead of straining them with crying.

When she saw the body and was in front of the Magistrate, it is said she looked sad. The author of the murder pamphlet took a different approach and wrote that she did not feel sad or scared, and that her brain was dry and would not create tears for her eyes to cry. This illustrates how the author felt about Margaret as well as the picture he was trying to paint of her for his audience. She was asked many questions but was so clear and consistent about her innocence she was not suspected at first. It was only when her servant boy began answering questions that suspicion grew. Her servant was unrestrained. He described her life as an 'abomination' and said she was often angry and forceful, threatening, and malicious. He also told the authorities that since her marriage, she had maintained an alleged adulterous relationship with a young man who had subsequently departed. She had also sold off all of her and Anthony's belongings before she heard of the murder, so she could join her paramour. Margaret's neighbours testified to similar goings on, so she was taken for questioning a second time.

During this more intensive round of questioning, she maintained her innocence very convincingly but was still committed to White Lyon Prison in Southwark. The pamphlet author takes care to write about how Margaret spent her time in prison awaiting her trial, which gives us insight into her character. She did not use the time to reflect on her malicious criminality or make improvements in her behaviour; she instead was indignant, created uproars, was unpleasant, and provoked and scolded the other prisoners instead of being cordial. He writes that she deserved the title of bawd she had previously received. During her trial, she once again pleaded not guilty.

There were several witnesses who spoke against her, discussing her immoral living and past. They pointed out she had previously attempted to poison Anthony, and that she seemed unconcerned with his demise. This was all strong information against her, but the most damning evidence came from two bargemen (sailors) who had once stayed at her brothel. On this night in question, Anthony had also decided to stay, and he and Margaret were in the room next to the sailors. The men overheard them arguing about Margaret's profession and sinful life; eventually she yelled at him and stormed out.

Subsequently, Anthony heard the sailors in the next room and went to see who was there. Taken unaware of their presence, he demanded they leave and not return, or there would be consequences. When asked what authority he had, he asserted he would be the master of the house if it weren't controlled by Margaret, 'a devilish woman' engaged in a sinful profession. Furious upon learning of this exchange, Margaret exclaimed 'ha(n)g him sla(u)e and villaine: I will before God bee re(u) enged of him (nay ere long) by one meanes or other, so worke, that I will bee rid of him'. (Hang him, slave and villain! I will, before God, be revenged of him, nay, ere long, by one means or another, so work that I will be rid of him.) Following this testimony, Margaret was found guilty and sentenced to be burned for petty treason.

She returned to White Lyon Prison until her execution date. During her time at the prison, she remained disruptive and scornful until three gentlemen, also prisoners with troubled pasts, heard of her history. They approached her to share their stories of repentance, reformation, and acceptance, hoping to inspire her to do the same. Eventually, she felt compelled to confess and repent about her former life, which the author documented. Margaret admitted to being a sinner and having worked as a prostitute since a very young age. As she got older, she chose to become a brothel keeper and recruit young women into her trade. Managing about ten women, some of whom were married, she confessed to persuading them by claiming they were not loved or appreciated by their husbands. She made them pay her 10 shillings per week, threatening to disclose their activities to their husbands if they didn't. Margaret also confessed to receiving stolen goods and acknowledged deserving death for her actions; despite all this, she maintained her innocence regarding the murder of her husband.

On the last day of February 1608, she received the news that her execution would take place that day. A preacher was sent to help prepare her and her soul and attempted to get her to confess. She denied her involvement once more but showed repentance for her life's sins. When brought to St. George's Field for execution, she wore a canvas kirtle over her own smock and a white sheet over that. Women on each side led her by the hand towards the stake. After being tied to it, the preacher asked once more if she would like to confess, she was steadfast in her answer of not guilty. Reeds were placed around her and lit. After a few short minutes, she was dead.

Women who earned their money as prostitutes or brothel keepers were looked down on by society as shameful sinners. Regardless of their manners, they were automatically assumed to be of loose morals. Margaret might have been ill-tempered, but her past and chosen profession may have coloured the testimonies and opinions about her. The supposed facts, even from Margaret herself, paint her as a less than cordial woman. The evidence was damning, and she had a reputation for being ruthless, of loose morals and unruly, but her consistent denial of her guilt in the murder raises questions. Was she actually guilty? Did she hire someone else to murder Anthony, so she could claim innocence? Did her lover commit the crime? We don't have answers because crime solving methods were not as definitive as they are today, especially in terms of forensic evidence. That would not become crucial for solving murders for another few centuries.

SARAH ELSTON (C.1632–1678)

The tale of our second seventeenth century lady begins in Southwark in an area called Fishmongers Alley. Here, Sarah Elston lived with her husband Thomas, a hatter. In their forties, they had been married a long time. Apparently, their marriage was rather unhappy, filled with fighting and disagreements. Some say that Thomas was abusive, always angry, proved disagreeable company, and committed other actions against Sarah that were deemed too unpleasant to discuss within the pamphlet about the incident. Some of Sarah's neighbours and friends mentioned they had heard her threaten his life many times, and in the pamphlet, Sarah was described as an unhappy woman; whether that was from informants or personal observation is hard to know. It sounds like they were not content as a married couple.

This unhappiness unfortunately came to a head on 25 September 1677 when they were having another heated argument. This argument may have begun during their visit to the local alehouse where they had a few drinks and continued once they got home. One record curiously describes Sarah as feeling lightheaded, even though she hadn't had much to drink. The argument may have been about Thomas withholding some of Sarah's goods and threatening to give them to another. Sarah said she was going to look for them, and according to some neighbours, Thomas hit her with a shovel; another record simply states that he beat her. One story says she sat up and attempted to give him time to calm down by taking a pair of scissors outside to do some work with them, something she often did. When he approached her, she held the scissors up to protect herself, and he walked into them. Another version of the story suggests that she grabbed the scissors to defend herself, and before either of them could realise what was happening, the scissors were plunged into the left side of his chest. He died quickly, indicating the scissors more than likely punctured his heart. While one record concludes at this point, the second report states that, upon witnessing the tragic outcome, she tried to administer some medicine. However, realising that he was dying, she fled to Whitechapel and informed locals of the unfortunate incident.

Sarah was indicted and had to wait many months for her sentence. During her trial, she pleaded guilty; not once throughout the entire process, did she deny what she had done. She did, however, continuously, and passionately exclaim she never meant to kill him, only to harm him to get back at him for beating her. If this is true, then the second theory about how the murder played out, where she grabbed the scissors in defence, sounds more accurate. She was convicted at the Surrey Assizes for petty treason, and on Tuesday, 26 March 1688, was sentenced to be burned at the stake. The date was set for Wednesday, 24 April 1688.

In the weeks that led up to her execution, it was written that Sarah often begged for more time to prepare herself and her soul. She never really went to church before the incident and did not have much knowledge of the Bible or church teachings. While awaiting her fate, however, it was written that she became incredibly penitent and receptive to what she was being taught by the ministers and other Christians who came to see her. She spent most of her time in prayer, with her ministers, or reading, and often lamented with tears how she had previously behaved. She admitted that she frequently acted with rage, snide comments, and teasing, which she believed more than likely provoked her husband to be more violent than he otherwise would have been. The author of the pamphlet about her case said she seemed willing to die and even stated that since she had killed her husband, she had lost the will to live; that she was even looking forward to death after hearing teachings about the wonders of Heaven.

On Wednesday, 24 April 1688, at Kennington Common near Southwark, Sarah was brought to the stake on a hurdle wearing all white with many attendants around her. She had quiet prayer with herself and once more reiterated vehemently that she never meant to kill Thomas, that she loved him and that she felt such horror, confusion, and surprise after he had been stabbed, she was not even sure if he ran into the scissors as she was defending herself, or if she actually stabbed him. Regardless, she said that even after everything he did, she would give her life to save him. She used her situation to leave a message for her fellow women and wives; that they should use her as an example and be warned what might happen if you don't live harmoniously with your husbands. She told the women to live peacefully with them if possible or at least not to aggravate or provoke them into acting violently, as she wrongly did.

The general message of living harmoniously with your spouse was positive, but the rest of her speech was very misogynistic, expecting wives not to upset their angry husbands. Sarah herself was not misogynistic, but this was the way everyone in early modern British society was brought up to view the relationship between wives and husbands and the accepted behaviours of men and women. The mention of the words 'if possible' illustrates the standards of seventeenth century society. Husbands were known to be violent and rough with their wives, making it possible that the only way for women to live peacefully was to stay out of their husband's way. This reality placed many early modern women into precarious positions, where they had to lead a silent life, bending to their husband's constant will and avoiding aggravation. If these women talked back, they risked being beaten, injured, or even killed. If they retaliated and defended themselves, their husbands might end up dead, and they would be burned for it. Pleasant options were scarce.

Sarah concluded her speech by reiterating the societal beliefs and hierarchies of the sixteenth century, emphasising that women needed to remember that their husbands were their heads, whom they had to obey, regardless of their behaviour. She then prayed for God's pardon for her misgivings and asked the spectators to pray for her, seeking strength and faith to endure the execution and guide her soul into heaven. As these final words were spoken, the fire was lit beneath her. As it crawled its way up, she emitted three high pitched shrieks and soon succumbed.

The referenced pamphlet, titled *A Warning for Bad Wives*, was written on the day of Sarah's execution. It explains the events leading up to that day, although some opinions, especially about the defendant, may carry bias, given the pamphlet was written by a man. Earlier, female killers defied the gender standards of early modern and medieval life, provoking shock and spectacle. The author's description of women as the weaker sex and referring to Sarah as a 'poor creature,' vividly illustrates the prevailing sentiments towards women during the seventeenth century.

Another record, titled '*The Last Speech and Confession of Sarah Elestone…*' and written in 1678, provides an interesting contrast to the other accounts about Sarah, exemplifying how some narratives might be biased, exaggerated, or only partially true. '*The Last Speech and Confession of Sarah Elestone…*' paints a much darker picture of Sarah before the murder took place as well as a different instance of murder all together! The author begins by reminding readers that people who murder those they are bound to obey, cherish and honour (wives to husbands) are breaking the laws of nature and deserve God's punishment. Describing Sarah as a wretched woman, the author asserts that she met with a deserved punishment.

In this version, the couple lived on a different street than the other records suggest, and their relationship was amicable until Sarah started associating with inappropriate women and developed a fondness for drinking. She began swearing and behaved unpleasantly, prompting

Thomas' friends to plead with him to help her break her habits. Claiming he could not stop her due to her obstinacy, Thomas hoped God would intervene. To curb her behaviour, he restricted her money. She borrowed money instead, which in turn accumulated debt for him. Thomas then restricted her from acquiring more loans, leading her to retaliate by selling their goods until they had almost nothing. (This might explain why he withheld her goods.) Resorting to physical violence, Thomas beat her, and their fights became frequent, often requiring intervention to separate them. This took a toll on both, with Thomas expressing regret over marrying her, and Sarah frequently threatening to kill him.

The author then proceeds to describe the murder, which differs significantly from the accounts found in other records. According to this retelling, Sarah had returned from drinking excessively with her friends and demanded money from Thomas, threatening to be the death of him if he didn't comply. In response, he took her and threw her down the stairs, locking the door. After some time, he went downstairs for a drink, and she was waiting at the bottom for him, with a pair of shears. She forcefully stabbed him, causing him to die quickly. Sarah fled, and soon Thomas was discovered, leading to the raising of the hue and cry against her. She was found and imprisoned until her trial. The weeks before her execution in this version are fairly similar, except it mentions that she initially showed indifference to the ministers' teachings and only began to listen and learn a few days before her trial. The account then mirrors the original story of her praying to save her soul, and reciting prayers as she was led to the scaffold until the flames began.

The original tale of the murderous event appears more accurate, comprising two different records that recount stories with similar tones and results. This isn't to say there aren't bits and pieces of the different retelling that might have some validity. The first story mentions Sarah's drinking but doesn't portray her as a drunk or a disturbance. Both original records convey the idea that she was defending herself, and that he walked into the scissors, or that she only meant to wound him, not kill him. They also describe Sarah as a much more passive person than the final record suggests. It is challenging to determine exactly what happened and what led to Sarah stabbing Thomas. Did she plan it and act innocently? Was she angry but only meant to wound him in retaliation for hurting her? Was she merely defending herself? We might never know the truth, but if she did not intend to kill him, or was simply defending herself, Sarah becomes another female victim of the harsh, gender-biased criminal justice system of the early modern period.

Mary Aubry (–1688)

The case of Mary Aubry or Hobry, as it is written in some records, is undoubtedly one of intrigue. According to one piece of literature, the murder had consumed and tainted the people more than any other tale of murder before. One can't help but feel sympathy for Mrs Aubry and the situation she was put in and had to endure. Mary was born in France, and when she came to England, married a man named Denis Aubry. A midwife by trade, they lived in the parish of St. Martins in the Fields in Middlesex. She had at least two children from a previous relationship, a son, and a daughter.

Mary and Denis had been married for about four years, but the marriage was far from happy. Denis was extremely abusive towards Mary, frequently yelling at and beating her. Mary often contemplated killing him to end her suffering. She attributed this desire to Denis's denial of their marriage despite the church ceremony, and his blatant expression of disappointment with her and their life together. Denis coerced her into engaging in activities she found uncomfortable, describing them as 'villanies contrary to nature'. When Mary refused, Denis became upset and abusive, instilling fear in her every day. Mary unwisely confided her desire and even a plan to a few neighbours. In a poem about Mary's life, Denis' treatment is labelled 'inhumane', depicting her escape to a private room in the house to evade his abuses.

Denis travelled frequently to France, and each return brought Mary's pleas for better treatment, to which Denis promised change, and at one point he even begged her to be with him, swearing that he would be kind and faithful. She believed him every time, and every time he quickly reverted to his abusive ways. Despite Mary's pleas for a separation, Denis refused, threatening to be her ruin.

On his final return from France, Mary warned him that it was his last chance to treat her properly, or she might retaliate. Denis promised to change. When he came home a few weeks later, he said he would treat her right if she could provide him with new clothes. She told him that she barely had any money for her own debts and didn't have enough to buy him clothes. Furious, Denis threatened Mary and the abuse continued. Frustrated and desperate, Mary confided in female friends and her cousins, Denis and John Favet, who also disliked Denis, discussing. ways she could be rid of him.

The tumultuous and violent relationship continued, with Mary admitting to contemplating killing Denis on several occasions. Mary even admitted to him that there were nights where she planned to kill him but resisted. His actions and indifference slowly wore away her resolve until the 27 of January 1688. Denis, heavily intoxicated, returned home and violently attacked Mary, punching and squeezing the air out of her lungs. In pain and fearing for her life, Mary, breathless and bleeding, screamed for her landlady. When she failed to appear, Mary told him she was going to the neighbours to tell them what was happening to her. He then threw her roughly back onto the bed and bit her. Shortly thereafter, he fell asleep, passing out from the liquor.

Mary, filled with rage and pain, and worried this would only end with his death or hers, took his garter, a cord made from hemp, made a noose, and threw it around the passed-out Denis' neck. She proceeded to choke, strangle, and eventually, after fifteen minutes, kill him. Immediately, she regretted what she had done and hoped he was not dead. She tried to revive him with brandy, but to no avail. After this horrible event, Mary was unsure of what to do. She was in a state of disarray and remained so for a few days until, on the following Monday, after people inquired about her husband's whereabouts, she sought her two cousins' assistance.

They refused involvement in the actual murder; they eventually assisted her in the aftermath when she asked them to inform people, they had sent him away to the Indies. She then fetched her son John Desermeau, who was only thirteen years old, from his place of employment as a servant and brought him to her lodgings to show him what had occurred. The boy was faint at the sight but swore he would remain silent about what had happened. Mary couldn't move Denis, and John refused to help, so Mary ended up cutting off his arms, legs, thighs, and head, leaving his torso intact. She hoped this would make it more difficult to identify him. With John by her side providing company and assistance as a lookout, she disposed of the head, arms, legs, and thighs into nearby public toilets and placed his torso in Parker's Lane.

Mary returned to the lodgings of some of her female friends, and when asked if she had dispensed with her husband, she replied, 'Yes'. Mary explained falsely that she and her cousins had devised and executed a plan, getting Denis very drunk and paying for him to board a ship to the Indies. They even claimed to have bribed one of the shipmen to keep an eye on him, joking that he would bring back diamonds. After the murder, Mary also went to another friend's house for dinner. Confiding in her friend about the crime, Mary was met with yelling and a stern command to leave. Despite crying that she didn't know what to do and felt lost, her friend still insisted she leave. Later, she falsely informed the same friend that she buried him. It's challenging to ascertain the genuineness of Mary's distress while she was lying about the details of the murder. Considering her personality and behaviour, it appears likely she was indeed anxious and fearful, with good reason. It's also puzzling why she would tell the truth to her friend about murdering him but lie about cutting him into pieces. Perhaps she wanted to protect herself from the even harsher judgement, but the exact motive remains uncertain. The following day, Mary's daughter visited and asked about Denis, having heard he had left for the Indies. Mary initially avoided the question but eventually disclosed everything to her daughter. The daughter promised to remain quiet about the murder and assured her mother she would never turn her in.

When the body was discovered, an inquest was initiated. Mary was sought out and found residing in a house in Phoenix Alley after some neighbours had enquired among themselves if the body might be Denis', as they had heard Mary threaten him before. One man confirmed that, as he pestered her in the streets, Mary had hinted at the deed, prompting them to find a constable who located her. She was staying with a patient who was almost ready to go into labour but it is also possible she was seeking a safe place away from her house. When questioned about her husband's whereabouts, Mary quickly confessed that the body was his and requested the constable and his assistants not make a fuss; she would obediently go with them.

She was indicted for the murder, and because English was not her first language, she had to have a translator. Mary's son and daughter mentioned to the court that they had heard Denis say many times he would be the death of Mary, and that Mary herself had confirmed this. Her daughter also disclosed to the court that Mary had never mentioned killing her stepfather. During her trial when she was asked how she wanted to plead, Mary admitted she was guilty. The court reminded her that if she pleaded guilty there would be serious consequences. They must have felt slightly sympathetic towards her situation as the court offered Mary a fair trial if she desired one, but she rejected the offer and again pleaded guilty.

Her cousins Denis and John were indicted as accessories before and after the fact, but the evidence against them was insubstantial. Upon the court's request, they found guarantors to vouch for their good behaviour and were let off. Mary's son John was indicted for accessory after the fact but was fortunately acquitted. Mary was sentenced to be burned until dead; the usual punishment for petty treason in seventeenth-century England. This tale of a poor abused woman who finally reached her breaking point, and realised that her husband had to die or she definitely would, is deeply upsetting. The fact that Mary was burned at the stake for it again sheds a glaring light on the profound inequalities of the early modern criminal justice system and what was deemed acceptable behaviour within a marriage, to the detriment of women.

There is a detailed and charming ballad written about Mary and her situation titled *A Warning Piece To All Married Men And Women*. From the title it speaks to men and women, almost as equals. It isn't 'A Warning for Men' about rogue wives or something to that effect, which is more frequently seen in broadsides and pamphlets about female crime. The poem's tone also favours Mary's situation, clearly painting a picture of the dreadful circumstances she faced and illustrating her struggle about what to do to help herself. There is a feeling of sympathy portrayed, however, it still calls her evil and warns women not to behave as she did. This is very different from a pamphlet written about Mary, as you can tell from the title: *A hellish murder committed by a French midwife on the body of her husband*. It already sounds more biased against Mary and sympathetic to the deceased. It barely mentions the abuse Mary sustained and rarely refers to her by name, and instead calls her 'the midwife.' The author finishes the pamphlet by referring to Mary as 'the Miserable Creature herself,' clearly repulsed by the crime and bold enough to show it. The author shows no true compassion towards Mary, whom he calls an 'Unhappy Wretch,' and illustrates, unfortunately, many early modern men's thoughts towards women who did not obey, submit to, and suffer under their husbands.

The verses from the ballad written about Mary reflect that the author understood what she went through and didn't want to hide it from the public.

ALL you that Married Men and Women be
Give Ear unto this woful Tragedy,
That now befell a *French man* and his *Wife,*
Who liv'd together in continual Strife;
One *Denis Hobry* about Four years since
Took to his Wife a Woman Born a *French,*
Whom he Abus'd at such inhumane rate,
That she a thousand times wish'd him ill Fate,
And thought within herself to end the Strife,
If she were forc'd, to take away his Life:
The cause that mov'd him to those Tyrannies,
Was her aversion to his Villanies …

What shall I do, (said she) must I, now Die?
Or Murther him that makes me, thus to Cry?
With that she started full of Wrath and Evil,
Being thereto Spurr'd by th' instinct of the Devil,
And pull'd his Garter off his Leg in hast,
Being a Pack-thread, which she thought no wast,
And doubling it about his Neck she drew
The ends so fest, that she him quickly Slew;

But soon Repenting, hop'd he was Alive,
And thought that Brandy would him then Revive:
When all was done, her labour was in Vain,
For Life once lost, can ne'er be had again …

The Corps being found, and all the truth well known.
She did her self no word of it disown;
But did confess that no untruth is here,
For God will not let Murtherers go clear.
She is now Burn'd, and beggs of all Mankind
And Women too, Wisdom by her to find.[1]

MARGARET MARTELL (–1697)

The final seventeenth century woman featured in this chapter is Ms. Margaret Martell. Margaret was a French woman living near St. Martins in the Fields. She was the acquaintance of Mrs Elizabeth Pullen, wife of Paul Pullen, Esquire. They lived at the Pine Apple in Suffolk Street and were relatively wealthy, much more so than Margaret. There is little information about Margaret's life before the late 1600s, but she was Roman Catholic and none of the records mention children or a husband. Margaret's life took a grim turn when on 29 June 1697 she robbed and killed her acquaintance Mrs Pullen.

Margaret arrived at the Pullens' house around dinner time and Mrs Pullen's maid answered the door. The maid allowed her in and she led Margaret to her mistress. Shortly thereafter, the maid brought in meat for them to eat, and Mrs Pullen sent her away to get some drinks.

---

[1] A Warning-piece to all married men and women being the full confession of Mary Hobry the French midwife, who murdered her husband on the 27th of January 1687/8 (as also the cause thereof), for which she receiv'd the sentence to be burnt alive, and on Friday the second day of March between the hours of ten and eleven in the morning she was drawn upon a sledge to Leicester-fields, where she was burnt to ashes, London, George Croom, 1688, in Early English Books Online [online database], (accessed May 21 2023).

When they were sitting Mrs Pullen asked Margaret why she was wearing slippers, Margaret replied that she had scalded her foot, and it was too painful to wear proper shoes. For her plan to work, Margaret needed to get rid of the maid. She asked the maid if she could deliver a letter that Mrs Pullen needed posting. The maid agreed and was away for a while, giving Margaret time to commit her heinous act. When the maid had left, Margaret attacked Mrs Pullen, slitting her throat with a knife, causing instant death for the poor mistress. She then hid her in a closet, closed the shutters and locked both the closet and the room. She may also have used some of the alone time to steal from them.

When the maid returned, Mrs Pullen was nowhere to be seen. Margaret informed her that Mrs Pullen had gone out and would return around seven o'clock. She also mentioned that before leaving, Mrs Pullen had locked one of her rooms and taken the key with her. The maid proceeded upstairs to continue her work, with Margaret following her, instructing her to pause her work and participate in a trick. She claimed that by sitting on the chair, holding the key, and closing her eyes, the maid could envision the person she loved. This seems like a ploy by Margaret to create an opportunity to pilfer some of the Pullens' belongings. After completing the trick, they returned downstairs and Margaret sent the maid out twice for drinks, again creating an opportunity and time to steal more items. Margaret then departed, saying she was going to go buy some shoes. When Mr Pullen, the maid's master, arrived home, she informed him that her mistress was out and had locked one of the rooms before leaving. Mr Pullen, unsuspecting of anything nefarious, nodded and retired to bed around ten at night.

Around the same time, Margaret returned, raising questions about her motives for revisiting the scene of the crime. Perhaps she sought to divert blame away from herself? She asked the maid to light a candle and mentioned needing buckles from Mrs Pullen to trim her stays.

(Stays are a type of corset made by two pieces of lace coming together supported with whalebone). The maid inquired about some blood on Margaret's petticoat, but Margaret ignored her. After a while, Margaret declared her intention to leave, saying it seemed doubtful Mrs Pullen would return that night and promised to come by in the morning.

Around midnight, the maid became worried, so she told her master that Mrs Pullen had yet to return home. She went to look for her nearby but could not find her. One of the neighbours asked the maid if she could open the locked room. The maid replied yes, and both went in to investigate. When they entered, the shutters were closed, making the room very dark. They opened them and noticed a lot of blood on the floor, accompanied by the footprint of a slipper. They immediately called for a constable and went to the closet. Upon opening it, they found Mrs Pullen with her throat cut six inches. The maid said that Margaret was the only person who had been to the house. Not long after, Margaret was found and arrested on Rupert Street, and when the authorities searched the trunk in her house, they found most of the stolen belongings and a bloody slipper.

Margaret stole: a silver tankard, two silver candlesticks, four gold rings, a silver porringer, three spoons, two gold watches, six pairs of silver buckles, and other items. When she was being apprehended, Margaret told the authorities that Mrs Pullen had gifted them, but during her trial, changed her story twice! She first mentioned that two men arrived at the house, and while one went to Mrs Pullen and killed her, the other held a pistol to her and said she was forbidden to mention anything until the next day and proceeded to give her the stolen items. She then said that Mrs Pullen had given her the items to reduce her debt, that her dirty slippers were bloodied at the market, and her blood-spattered petticoat was blood from meat she was preparing. She insisted she was innocent of the murder. The lengthy trial consisted of a half French, half English jury who after four hours of deliberation decided she was guilty of wilful murder and of robbing the Pullens. She was sentenced to hang. Margaret, now facing a desperate situation, pleaded her belly, and a jury of matrons was summoned to examine her. They did not find her pregnant, so her sentence was confirmed.

While she waited for her execution, she spoke to someone who spoke French and knew about the crime, while the Ordinary of Newgate took notes. She told the Frenchman she did not care for his advice as he talked with her about the crime, and both tried to extract a confession. It is more than likely that both men, and the church she was in, were Protestant, as that was the primary religion in England during the reign of King William III. They may have been promoting Protestant ideals and frowning upon her Roman Catholicism. She assured them she had been a Roman Catholic since birth and would die that way.

Initially, she acknowledged being a great sinner but refused to confess to the murder. However, she eventually admitted to killing Mrs Pullen and expressed remorse. She initially told the Ordinary that she would listen to their teachings to prepare her soul. However, the Ordinary writes that she later decided to maintain her Roman Catholic views and principles. Margaret's speech at her execution was filled with prayers and pleas to God for the salvation of her soul. She acknowledged deserving the punishment she received and hoped for redemption and mercy. She was hanged on 16 July 1697 at Tyburn. The case, involving the killing of a wealthier individual for their belongings and money, was not quite as prevalent as murders involving husbands or children/infants when it came to female perpetrators. Nevertheless, it did occur, as exemplified by the Wilson and Pullen murders.

During the seventeenth century, women who committed murder increasingly became subjects of spectacle and arguably faced far harsher treatment when challenging gender norms. The early modern period witnessed the solidification and heightened valuation of gender norms. Consequently, when a woman deviated from societal expectations, it instilled fear, confusion, and curiosity, and led to severe prosecution as a deterrent for others. With the popularisation of murder pamphlets and broadsides, the wider population of all classes of society, knew of criminals and crimes, and were captivated by the excitement and dramatization the crime literature brought. These publications presented a multitude of opinions that no doubt shaped the population's ideas, but also likely influenced public perception and prompted contemplation on the real reasons behind such atrocious incidents.

One of the most significant events of the seventeenth century that disadvantaged women endured was the witch craze. Hundreds were burned at the stake for suspected malicious actions, though it was more likely to be that women simply deviated from the societal norms, and expectations demanded of females. Infanticide was common due to societal ideas and repercussions of illegitimate children, and women were prosecuted harshly, especially with the introduction of the 1624 statute. Magistrates, however, were slowly beginning to show leniency towards women indicted for infanticide, but this would only become noticeable the following century. In some cases, it might be understandable why these women resorted to murder. Women like Mary Aubry were abused, attacked, and almost killed themselves, so they put an end to the brutality. Of course, some women were brutally malicious, while with others it's hard to tell whether they were victims or not. The eighteenth century holds more innovation, dastardly crimes, and intriguing women, as Britain enjoys the Enlightenment and moves closer to modernity.

Chapter Four

THE EIGHTEENTH CENTURY

The eighteenth century ushered in a new era of exploration, discovery, learning, questioning, knowledge, and beliefs. The Enlightenment transformed British society and culture by reshaping the way people thought about themselves and life. There were advancements in the ideas of individualism, rationalism, scientific method and thought, industrialism, and commercialism. This progression had ramifications within the criminal justice system too, including growth in crime related science and medicine and changes in punishment. There was also a surge in print culture regarding crime, especially because the British population was slowly reaching mass literacy; by 1720, fifty-six per cent of women in London could sign their name. The creation of Britain in 1707 with the joining of England, Scotland, and Wales was one of the most significant political developments of the eighteenth century. The middle class began to grow and form a separate and dominant section of society. Due to these many progressions over the century, there were many changes regarding the attitudes towards women and crime.

From the end of the seventeenth century to around 1735, London and other metropolitan areas saw an increase in female felonies. This is most clearly seen in respect to theft prosecutions, but is still present when viewing indictments for murder at the Old Bailey. Between 1690 and 1735, there were thirty-eight prosecutions for murder by women, who were found guilty and sentenced to death. This is slightly higher than the previous years, which from 1674-90 had thirty-four prosecutions. More startling is how much higher the figure is than the following twenty-five years. From 1735-1760, there were only seventeen women prosecuted under the same categories! Less than half of the previous decades.

As was discussed in the previous chapter, between the years 1674-1713, there were fluctuations in patterns of female homicide corresponding to the increase in female felonies overall. Women, though not as frequently as men, were occasionally involved in brawls; some of which ended in fatal blows. The perpetrators were often indicted and hanged for these incidents. Most cases involving brawls would be deemed as manslaughter, but some, such as the case of Elizabeth Armstrong, were decided otherwise. In 1735, Elizabeth fought in the streets with shop owner Patrick Darling, who had made fun of her cousin Mary Price's legs. Patrick later died from his injuries, and Elizabeth was convicted of murder, and hanged. Elizabeth and Mary claimed Patrick was making sexual advances towards Mary. Unfortunately, those types of allegations in early modern murder trials did not carry much weight, and women could be hanged for supposedly defending themselves or others, like Elizabeth was. There was sympathy expressed for abused women on trial, but this did not usually sway the magistrates or jury.

Another shocking discovery is that women accounted for forty per cent of the individuals prosecuted at the Old Bailey for all felonies from 1690-1735. When analyzing the previous decades, women only accounted for twenty-seven per cent. This includes more than murder charges but still illustrates a sharp increase in female crime, or at least its prosecution. It was more than likely due to a combination of both factors, an idea proposed by Robert B. Shoemaker in his article *Print and the Female Voice: Representations of Women's Crime in London, 1690–1735* (2010). Even with the spike in female offences, women still didn't commit homicide at the same level as men. Records from the 1700s reflect female offenders as fifteen per cent of the male total. When women committed murder, around fifty-eight per cent of their victims were men, which illustrates the continued prominence of husbands being the victims of their wives' ferocity. Eighteenth century women used all sorts of methods for murder and were not limited to any one weapon. Cases from Surrey during the period include women who wielded knives, witchcraft, a club, poker, iron spit, pewter pot, pistol, throwing a man out of a window and beating by punching and kicking. These were just a few ways in which early modern women committed murder in one town. They also slit throats, drowned people, strangled, tortured, poisoned, and starved their victims. There is no way these women could be pigeonholed by saying their methods were gender specific.

As discussed in the chapters for previous centuries, similar to England, women in rural Scotland did not commit crimes as frequently as women in cities. This theme continued into the eighteenth century and is thought to be because in rural areas, women did not have the same opportunities or freedom as women in cities. The gender gap, though still present, was lesser in populous cities allowing for women to participate in male centred activities more easily, which were more likely to result in mischief. Metropolitan areas throughout Britain have been described as having an equalising effect with regards to gender and crime.

The homicide rate in Enlightenment Scotland was dominated by male perpetrators, but women still participated in especially devious and brutal murders throughout the country. Anne-Marie Kilday estimates that between 1750 and 1815 women were responsible for approximately twenty-one per cent of the homicide convictions in southwest Scotland. During the Enlightenment, Scottish murderesses tended to kill within the family, as this is where they spent the majority of their time. Records depict that eighty-eight per cent of women charged with murder, killed someone within their family, and more often than not it was their husbands. Interestingly, contrary to what happened in Wales, Scottish murderesses often worked alone rather than in groups or duos. To understand the scope of Scottish murderesses during this period, between 1740 and 1834, seventy-nine women were successfully convicted, of which thirty-six were for murder. Twenty-three of these convictions were for murdering their own children, five of the victims were strangers, four were husbands and four were other family members.

Poison was often the murder weapon of choice for Scottish women during the early modern period, similarly so for English murderesses, though not favoured in Wales. Poison was easy to conceal both in administration and in postmortems, and therefore was used frequently. Poison was greatly feared due to these factors as well as the idea of a secretive and devious woman, so cases of poisoning were usually dealt with seriously. Until the late nineteenth century, it was difficult to determine the use of poison for murder, as the medical expertise needed remained undeveloped. In consequence, there were more than likely several deaths by poison that went unnoticed because in order to gain a conviction, the use of poison had to be proven. It is not fair, however, to say that women favoured poison because it required less physical strength. Women may have enjoyed the stealth and accessibility of the process, but women had no problem using physical strength to murder. Strangulation was another popular *modus operandi,* as Kilday puts it, for Scottish women, as well as other violent acts such as drowning, beating, slashing with razors, stabbing, bashing heads in with pokers and stoning. So, despite what some historians have said about women taking a less violent approach to homicide, they didn't hesitate from using violent methods to commit their dastardly deeds.

In eighteenth-century Wales, according to Katherine D. Watson in her paper *Women, violent crime and criminal justice in Georgian Wales* (2013), women who committed murder were often treated with leniency instead of severe punishments, and Wales had its own unique approach to the criminal justice system. Women in the Welsh courts were frequently shown leniency, but if a woman committed a deliberate murder, the likelihood of execution was probable, as that act was far beyond the expected behaviour of an eighteenth-century woman. For women who committed infanticide, however, there was a greater chance of receiving a pardon, as that was considered less threatening to society.

The number of Welsh women who committed murder throughout the Enlightenment was smaller than both England and Scotland, but what was especially miniscule, was the number of actual convictions. The Court of Great Sessions in Wales records sixty-four women being accused of murder between 1730 and 1830. This number is an approximation and does not account for unreported crime or infanticide cases. Out of these women, however, only two were sentenced to death, and two imprisoned; three were considered insane, and thirty-four were found to be not guilty; it does not say what happened to the rest. Records show that when violence was committed, it often took place within the home or in partnership with men or other women. The homicide cases that involved adult victims often included beating or hitting them with an object. The use of strangulation and suffocation was habitually used against children. For these few Welsh homicides, husbands and children constituted the majority of the victims.

By the end of the eighteenth century, parliamentary frustration began with regards to the Court of Great Sessions, which brought English law to the Welsh courts but was still a separate identity than the English assizes. The English members of the court, which included the majority, wanted to escalate and bring Wales into the English assize court system. This, to Welsh disappointment, eventually happened in the early 1800s.

The 1700s brought an ever-increasing surge of print culture coupled with a steadfast public fascination with crime related stories. Rather gruesomely, crime tales and public executions were considered entertainment for people. During the eighteenth century, coffee houses, newspapers and tea houses became intrinsic to society and culture and would have helped to popularise and spread printed materials and subsequent gossip regarding their contents. Particularly interesting cases from the Old Bailey and assize courts from around Britain would be featured in all sorts of printed media, even bringing a type of celebrity to some of the defendants whom the public found cunning and admirable. The ones who were considered brutal and wicked were still intriguing but garnered a more infamous reputation. There were even some female convicts who received the opportunity to write their own crime story and get it published, so the public heard the story directly from their side. Sarah Malcolm in 1733 was the first woman to have this opportunity.

Not many women received an opportunity like this however, and instead had their tales written with an extra flair of the dramatic. Broadsides, murder pamphlets, and ballads were often written in a way that stripped the women of their individuality, personal circumstances, and feelings, as Vanessa McMahon said in her book *Murder in Shakespeare's England* (2004). Instead, they made the crime all about female violence and sexuality. Women were often depicted as victims who were not in control of themselves, weak, and at the mercy of men or mental illness. These actions led to many women being described unfairly or incorrectly, especially as most writers were middle to upper class males. These printed materials reflected contemporary feelings regarding women and crime. All forms of this 'media' were immensely popular in Britain throughout the century, and murderesses received particular attention, receiving twice as much coverage as male criminals in the late eighteenth century.

Over the course of the 1700s, the level of detail in which cases were recorded, especially felonies like murder, increased immensely. The Old Bailey frequently documented murder cases with full trial transcripts and Ordinaries accounts providing personal and witnessed details of the convict, their crime, and the proceedings. Both of these would have provided a fairly accurate account of the offence and trial, but the Ordinary's account would have some bias from the Ordinary's own opinions. For cases outside of London and Middlesex, court documents were still copied in great detail and for cases all over Britain, printed resources like broadsides covered the key elements of the event and sometimes a brief background of the crime and convict. The public only had access to the biased materials, which, in turn, impacted their thoughts and perceptions on the case and the convict.

Infanticide during the eighteenth century was still the most common type of homicide committed by female offenders. That being said, the rate at which these murders occurred was relatively low. There were only sixty-one trials for infanticide at the Old Bailey between 1730 and 1774. This totals to less than two per year, and these numbers were on the high side for England, with most counties having 0.5-1.5 per year. When women committed this desperate and dreadful crime, they were subverting the revered and expected role of women as loving and caring mothers. This unexpected deviance resulted in shock, fear, and disgust throughout society, though opinions were slowly starting to evolve.

There was a growing sense of mercy within the court systems of England and Wales when dealing with infanticidal mothers. This shift possibly stemmed from the realisation of the circumstances that many of these women were facing, and the unwillingness to harshly prosecute desperate mothers. A new thought process emerged regarding a woman's guilt, questioning not *if* she concealed it but if she *intended* to conceal it, combined with the already established evidence of innocence, including preparing for the baby, helpful witnesses, and medical opinions. Medical investigators searched for evidence of violence on the child and if none could be found, it would have been evidence towards an acquittal. These opinions continued and developed in the nineteenth century, although punishments were still carried out, as it was still regarded as a horrible and despicable act that all European societies wanted to end. There was also an increase in the mentioning and involvement of the father of the said infant during trials, though they would not have to suffer any physical consequences unless they had a hand in harming the child. In 1702, the father of Christian Russell's baby had told her he would marry her after she became pregnant. Later, he withdrew his promise and left her, and Christian ended up killing the infant. Christian was hanged for her crime while her baby's father was simply chastised about his actions and the ramifications for his soul.

The plea of insanity or the determination of insanity was used on occasion to acquit a woman of responsibility for the murder of her child. This status or plea of mental instability was used in other murder cases too and gained traction in the following centuries as the main cause of criminality. If a woman claimed to be insane, it was unlikely she would be found insane. Insanity cases that succeeded were more often than not the ones where, after hearing evidence, the court deemed them mad, unstable, distracted, or insane. The ideas of post-partum depression and depression-related mental struggles (though they weren't called depression) were known to people and sometimes recognized by the court as possible contributors to infanticide cases. The understanding of said health issues in relation to crime, especially women's crime, continued to evolve over the next two centuries. If a woman was considered insane by the courts, she would be acquitted since there was no established procedure for determining the defendant's sanity at that time.

Similar to Ann Philmore in the 1600s, in the 1700s there were cases where women who should have been considered mentally unfit and treated accordingly, were despised and condemned as poor, evil, and lacking proper religion. This occurred with Ann Walson in 1752. The court should have recognized her mental struggles brought on by the past emotional trauma of her husband dying and all that followed, were clearly the cause of her poor decision making. She was destitute because of her husband's death, and the parish was unwilling to help her with her child unless she gave up all her belongings too. No wonder she wasn't thinking clearly. Even the Ordinary mentioned that she was behaving madly, but the court still regarded her in proper mental health. Her claim, however, that the child died of convulsion was accepted, and she carried on, with the guilt of that act weighing on her so heavily, she tried to commit suicide twice, and eventually killed her employer's fourteen-year-old daughter so she would be sent to the noose. This woman was obviously suffering, and because no one realised how much, she resorted to extreme measures and went to distressing lengths to first survive and then later to seek penance for her first deed. If poor relief and mental health had been higher priorities, Ann and her victims might have been rescued.

Throughout Britain, female servants were often the unfortunate recipients of illegitimate pregnancies and subsequently faced with unimaginable choices, consequences and the possibility of shame, homelessness, and poverty because of their situation. This can be slightly contradicted concerning Wales, when records of depositions at trials indicate that some employers were relatively understanding and willing to help their employees who had fallen pregnant. However, this evidence does not lessen the challenges faced by many women in England and Scotland who were not as fortunate. This correlates with the data showing most women accused of infanticide were unmarried, and likely feared the thought of bearing an illegitimate child. Like the seventeenth century, this does not mean that married women did not commit infanticide, only that it was less frequent, and easier to conceal and carry out within a private household. Additionally, if a married woman was found guilty of infanticide, she would have been presumed insane until the courts could prove otherwise.

England and Wales seemed to be relatively similar in their treatment of murderous mothers, with their general acceptance of necessary punishment but an increasing sense of mercy. This differs from Scottish treatment, which at this point in time was more severe. Suspected infanticidal mothers were treated differently in Scotland due to the increasing condemnation of illegitimacy, and desire to control society's sexual morality. This was a sentiment growing throughout Europe. In Scotland, it wasn't just the desire to control immorality that caused the illegitimacy but also the economic strain illegitimate children placed on the state. Historians have postulated that it was the economic burden, rather than the distaste of illegitimacy and the subsequent killing, that spurred the development of a new Act titled 'Act Anent Murthering of Children', resulting in a severe capital conviction for any woman accused of infanticide, whether there was evidence of murder or not.

To be accused of infanticide, courts would examine if a woman had concealed her pregnancy, did not call for help during her delivery, and then ended up with a missing or dead infant. This was the basis for indictments and trials from 1750–1815; after 1752, women convicted of infanticide were treated like vicious homicide perpetrators, receiving punishments like public dissection and anatomisation. As Anne-Marie Kilday accurately summarises in her book *'Women and Violent Crime in Enlightenment Scotland'*, the decision to act so harshly reflected the thoughts that officials had about violent women and mothers. The unforgiving treatments and opinions were mirrored in European countries too.

In 1787, Janet McGuffog was indicted by Scotland's South Circuit Court. She supposedly strangled her newborn son so viciously that he turned blue, and his neck bones splintered. Throat cutting was another common method of infanticide exemplified by Sarah Quarrier in 1752, Jean Stewart in 1755 and Isobel Perston in 1798. Many Scottish murderesses also used battery as their weapon like Janet Cooper in 1768 and Lilias Miligan in 1774, both of whom smashed their child's head off the ground, or Hannah Main in 1793, who killed her son with a hammer.

In Wales between 1730 and 1830, the Court of Great Sessions records approximately 186 females accused of infanticide, though it is highly probable the actual number is higher, considering the near certainty that some went unreported. The reality that women sometimes gained reprieves for committing infanticide, represented an increasing lenience towards criminal women. Most accused women, similar to England and Scotland, were single mothers delivering illegitimate children. Though 186 indictments sound like a lot, seventy-seven of these women were deemed not guilty, only three received the penalty of death, and fourteen, imprisonment. Two women were also found to be insane which would more than likely lead to an acquittal.

There is an interesting gap between infanticide numbers in South Wales compared to North Wales. Attitudes about infanticide varied so greatly between different parts of Wales, that one county might condemn a woman to death, when another would not even indict her. Some historians have postulated this could be due to different population numbers, relationship and lifestyle values, or ideas about violence. Akin to Scotland and England, any strictness in the latter half of the century was probably due to the likelihood of unmarried mothers and their progeny putting more strain on the already high cost of poor relief. They were seen as morally and financially burdensome, and attitudes towards the poor were already negative and ignorant.

There was an increasing use of medical testimony during infanticide trials to determine if the child had been born alive or not. This required medical experts like surgeons, midwives, and coroners, though their observations were not always reliable to determine a clear or accurate verdict. Midwives especially, began to testify more, even if they hadn't been present at the birth. In sync with the court throughout the eighteenth century, they were getting increasingly sympathetic towards accused women and used their testimonies to express that. The need for medical testimony continued to rise throughout the nineteenth century, becoming commonplace and often relied upon for most murder and infanticide cases.

Mercy Hornby of Stoke-Newington was indicted in March of 1734 for murdering her newborn child, referred to as a bastard, indicating Mercy was unmarried. This subjected her to insurmountable amounts of fear and stress. Mercy took her child and threw her into the nearby privy, where she was later found. During her trial, Mercy was found guilty of this horrible deed and sentenced to be hanged. In February 1737, Mary Shrewsbury was indicted for killing her newborn son. She took a sharp instrument, slit the child's throat, and proceeded to hide it in a hole in the closet, but told everyone she had thrown it down the privy. The child was eventually found, and Mary was indicted. It is mentioned that Mary was poor, and the local overseer referred to her as a 'poor creature' upon finding her crying in bed. This exemplifies how people were beginning to view these unfortunate incidents, still horrified but also with feelings of compassion for the woman who went to such lengths. Mary was found guilty and sentenced to hang for her crime. These women were two of the twenty-nine women found guilty and sentenced to hang at the Old Bailey for infanticide during the eighteenth century. However, some of these executions might not have proceeded as leniency was sometimes shown even after a woman was declared guilty, leading to a pardon.

Punishments for British convicts changed dramatically over the century. One of the most visible changes was the slow move away from using death as a punishment, and instead sentencing people to imprisonment. Other punishments, such as whipping, and the pillory began to dwindle in popularity too. Women were less likely than men to be sentenced to these and no woman was sent to the pillory after 1762. This progressive thinking about morally acceptable punishments reflected the changing values of people around Britain.

In eighteenth-century Scotland, women who committed petty crimes were often treated less harshly than men with regard to convictions and punishments. Geoffrey Elton, in *Introduction: crime and the historian* in J.S. Cockburn's *Crime in England, 1550-1800* (1977), believes this may be due to an intrinsic chivalry within men when faced with a woman in trouble, leading them to automatically respond with pity for these women rather than seeking justice. However, this did not apply to felonies. When a woman stepped far outside the realm of female characteristics and expected behaviour, they were convicted and severely punished to deter further behaviour and exemplify how unacceptable those actions were to society. Kilday describes how violent women were seen as 'abnormal, unnatural, animalistic…and certainly unfeminine.'

In Scotland, most female murder cases involved husbands, and magistrates tended to treat these women unforgivingly once convicted. Overall, women in Scotland seemed to receive stricter and less sympathetic treatment than elsewhere in Britain. Approximately sixty per cent of women indicted of murder were convicted, and a staggering two-thirds of these women were hanged! These are large numbers when compared with England and Wales (especially Wales). This rate was higher than the rates of conviction and hanging for Scottish men in the eighteenth century. Women were seen as traitors to their proper female behaviours and qualities and were punished for it.

Welsh juries were, for some reason, more unwilling to prosecute murderous women than in England or Scotland, possibly because they believed they were not fully accountable for their actions due to circumstances out of their control, or mental instabilities. If it was, this idea was not yet shared in the same volume in England and Scotland. Not many women were sentenced to death for homicide, and only a few were executed, imprisoned, or transported for serious crimes. However, there was no shortage of Welsh women receiving corporal punishment, like being pilloried or whipped. This happened far more frequently than in England. Overall, Wales seemed to be reluctant to execute women.

The punishment of transportation, which began in the seventeenth century, was used more frequently during the eighteenth century, especially to Australia, but also to the colonies in North America. During the American Civil War, convicts could no longer be sent to America, so instead, were sentenced to hard labour working on improving the Thames. Burning at the stake was still a punishment for women who committed petty treason in England, but it was used less and less, with Mary Bailey being the last woman burned for petty treason in England in 1784, and the last woman burned at the stake for any crime in Britain was Catherine Murphy in 1789 for coining offences. This ended one of the most brutal punishments that women endured for centuries, simply for diverting from expected gender roles and norms. In Scotland the burning of women for petty treason had already ended by the 1720s, with women being hanged instead.

In 1783, public hangings moved from Tyburn to Newgate prison, but public executions lasted into the nineteenth century. Convicts could petition for a Royal Pardon or reduction of punishment, and women still regularly pleaded the belly. They would subsequently be examined by a jury of matrons and if found to be 'quick with child' they would have their punishment respited until after the birth. Many women received full pardons after this, as during the eighteenth-century judges and juries became more sympathetic towards convicted mothers. This plea declined over the century, with half of convicted women using this at the beginning of the century, compared to only two per cent of women using it at the end of the century. The courtroom experienced a significant development in 1737 when the jury was brought together to sit to the right of the defendant, so they could easily discuss their thoughts and determine a verdict without leaving the room.

One of the most momentous developments in crime legislation in Britain during the eighteenth century was the implementation of the Murder Act in 1752. The Act, aimed at 'better preventing the horrid crime of murder', was put in place and remained unchanged for eighty years. It standardised the procedures used for execution and post-mortem punishment. This act mandated for anyone convicted of murder, regardless of race, class, or gender, to face execution by hanging. Additionally, as an extenuation of their punishment, the bodies of executed murderers would be taken either to the surgeon and medical students for anatomisation and dissection or were hung in chains or 'gibbeted'. Both actions were made public spectacles intended to bring shame and humiliation to the convicted person and serve as a deterrent for others. The increased speed of these processes made it more difficult for convicts and their families to petition for pardons. Overall, this Act played a major role in the development of the medical field and was ultimately used as a form of social control. Although this Act was nationwide legislation, its enforcement was more prevalent in London and its surrounding areas, as well as in the east of the country.

During the eighteenth century, prisons were becoming increasingly crowded, especially as judicial policies shifted away from harsh public punishments and torture. Instead, more criminals were sentenced to imprisonment, hard labour, or transportation, reflecting a growing belief in the value of hard labour. This approach was equally beneficial for the state, providing workers for Britain's economic endeavours. The British prison faced a crisis as immeasurable overcrowding led to disease and death, prompting the rebuilding of prisons nationally and initiating the era of prison reform.

The criminal justice system of the late seventeenth century and the eighteenth century was relatively centralised in London, with local policing by watchmen and constables. Other cities and towns also had local constables patrolling the streets. Stemming from the medieval community effort of policing and policies like the hue and cry, people were expected to help protect the safety of individuals in their communities. Anyone was allowed to and expected to stop, report crimes they witnessed, and even begin a prosecution if they chose to. This attitude prevailed throughout the sixteenth and seventeenth centuries but began to change during the eighteenth century. People, especially in London, were reluctant to involve themselves with criminals, and prosecution was a relatively expensive process. As a result, many people not directly involved in the crime avoided such involvement, even with government incentives. The roles of thief-takers and informers became more popular, gradually replacing local citizens who interacted with confronted criminals.

Night watchmen who patrolled specified areas of town overnight, and constables, were unpaid positions during the sixteenth and seventeenth centuries. They continued as such into the eighteenth century but were often replaced by hired officers or deputies. By 1800 due to the taxing of the parishes, most watchmen around London were paid. In rural areas, standardized, paid forces developed a little slower, but developed, nonetheless. The distinguished High Constables of Edinburgh continued to patrol the streets, deterring petty crime, and assisting with the preservation of the streets of Edinburgh. The carrying of batons was introduced in 1700 and continues to this day. The use of lawyers in the courtroom was becoming popular in the eighteenth century though not frequently used for prosecution until the 1730s. They weren't used for defence cases nearly as often which was seen as unfair, so lawyers were used in defence cases too. By the late 1700s council for prosecutions was relatively inexpensive and one could attain a defence council for free, which allowed for poorer members of society access to lawyers.

These improvements to general policing, including the establishment of the Bow Street Runners in 1749, was bringing the professionalisation of a police force closer, and with it the founding of the Metropolitan Police in 1829.

Eighteenth-century Britain holds many stories of women who killed, whether it be their apprentices, masters/mistresses, lodgers, parents, husbands, or children. Isobel McLean's tale takes us to Glasgow, Scotland and reinforces the idea discussed by historians like Anne-

Marie Kilday, that Scottish murderesses could be extremely brutal and ferocious. Isobel Mclean lived in Glasgow with her husband Henry Small, a shoemaker by trade. Not much is known about them or their lives except for the incident that turned everything upside down. On 30 July 1787 an argument erupted between them, and Isobel, becoming so upset, took a knife or sharp instrument and stabbed Henry.

The records report she stabbed him multiple times and delivered several blows with her fists and feet, stomping and kicking his stomach and other parts of his body. This alone suggests brutality and rage. One publication mentions that she even cut off his genitalia during the attack, although this detail could not be found in the court records. However, the records do state that she stabbed him in his 'upper thigh' when he moved to avoid her stabbing his stomach. Could this be the court's way of concealing a nastier wound? This resulted in significant blood loss, and she threatened to kill him then and there after he attempted to avoid one of her blows. Henry, who was still alive at this point, was assisted by neighbours coming to help, and gently placed on his bed.

After they left, Isobel took the opportunity to continue and grabbed him by his hair, dragged him out of bed, threw him onto the floor and proceeded to bite and tear at him with her teeth until she finally had enough. Due to his extensive injuries, Henry died soon after. Interestingly, Isobel was indicted and sent to prison instead of being hanged for petty treason. This could have to do with the fact that at this point, Scotland and the rest of Britain were moving away from the death penalty and turning towards imprisonment as a punishment. The brutality of this attack leads one to believe that Isobel was deeply antagonized or had a tremendous amount of accumulated anger that eventually made her snap. It isn't clear what exactly prompted her attack on Henry, but the intensity showed that she was not playing around.

A similar, but less brutal case occurred in London in 1773 when Elizabeth Herring stabbed her husband in the neck with a knife while at a friend's establishment. Witnesses say they heard them fighting and then saw her thrust the knife into his neck; he died shortly after. Elizabeth said that he treated her horribly, stabbed her with forks, threw things at her, and abused her. She said she threw the knife at him in anger, and it accidentally stabbed him. Nonetheless, she was found guilty of petty treason and burned on 13 September 1773. She was one of the last few women to receive this punishment in Britain, as it was abolished eleven years later.

The case of Elizabeth Brownrigg was well known throughout Britain due to its brutality. The many accounts written about the incident illustrates its degree of popularity. A pamphlet written about the case during the same year of her execution gives great detail of the entire affair. This was printed in London and sold throughout England. Elizabeth Brownrigg lived with her husband and son in London in 1763; she was a midwife for her local parish, known to perform well at her job and to be a loving and devoted wife and mother. It is curious she would end up being indicted and sentenced for such abusive cruelty. She and her family took in young apprentices, but unfortunately this was an unhappy place for them. Mary Mitchell and Mary Jones were apprenticed to the family in 1765 and unfortunately were subject to frequent beatings and teasing. Regrettably, the beating of subordinates was rather common and relatively accepted in early modern society, but it sounds like Elizabeth and her family went beyond the accepted norm. Mary Jones attempted and succeeded in making an escape and fled to the Foundling Hospital, though nothing was done about the situation she described.

The following year Mary Clifford came to the house and the beatings continued. They were horribly brutal; she was stripped, choked with a chain, and even hung on a hook in the kitchen. These beatings were so deplorable they caught the attention of the neighbours who immediately alerted authorities. The poor girls were removed from the house, but Mary was too far gone, and died a few days later. Gruesomely, she was described by the surgeon as being one big wound. Elizabeth, her son, and husband were indicted but only Elizabeth was charged. Whether this was fair or not is difficult to determine, but in the least they were definitely complacent, as they were aware of what was happening. Elizabeth was executed by hanging at Tyburn on 14 September 1767 and her body was displayed at the Surgeon's Hall at the Old Bailey afterwards which followed the directions of the newly instated Murder Act.

Henrietta Radbourne's case is less frequently observed compared to other forms of homicide. She was a servant who killed her mistress. On 31 May 1787, when her mistress was sleeping, she snuck into her bedchamber and with a bayonet attached to the end of a stick, she stabbed and wounded her mistress, Hannah Morgan. Hannah languished with her injuries until 11 July when she died from them. As Henrietta's crime fell under the definition of petty treason, her act was described as traitorous, with a considerable amount of sympathy for her victim as she was killed when she was helplessly sleeping by someone she relied upon.

Due to insufficient evidence that lacked the exact parameters for the charge of petty treason, her charge was changed to murder. She was found guilty and sentenced to death by hanging and afterwards to be dissected and anatomised.

The use of poison for female murderers was becoming more and more popular during the eighteenth century and was one of the most common "*modus operandi*" for women of the nineteenth century. An example of a poisonous murder case is that of Elizabeth Cranberry from Twittenham, who in 1720 used white arsenic to poison her stepfather Thomas Biggs' porridge. The previous day they had had a fight and he had threatened to kick her out. He consumed the poison at breakfast, and by 4pm, was dead. There was damning evidence against her. The white substance was seen in the porridge pot, her family servant saw her with a parcel of it in her bed as well as one tucked away in one of her boxes, and the post-mortem found Thomas' stomach black and corroded, a clear sign of arsenic poisoning. Elizabeth was indicted, charged with murder, and hanged.

Mabel Hughes, Mary Price, Rachael Beacham and Margaret Williams (nee Morris) were all convicted and executed for killing children. They were not indicted for infanticide because the children they killed were not under one year old. Mabel Hughes lived in a workhouse and supervised young boys who wound silk. She was often teased and irritated by them, and in July 1755, she beat an eleven-year-old boy, Alexander Knipe so roughly by stomping on and kicking him, that she ruptured his hernia. He suffered in bed afterwards and shortly died. She was convicted and hanged. Mary Price from St. Martin in the Fields strangled three-and-a-half-year-old Ann Bickam in 1718 to get back at her stepfather (Ann's father) for taking away her tobacco box. It was given to her by a man she cared for, and little Ann found it and presented it to her father. For revenge, Mary took a leather cord and strangled Ann. She immediately seemed most remorseful and went to tell the neighbours what she had done. When indicted, she pleaded guilty so quickly without any prompt of evidence the jury was shocked and wondered if she might be *non compis mentis* (mentally unfit). They examined her and decided she seemed in the right mind, and she was sentenced to hang.

Rachael Beacham's crime could have had something to do with a mental lapse but surprisingly, despite the evidence, she was not deemed mentally unfit and fully charged and sentenced for her crime. According to people who knew her, she was a respectable woman and mother, but for some reason in 1752 she slit the throat of her lodger's five-year-old daughter named Henny. She did it in the presence of her own nine-year-old daughter. Rachael had recently gone through a long fever, which may have left her in a state of melancholy and delirium. Rachael described herself as restless and addled ever since and that she was unable to sleep as she was afraid she would be tortured by fears. Similar symptoms appeared and disappeared while she was imprisoned and waiting for her execution. She even told her husband she had thoughts of harming herself or her children (which she had never mentioned before), but nothing was done about it. It is surprising the jury and magistrates didn't take these statements into account when listening to what occurred. Today, symptoms like these would have been taken seriously and hopefully Rachael would have received the help she needed.

She was going through a crazed spell for a few days, and on the third day, she burst into the room where Henny and her daughter were, holding a knife and heading towards Henny. Her daughter questioned her, alarmed. Rachael dropped the knife and went to see if the child's mother was near, which she wasn't. She walked back towards the child, grabbed the knife, and slit her throat as well as stabbed her in the chest. The daughter cried out, which attracted neighbours and Rachael's husband. Rachael was declared sane, convicted of murder, and sentenced to hang. After her indictment she was described as being stupid and senseless. She could barely walk upstairs, was delirious and seemed unaware of things happening around her. It definitely seems like a mental breakdown took place, but no one took it into account. Instead, they focused on how sane and coherent she was when she explained how she carried out the crime, how horrible it was, and that she deserved her fate but worried about her children being without her. She was declared sane and hanged on 13 January 1752.

Margaret Williams (nee Morris) from Caernarfon, Wales killed her six-year-old stepson by beating him and pushing him into a river. She was sentenced in August 1774 but was found to be pregnant, so her sentence was respited for pregnancy. However, it was carried out after she had her baby in either December 1774 or January 1775, and she was hanged. Due to the new legislation of 1752, the punishments of convicted killers were carried out very quickly after sentencing, leaving less time for them to try and change their fate. This development can be seen in a few of these cases like Elizabeth Brownrigg, who was tried on 9 September and executed on 14 September, Mabel Hughes who was tried on 10 September and hanged on 15 September, and Elizabeth Herring who was tried on 8 September and burned on 13 September.

The following featured women are a small sample of eighteenth-century British murderesses who supposedly stepped outside the law and suffered greatly for it.

ANNE FOGGET (–1716)

Anne Fogget lived in York with her husband Abraham during the early eighteenth century. She was a self-proclaimed Quaker and part of a local Quaker society. Quakers are a religious group devoted to peace, who reject institutional ways of worship. The specifics of Anne and Abraham's marriage are not well known except they were notorious for having frequent arguments. Given this criminal case, however, it was more than likely an unhappy marriage. In her final speech before her execution, Anne said the members of her religious group were not happy with her marriage to Abraham, but she married him anyway. It does not mention why they didn't like him. For some reason, Anne reached a point where she could no longer cope and took drastic action. In her last speech, she says she gave in to the temptation of the enemy of her soul when she committed her vicious crime.

One evening in the first months of 1715, Abraham Fogget came home rather drunk. In the broadside produced surrounding the murder, it says that Anne had already placed an axe in preparation for her husband returning home. Whether this is true or not is unknown. Nevertheless, Anne took an axe, and as Abraham was drunkenly getting into bed, she proceeded to strike him in the head. She continued to hit him several times, so much so that Abraham's body was described as mangled.

After the act was accomplished, Anne hastily wiped up the blood, took the disfigured body and threw it into a nearby well. All was fine until the next morning when Abraham's brother and a neighbour came by to see him. When they asked where he was, Anne was guarded with her replies and seemed a bit confused. The men became suspicious that something might have happened to him, especially when they remembered they often fought with each other.

They forcibly took Anne and tied her to a tree while they searched for Abraham. They procured an instrument designed to retrieve items from wells and threw it down. Unfortunately, they found Abraham at the bottom. Anne confessed to what she had done and was indicted and taken to York Castle to await her trial. She was afraid that her actions would reflect negatively on her Quaker kinspeople, whom she respected, so she gave a confession to absolve them. She expressed she was part of their organisation, had attended meetings and heard the teachings, but she did not listen or take the advice preached to her by God or her fellow Quakers about marrying Abraham Fogget. She further went on to say that if she had listened and not married him, she would not have been driven to kill him, and that her actions did not represent the actions or thoughts of Quaker people. She confessed that she was guilty and deserved whatever punishment she received. Anne continued and said that she hoped that her decisions didn't hurt her Quaker family and that they should look to her as a warning to not give in to ungodly temptations.

Her trial at the assizes was in March 1715, and she was found guilty of petty treason and sentenced to death by burning. Her execution, however, didn't happen until September of 1716. After she was sentenced to death, she pleaded, her belly and was found to be pregnant. After this revelation, she was returned to the castle to wait for her child to be born. After several months, she delivered a healthy child, but soon after, at the assizes on 6 Aug 1716, it was taken away and she had to accept her previous sentence. Anne was executed at York on 10 September 1716.

This trial and its subsequent execution gained popularity among the people of Britain, evidenced by the broadside printed about them in 1716 in Edinburgh. Interestingly it was printed by a woman, Margaret Reid, who took over her father's Edinburgh print shop. There were a few female printers in the early modern period, but it was certainly a male centred industry. This broadside also has a very simple title. There are no embellishments or descriptors of the participants, just *The Last Speech and Confession of Anne Fogget Burnt for the Murder of her Husband Abraham Fogget.* The title does not call Anne horrid, barbarous, or wicked which is often seen in other broadsides about female felons written and printed by men. This neutral attitude is reflected in the writing, and it raises curiosity to contemplate whether this was authored by Ms. Reid or another woman rather than a man.

Also intriguing, is that a newspaper that published the broadside information about Anne, and her crime, also wrote about four convicts (two women and two men) in the same piece. When they were listed together, the women had their crimes listed beside them and the men didn't. This action looks like the newspaper was offering more attention to the two women's crimes. Whether this was intentional or not is in question, but it would not be surprising if the newspaper hoped to entice more readers by highlighting misbehaving women, instead of men.

SARAH MALCOLM (C.1710–1733)

The tale of Sarah Malcolm is a complex one. Though she was found guilty and sentenced to hang for her crimes, reading the trial records, the Ordinary of Newgate's account, her written confession and witness statements, does not provide a clear verdict of her guilt. There is no damning evidence, only circumstantial, and though the evidence against her is compelling, her defence is convincing. There is also the question of how strong a role her gender, Roman Catholic religious beliefs, and Irish heritage played in her sentencing.

Sarah Malcolm was born in Durham around 1710. Her father was British and her mother Irish; they were fairly well off, but their fortunes took a turn, and her mother relocated them to Dublin, Ireland. Here Sarah was thoroughly educated and travelled back and forth to London quite frequently with her parents. When she matured, she moved to London and worked as a barmaid and servant in many establishments, always receiving positive feedback from her employers. Soon after, her mother died, and her father returned to Dublin, leaving Sarah to fend for herself. She ended up getting a job as a charwomen (house cleaner), and laundress in the Temple, an area around Temple Church in the City of London. She was twenty-two years old when things began to fall apart.

Previously, she had worked as a barmaid at the Blackhorse Alehouse, where she met the sly Mary Tracey, and subsequently the brothers Thomas and James Alexander, their dastardly recruits. Sarah told the Ordinary of Newgate that Mary and the brothers often encouraged her to rob or blackmail her well-off clients, given she had trusted access to their rooms and belongings. Sarah claimed to have often refused to do so, so it is curious what changed her mind when Mary suggested they rob elderly Mrs Lydia Duncomb, one of her former clients who lived in the Temple. Perhaps, her advanced age posed less of a threat to being caught. She also lamented the false rumours spread about her throughout London, often due to the Alexander brothers. She said they gave her a bad reputation and portrayed her as more misbehaving than she actually was. This theme, if she was innocent, unfortunately persisted for years after her execution. Despite her reservations, Sarah was not against the idea of robbing Mrs Duncomb, but she told Mary she wanted help. Mary enlisted the Alexander brothers, and the four of them set to work preparing a plan. Sarah was the mastermind, knew the building and tenants best. Lydia Duncomb lived with her two maids, an elderly one by the name of Elizabeth Harrison and a young girl named Ann Price.

The night of the theft arrived on 4 February 1733, and the four thieves were preparing for the burglary. They headed to the Temple and waited in the stairwell until Miss Price came down to fetch something to help Miss Harrison with her illness. They took their opportunity to gain access, as Ann would leave the door ajar because the other two were too unwell to rise and let her back in. James rushed inside, quickly concealing himself beneath one of the beds. The other three waited for several hours until James believed it was safe enough to join him. It was nearly 2am when he finally opened the door for the others. This is the point where conflicting details emerge. Sarah was adamant during her trial proceedings and discussion with the Ordinary of Newgate that she remained on the stairs while the other three went inside and carried out the burglary. Tragically, all three women were murdered. Ann's throat was slit, resulting in blood pouring everywhere, while Lydia and Elizabeth were strangled with a thin string - an easier task given their old and infirm conditions.

Sarah insisted that she had no knowledge of the ladies being murdered until the next day, and that her three accomplices did the killing. However, this contradicts certain pieces of evidence against Sarah. Sarah stated that when her accomplices emerged, they informed her that they had to silence the victims, but that was the extent of her knowledge. They divided their spoils and she received a silver tankard filled with money and clean linen as her share. They went their separate ways shortly after. Sarah said she returned to her master's chambers to hide the stolen items, and that all four planned to meet some time afterwards. This never occurred because Sarah was apprehended.

Now, the evidence against Sarah paints a different narrative. It suggests that Sarah, accompanied by her accomplices, participated in the killing of the three ladies, particularly Ann, as Sarah had blood all over her shift and apron, and that, after the gruesome act, Sarah left the scene with her accomplices and the stolen belongings. Her master, John Kerrel, discovered her in his chambers late the following evening, around midnight on 5 February, shortly after the three women had been discovered dead. Questioning her presence at such a late hour, Kerrel asked if she had heard about the murders. She claimed she knew of the murders but was unaware of the perpetrator. Noticing a bundle of linen on the floor, Kerrel asked about it. Sarah explained that it was her undergarments, which he found appalling and left on the ground. Suspecting that the culprit might be someone with access to Mrs Duncomb's rooms, Kerrel ordered her to leave and summoned watchmen to apprehend her. Curiosity led Kerrel to investigate further, with the help of a friend. They discovered more linen and a silver tankard with blood on the handle in his close stool (boxed toilet). Mrs Duncomb's clean linen and an apron were also found under the bed, some stained with blood.

Rushing to fetch the watchmen, Kerrel brought Sarah back and questioned her about the tankard and linen, both stained with blood. Initially, she falsely claimed ownership of both items, providing little assurance of her innocence. Throughout the trial, Sarah maintained her defence, asserting the bloody linen was due to her menstruation.

This defence was fascinating and unusual, considering that discussing menstruation was taboo and highly unconventional during the eighteenth century. It shouldn't have been, but it was seen as private and inappropriate; it was a subject that people only attributed to women with loose morals. Throughout the trial, Sarah maintained her defence, asserting that the blood on the tankard was from her cut finger, and the bloody linen was due to her menstruation. Sarah's persistence in using this defence, did not necessarily aid her case.

Sarah faced charges for burglary and for the murders of Lydia, Elizabeth, and Ann. The burglary alone warranted the death penalty, as the stolen money and belongings were valued at around £300. While awaiting trial, Sarah imprudently admitted to her fellow inmates that she stole the tankard and money, which she had on her. During the trial, she admitted to masterminding the theft. She was only tried for Ann Price's murder, and the court decided that if found guilty, the other murder trials would be declared unnecessary, as she would already be receiving the death penalty for killing Ann. In today's legal system, such logic would most certainly not hold. Sarah shared her version of events, confessing her guilt in the burglary but maintaining her innocence in the murders until the end. Witnesses provided their statements, and after deliberation, the jury found Sarah guilty of murder, burglary, and robbery, sentencing her to hang.

While awaiting her impending punishment, she provided her statement to the Ordinary of Newgate, who attempted to guide her in the ways of God and sin. Being Roman Catholic, she grew up with slightly different views than those popular in England at the time. The Ordinary noted that she listened and nodded but was not fully engaged, often glancing at her own book she carried with her. He observed that she often cried, and records indicated that she experienced fits and appeared unwell while waiting for her execution. Upon learning of the apprehension of Mary and the Alexander brothers, she expressed happiness and was requested to identify them. She complied, displaying anger towards them for their actions. In an unjust twist of events, after Sarah's execution, Mary and the Alexander brothers were released without charge.

The presence of Sarah's bloody clothing was the proverbial 'nail in the coffin' of her case, the primary reason she stood out among the rest. Even if her defence was true, openly and nonchalantly stating in court that the blood on her clothes was menstrual, unfortunately heightened suspicion about her character. If Sarah was innocent, these facts imply that she was prosecuted and subsequently executed because of her body and for being a woman. Jane Magrath, in her article '(Mis)Reading the Bloody Body: the case of Sarah Malcolm,' discusses this outrageous aspect of the case – the possibility that Sarah met with her fate simply because of her body, gender, and the court's discomfort with the notion of female menstruation.

She composed two letters to be read posthumously. One detailed her account of the crime, asserting her non-participation in the murders, and the second expressed forgiveness for those administering her punishment. It remains unclear whether the second letter genuinely sought peace, or if it was a final attempt to falsely promote her innocence. The night before the execution, she prayed with fellow inmates but declined having a psalm sung for her at the gallows. On the day of her execution on 7 March 1733, she was brought to Fleet Street near Temple Gate, the site of the murders. She was unhappy about the location as she did not wish to be seen by her acquaintances. Her execution became a spectacle, with stands set up for onlookers, some of which collapsed, injuring several people. Prior to her execution, she asserted that accusations against her, provided by Master Kerrel, were false and any evidence given besides what she wrote in her letter was untrue.

Determining whether Sarah was telling the truth remains a challenging task. She is branded as a wicked murderess who brutally killed three women, but is this narrative accurate? Her defence is compelling, but so is the evidence against her. The Ordinary of Newgate labelled her devilish, and William Hogarth, who famously painted her picture while she was in Newgate, coldly stated that he could discern from her face that she was capable of wickedness. Although the basis for this opinion is unclear, Hogarth's painting contributed to the enduring fascination with Sarah and her alleged crimes. Descriptions of her as cool during the investigation and proceedings added to the perception of her as wicked and unfeeling. Unfortunately, these ideas of her persisted even after her execution.

She was also characterised as melodramatic while waiting in prison and during her execution. She experienced fits of near mania during imprisonment, which, whether genuine or not, could have seemed excessively dramatic. During her execution, she was described as wearing all black and devoutly wringing her hands in an expressive manner. Based on the case record, Sarah was undeniably intelligent enough to plan and execute her actions, but the question of her guilt remains a mystery. If she was guilty, she was another cunning, and malicious murderess who maintained her resolve until her execution. If innocent, she became another unfortunate woman who fell victim to biased judges and juries, dying for a crime she did not commit. While she did commit a felonious burglary and paid the brutal price for it, if she was not a murderer, she shouldn't be remembered as one.

SARAH METYARD (1718–1762) AND SARAH MORGAN METYARD (1738–1762)

This next case unfolds as a double dose of murderesses, featuring a mother and daughter, both indicted and hanged for the murder of one of their servants, a thirteen-year-old girl named Ann Nailor. Residing together near Hanover Square in London, Sarah, the mother, operated a haberdashery, employing apprentice girls to learn sewing and crafting skills. On the surface, Sarah and her daughter, Sarah M, appeared cordial and polite, keeping mostly to themselves. However, the ensuing court case and testimonies reveals a starkly different picture.

In late September 1758, Ann Nailor, a servant working for Sarah and Sarah M, attempted to escape as the milkman delivered his goods. The two women pursued her, shouting for the milkman to intervene. He apprehended her, and she begged him to release her, and that if he didn't, she would surely starve to death. He ignorantly assured her that she would not and returned her to her keepers. Ann was already incredibly frail and weak, frequently denied meals for unknown reasons, confirmed by the testimonies of two servant girls who lived with her. These girls also detailed instances of Sarah's physical abuse, including beatings with a walking stick or hearth broom. On 29 September 1758, after her near escape, Ann experienced another episode of mistreatment.

After Ann was returned to her place of work, Sarah M roughly brought her to the room where she and her mother slept. While her mother held Ann by the head, Sarah M brutally beat her. Subsequently, she was taken to the foot of the attic stairs and tied there, unable to sit or lie down. She remained there, with no food and more than likely no water, for several days. Conflicting information arises, with one witness claiming three days, and the trial transcript stating until 4 October, totalling five days. Ann was untied each night to sleep and retied in the morning. After enduring days of beatings and deprivation, she appeared lifeless, doubled over and hanging from the door where she was tied. Alerted by the two apprentices, Sarah M tried to revive Ann by beating her with her shoe. Unsuccessful in her attempts, Sarah came, cut her down, laid her on her lap, and sent an apprentice to fetch some drops to aid her. After the apprentice returned, the young girls were sent away while the two women 'tended' to Ann. The girls claimed that was the last time they saw Ann. During the trial, Sarah refused to admit that Ann died in the house, and only confessed the truth after their conviction, though she continued to deny causing it.

Details become fuzzy here due to the conflicting and confusing stories. Sarah M, in her testimony, provided an account of the next twenty-four hours, claiming she had pleaded with her mother to provide more food for the girls and requested that Ann be given food that last night. It remains unclear if this is true as she had always been aware that some girls were being starved. She also testified that she took no part in the murder, although she had clearly beaten Ann alongside her mother and initially tied her up. The timing of Sarah M's account is uncertain, but if it followed the last time the girls saw Ann, Sarah told her daughter to take her upstairs to bed after giving her the drops to revive her. Sarah M related to her mother that she was afraid for Ann as she was very weak and unable to speak or walk.

The next morning Ann was still incredibly fragile and unable to speak. Seeing this, Sarah M approached her mother, who went to see Ann. When Sarah M saw them, Sarah was talking to Ann, telling her that if she apologised, she would forgive her. Ann was silent but begged with her hands and Sarah laid her on her bed. Later that afternoon, Sarah M was informed by her mother that Ann was dead.

The subsequent events are as devious and horrifying as the initial murder. To conceal the obvious signs of starvation and fatal beatings, the women (although Sarah M claims it was only her mother) hid Ann's body in the attic. In court, Sarah's claimed defence was that Ann was a sickly girl and had been extremely unwell. After nursing her back to health, she supposedly escaped with a milkman she fancied. Sarah repeated this to the other apprentices when they inquired about Ann's whereabouts after not seeing her for several days. After two months, as the body started to decompose, Sarah asked her daughter for help dismembering the body. Sarah M claimed she was crying, and her mother scolded her not to let the others see her upset. After finishing the gruesome task, Sarah disposed of the body parts in a sewer drain on Chick Lane. Though Sarah M was equally culpable for assisting, beating, and ignoring the girl's suffering, the young apprentices revealed that she sometimes provided them with money or food without her mother's knowledge. They stated that Sarah was awful to her daughter as well; that she beat her, and the two often fought.

The body of Ann Nailor was discovered approximately two months later when two watchmen spotted it in the drain. They alerted a parish official, and the three men retrieved the body pieces. They claimed all parts of the body that were there except for the hands, which Sarah had previously burned due to some distinctive markings. The coroner examined the body and granted permission for Ann to be buried, though sadly no one knew her identity.

Fast forward four years: having carried on with their lives since the incident though not peacefully, they were finally exposed due to their own slip of the tongue. Additionally, since Ann's death, two more servants had died 'mysteriously' within the house, including Mary Nailor, Ann's younger sister. The women were indicted for Mary's murder too, although not tried for it, as they were already found guilty of killing Ann.

About two years before their exposure, a lodger named Mr Rooker stayed at the women's house. Witnessing the poor treatment of the girls and Sarah M's mistreatment, he decided to move out. When Sarah M practically begged him to take her with him as a servant, he agreed. Sarah M lived and worked for Mr Rooker for two years, both in the city and in the country. She claimed she was attempting to break away from her mother and earn her own living. However, her mother continuously dropped in to see Sarah M, leading to heated arguments. Fearing their secret might be revealed, Sarah tried to persuade Sarah M to return home. Sarah M threatened to disclose their secret unless her mother backed off. In response, her mother threatened to tell people first and blame it on Sarah M, leveraging her status as the mother. This escalated into a frenzy, and Mr Rooker heard Sarah M yell 'murder!' from the kitchen. Rushing down, he noticed Sarah M's headscarf had been ripped off, and that Sarah had just dropped a knife to the floor, which had apparently been at Sarah M's throat. Sarah muttered something about the Chick Lane story, and Sarah M. retorted that her mother was the Chick Lane ghost, reminding her of the drain where they disposed of Ann's body.

On 9 June 1762, Sarah visited Mr Rooker, and in a heated encounter, he expressed regret that she wouldn't behave better. Feeling offended and concerned that he might disclose what he had learned from the women's numerous arguments, she wrote a threatening letter to his sister, which she promptly showed to Mr Rooker. This backfired for Sarah, as Mr Rooker immediately demanded that Sarah M disclose the entire story. She proceeded to share the details about Ann, although some embellishments might have been present. After the revelation, Mr Rooker reported the incident to the proper authorities, leading to Sarah's prompt apprehension. Sarah M, thinking she could distance herself from the crime, portrayed herself as an innocent and scared victim in her narrative. However, when testimonies revealed truths about Sarah M, she was indicted for the murder too.

Held in Newgate, their mutual fury led to their confinement in separate areas of the prison. Their dispositions in prison differed, with Sarah M displaying terror, sadness, and victimhood, while Sarah exhibited a reserved and almost flippant attitude. During their trial, strong evidence was presented against both, prompting heated exchanges and claims of innocence. Despite their protests, they were found guilty on 17 July for the brutal murder of Ann Nailor and sentenced to hang. They returned to Newgate to await their execution.

As they faced their impending fate, both distressed and terrified, they persisted in blaming each other with extreme disdain. Sarah M, pleading for her life, even invoked the possibility of pregnancy, but it was dismissed. Sarah, equally unhappy, adopted a quiet, dejected, and impertinent demeanour. Ironically, she attempted to starve herself before facing the gallows, nearly succeeding as she fell ill and had fits as the execution day drew nearer. On the morning of their execution, Sarah M, remained distressed, denying direct involvement in the murder while acknowledging her role in hiding it. She lamented her mother's negative influence since her early years, citing practices of illegal trickery that her mother encouraged, which impacted her later misdeeds. Sarah, still weakened from her self-induced starvation, continued to suffer fits.

At approximately 10am, they were led to the scaffold, where large crowds had gathered to witness the execution, making it challenging for the Ordinary to approach the women. Sarah M displayed intense anxiety, and her mother, Sarah remained relatively unconscious. Sarah M appealed to the crowd, asking for forgiveness for her mother and her prosecutors and requesting prayers for herself. On 19 July 1762, they were hanged at Tyburn.

MARY BAILEY (C.1735–1784)

Mary Bailey's story holds great significance in the history of female crime, as she became the last woman in Britain to be burned for petty treason. Collaborating with her lover, Mary orchestrated the murder of her husband, Cornelius Bailey, by beating him to death.

Mary and Cornelius both hailed from Longford, Ireland, and their paths crossed when Mary, at the age of fifteen, accompanied her soldier father to his posting in Gibraltar. Cornelius, a Marine, arrived in Gibraltar around the same time, and the two, being fellow Irish natives, quickly formed a friendship. They married in 1751, had a child and enjoyed what was described as a happy marriage. However, Mary was noted for her flighty nature and penchant for swearing, qualities not typically associated with a 'proper' woman of the eighteenth century. Over the next two decades, they expanded their family to fifteen children, and by 1771, they relocated to Oakum-Bay in Portsmouth.

Once in Portsmouth, Mary's life took a morally ambiguous turn as she engaged in an affair with John Quin, a private in the Portsmouth Division of Marines. The affair strained her marriage, leading Cornelius to leave her and move to another part of town. During his occasional visits, her involvement with Quin still fuelled quarrels and fights.

The fateful day of the murder arrived in 1784 when Cornelius went to see Mary. Strangely, she questioned him about whether he had come to murder her and her family. Cornelius denied any harmful intentions, just as Quin walked in. Their mutual presence triggered a heated argument. Quin, being more aggressive, overpowered Cornelius, and subjected him to a brutal assault. Mary joined in, further incapacitating Bailey. Despite Bailey's attempts to escape, he was relentlessly beaten by Quin. He was grabbed by Quin and thrown onto the floor which gave him a serious and bloody head wound. Quin pulled Bailey downstairs where he and Mary continued to beat him. Eventually Mary and Quin became tired, and Bailey took this opportunity to escape into the street. His neighbours came to his aid, returned him to his lodgings, and asked what had happened. Cornelius relayed that Quin, and his own wife, were responsible for the assault. He was brought to the poor house in the hopes someone could attend to his needs. He died there three days later.

Mary and John were indicted following a coroner's inquest, and they were immediately taken to the gaol for trial at the Winchester Assizes. During their trial, John falsely claimed that Cornelius had instigated the fight, and insisted that he only used his fists. Witnesses contradicted this, attesting to John's vicious kicks and jumps on Cornelius. Mary, in her defence, lied about Cornelius not being her husband, a falsehood refuted by a witness present at their wedding. John eventually admitted guilt, but Mary persisted in denying her involvement. Both were held responsible for Cornelius' death, which resulted in Mary being burned for petty treason and John being hanged, dissected and anatomised as per the new Murder Act. On 8 March 1784, they were executed in front of hundreds of onlookers. The sensational tale inspired the creation of a murder ballad depicting the deadly love triangle.

I hope that none will be severe
And twit her guiltless children here
Nor tell them of their mother's deed
And cause their aching hearts to bleed

Right: An engraving of the Old Bailey Sessions House in 1779. (fleuron.lib.cam.ac.uk)

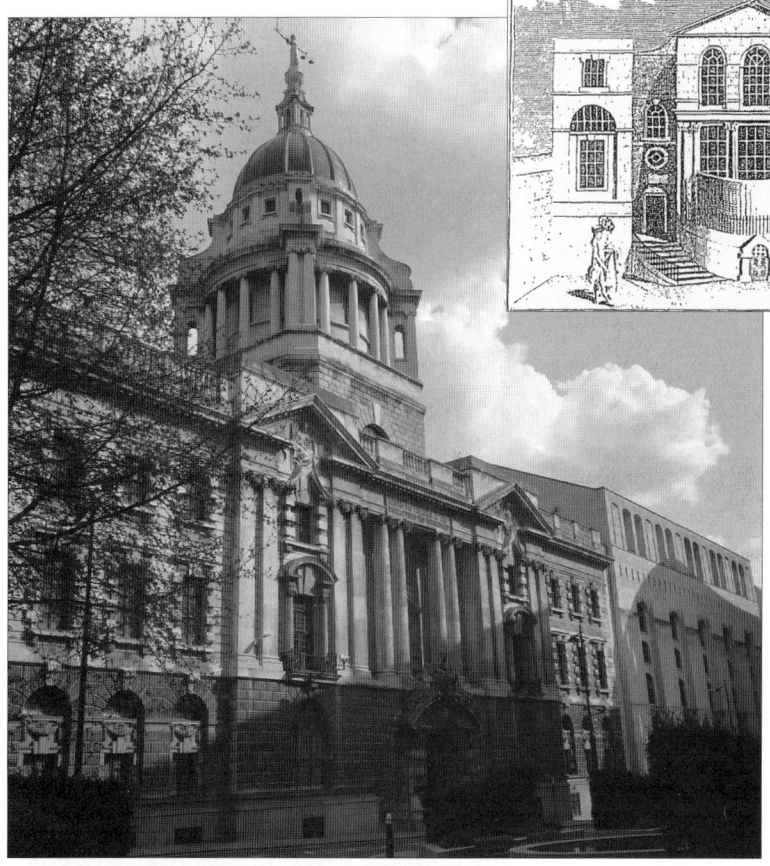

Left: The Old Bailey, Central Criminal Court in London, 2020. (GrindtXX)

Below left: Portrait of Sarah Malcolm while imprisoned by William Hogarth, 1733. (British Museum)

Below right: The Marble Arch, now situated on the site of the Tyburn Tree, London 2023. (Erin Fetterly)

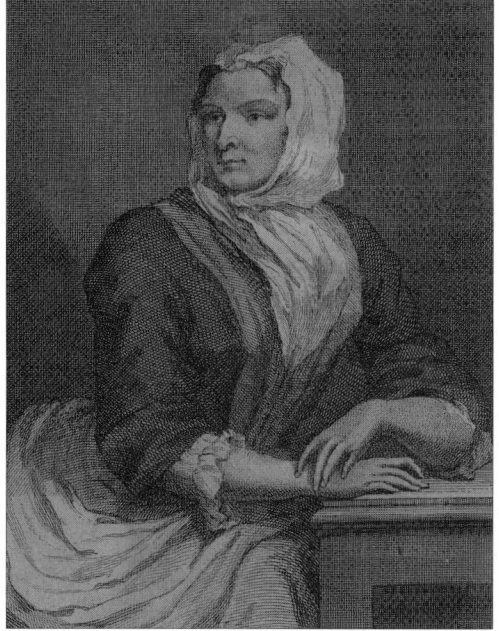

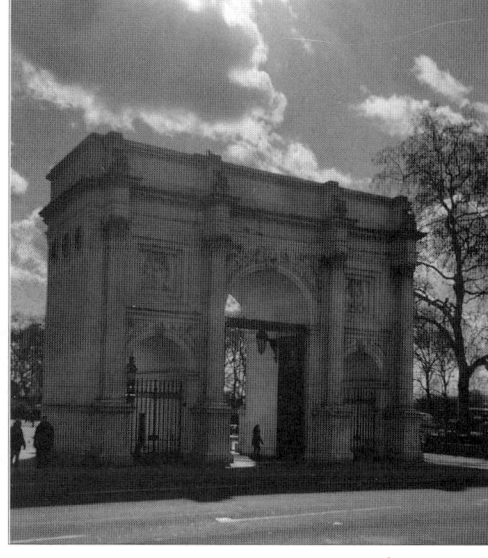

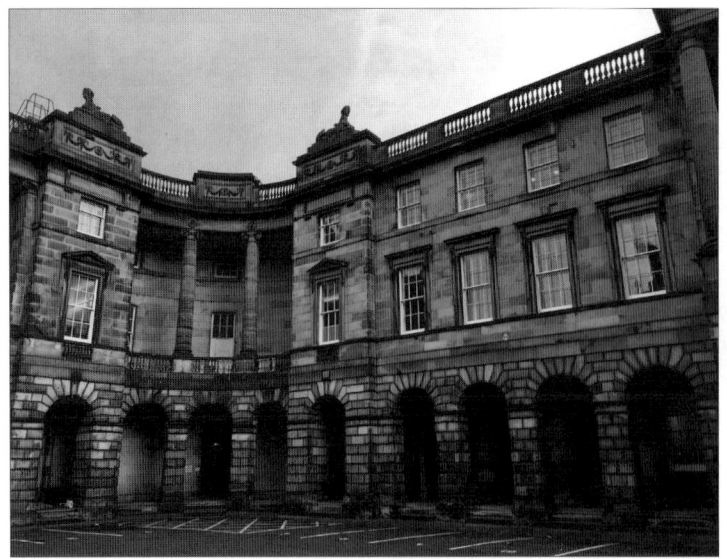

Top left: High Court Justiciary and Sessions Court, Edinburgh, 2017. (LornaMCampbell, 2017)

Centre left: A drawing from the *Illustrated Police News*, 1879, of the trial and conviction of Kate Webster. (*Illustrated Police News* 1879)

Below: A drawing of Newgate Prison in the City of London c. late eighteenth century. (Wellcome Collection)

Opposite page, botton left: An etching by G. Terry of several people being burnt at the stake including three women: Cicely Ormes, Margaret Thurston and Margery Austoo, sixteenth century. (Wellcome Collection)

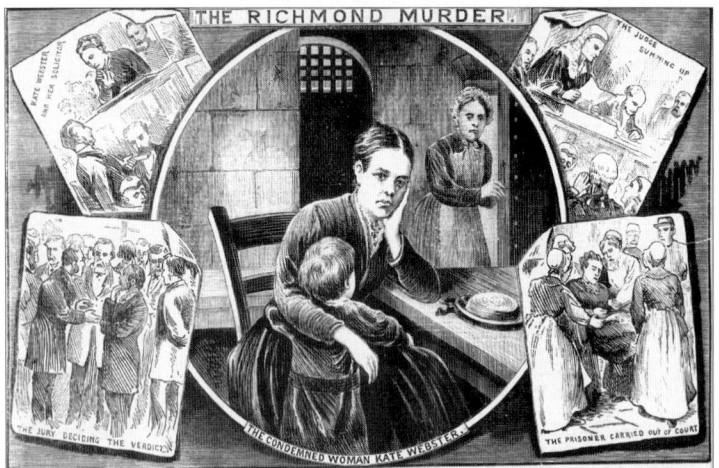

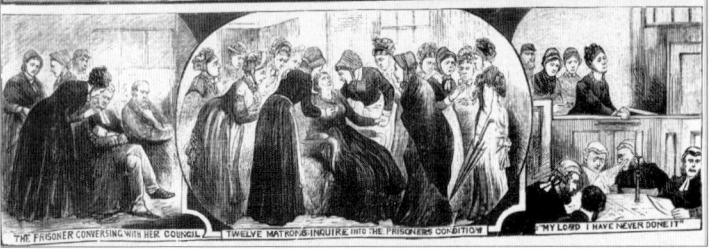

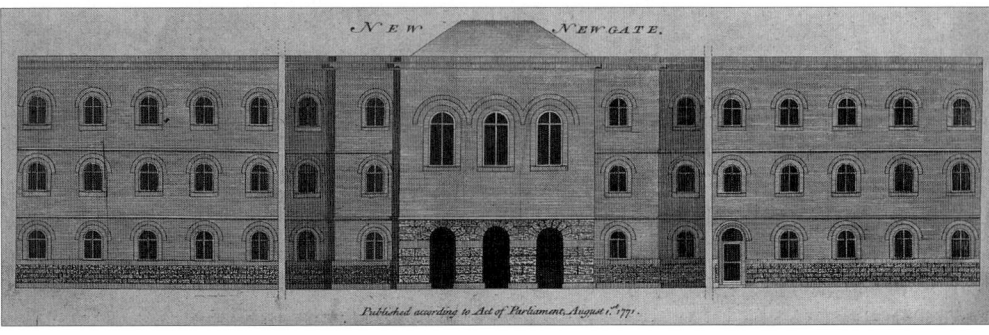

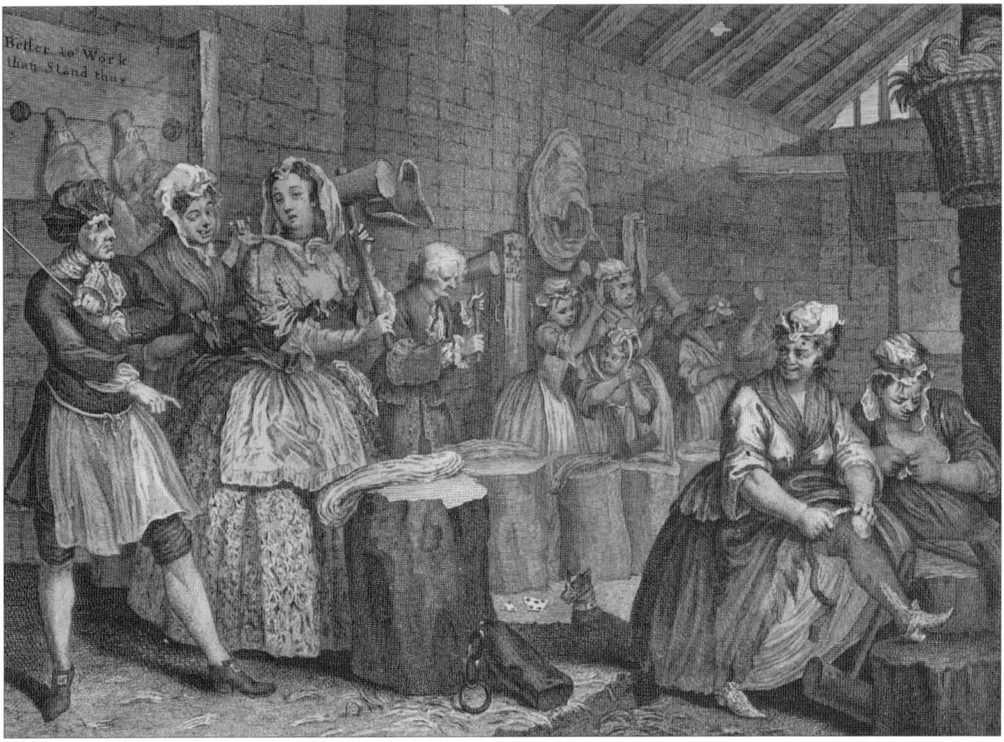

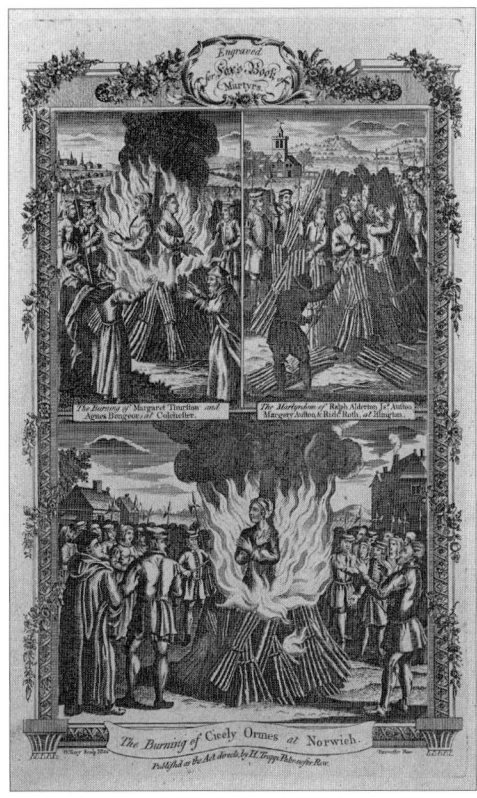

An etching and engraving of female inmates in Bridewell prison, beating hemp while under the supervision of a warder, 1732. (British Museum)

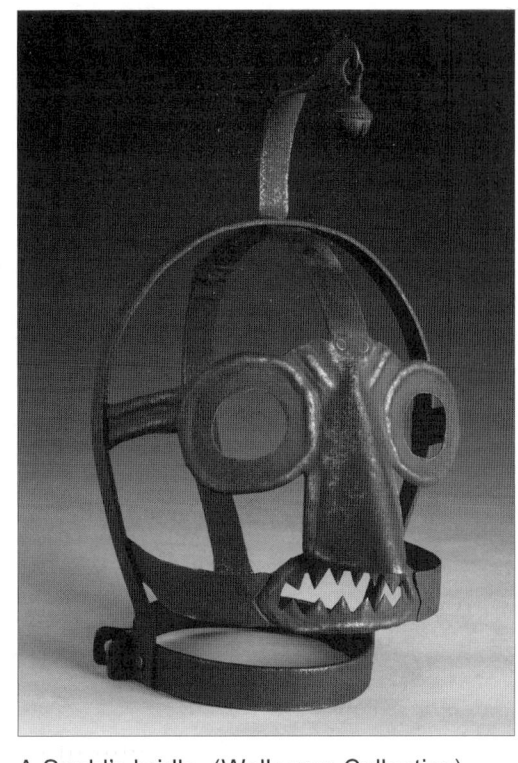

A Scold's bridle. (Wellcome Collection)

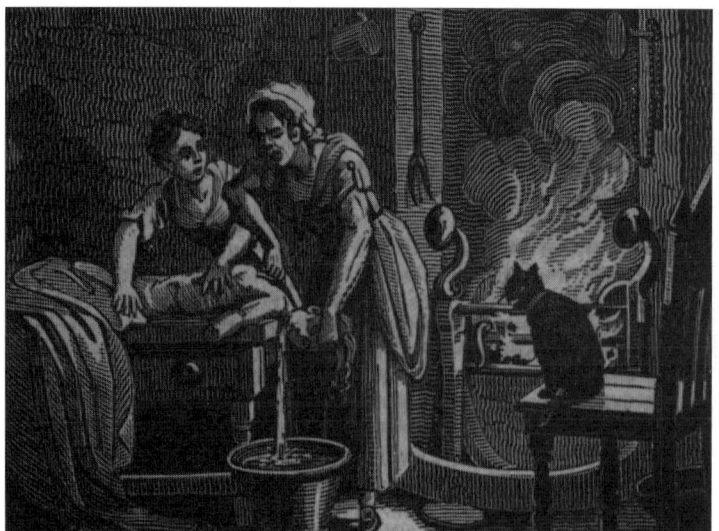

Top left: A drawing from a nineteenth-century book of Sarah Metyard and Sarah Morgan Metyard dismembering their servant Ann Nailor after killing her in 1758. (Courtesy of HathiTrust)

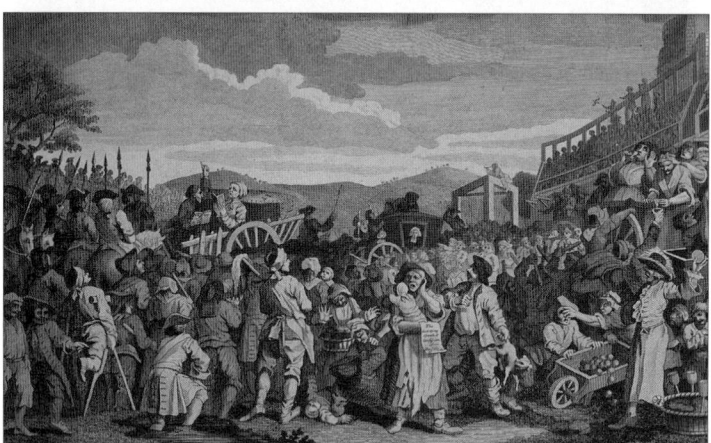

Centre left: A crowd of spectators gather around the Tyburn Tree to watch as a hanging takes place, 1750. (William Hogarth)

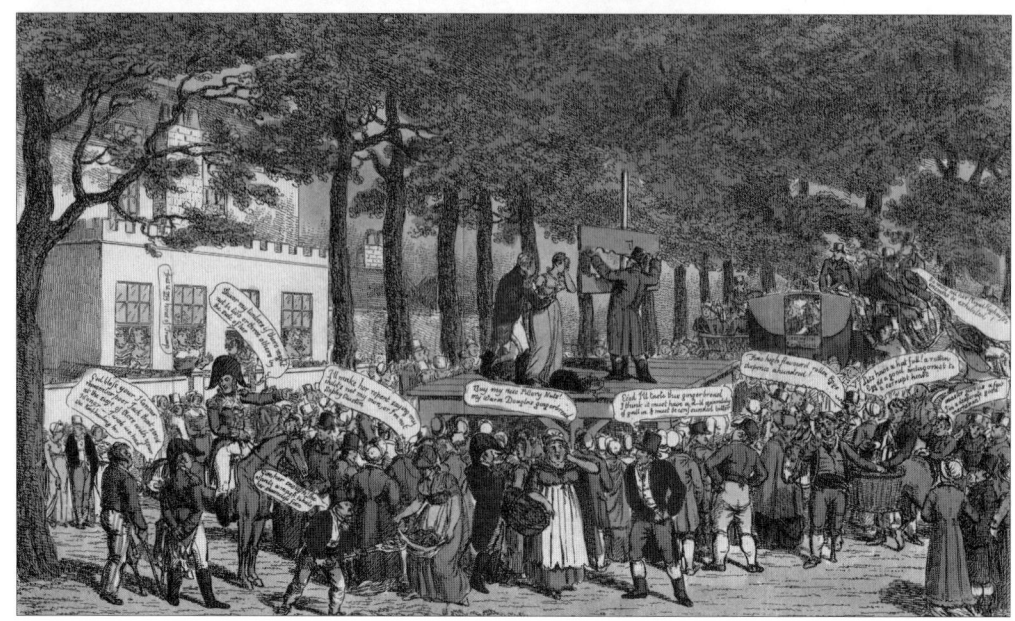

Below: A satirical cartoon from 1813 depicting Sir John and Lady Douglas, being placed in the pillory for providing evidence against Queen Caroline, and the community gathering around such an event. (British Museum)

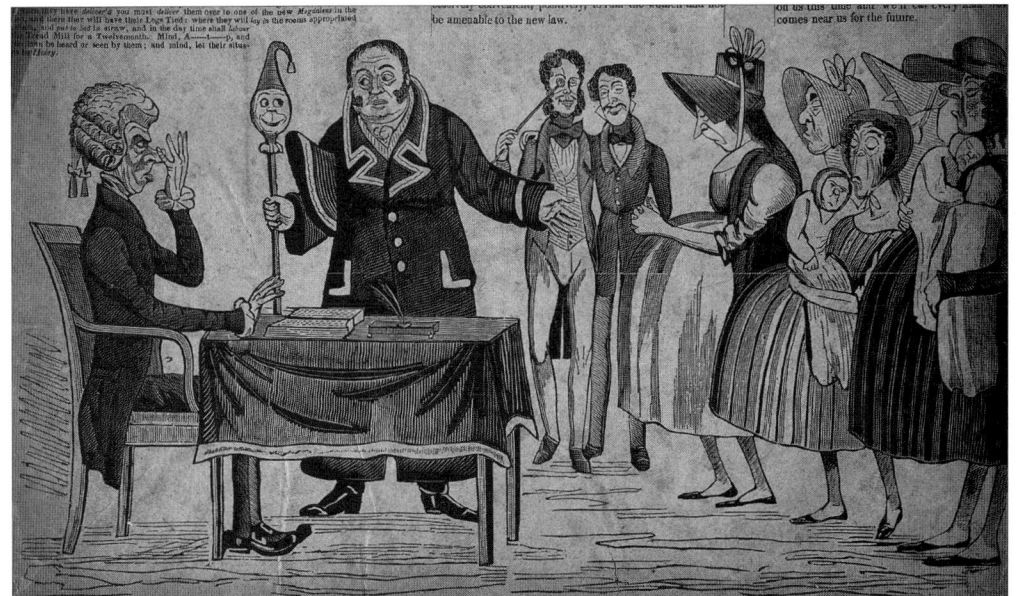

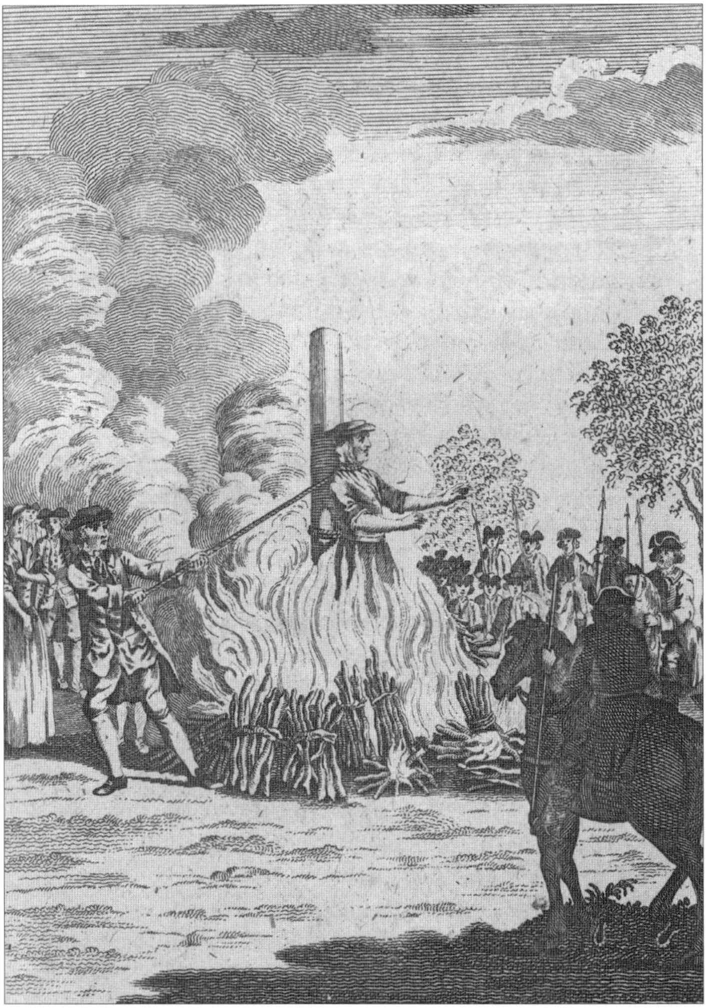

Above: A cartoon of unwed mothers being brought before the court and judged harshly after the introduction of the New Poor Law and its legislation on bastardy. This illustrates the pressure that unwed mothers faced from society, c.1834. (Wellcome Collection)

Left: An etching of Catherine Hayes being burnt at the stake in 1726 for the murder of her husband. Found within the Newgate calendar published in 1795. (Wellcome Collection)

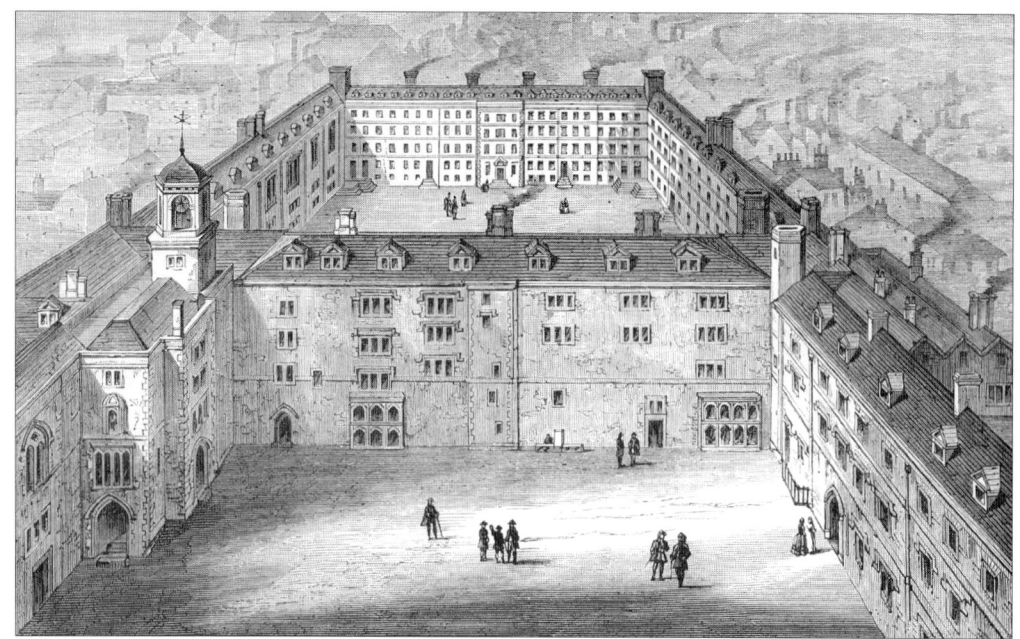

A print of Bridewell prison/hospital, 1889. (Walter Thornbury)

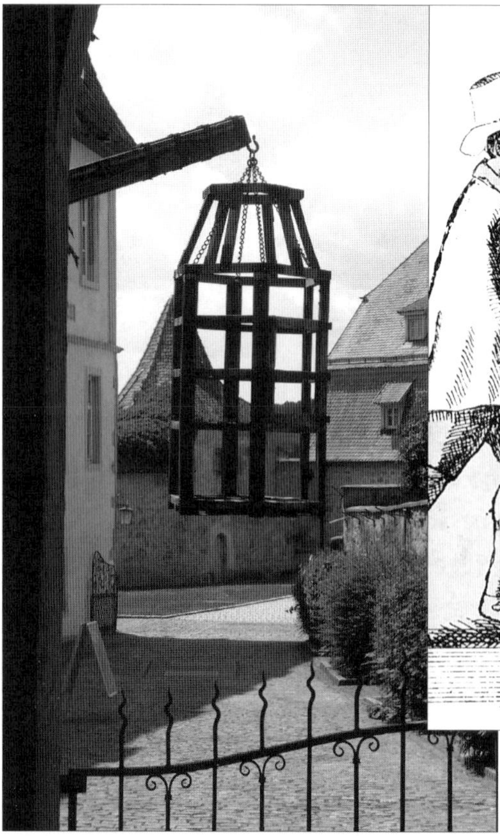

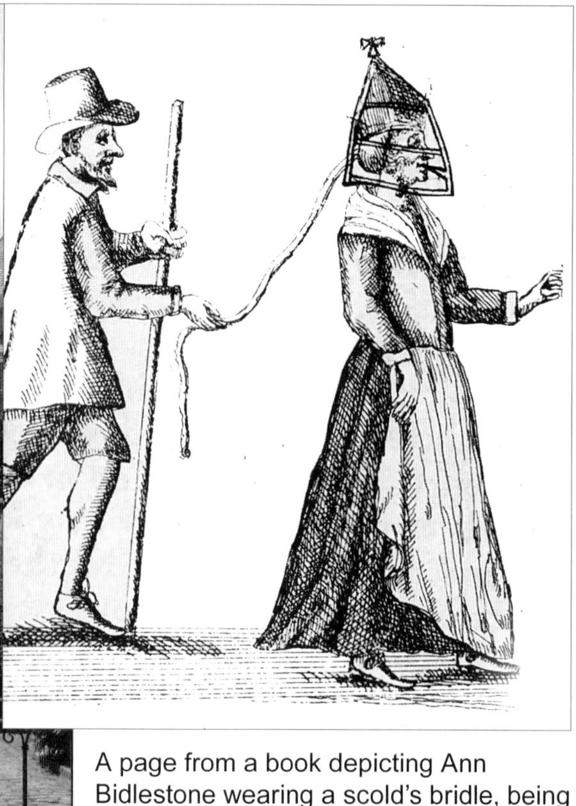

A version of a medieval ducking stool. (Unknown)

A page from a book depicting Ann Bidlestone wearing a scold's bridle, being driven through the streets by a man named Robert Sharp. Likely from the sixteenth century. (4.0 International)

Top right: A man is in a version of the pillory in Switzerland while he is subjected to public ridicule and stones thrown at him, likely eighteenth century. (Wellcome Collection)

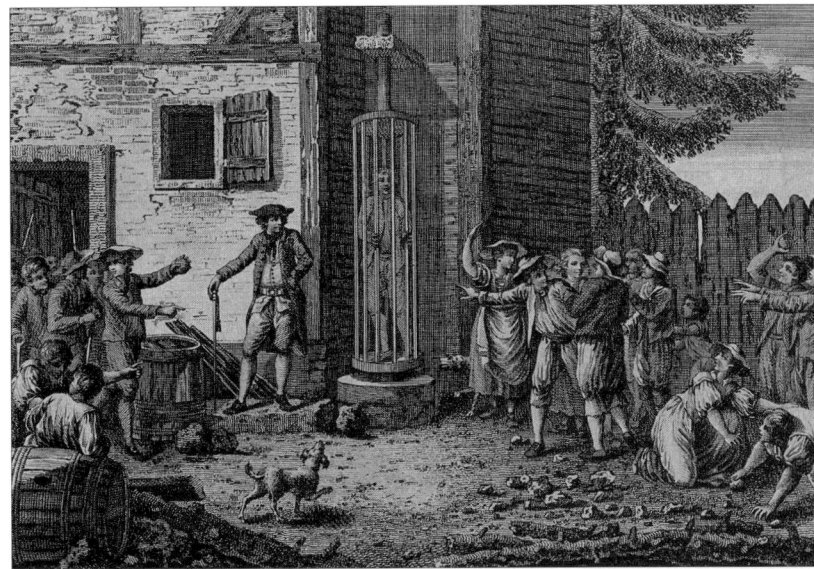

Centre right: An engraving depicting a London street during the eighteenth-century gin craze, 1751. (Wellcome Collection)

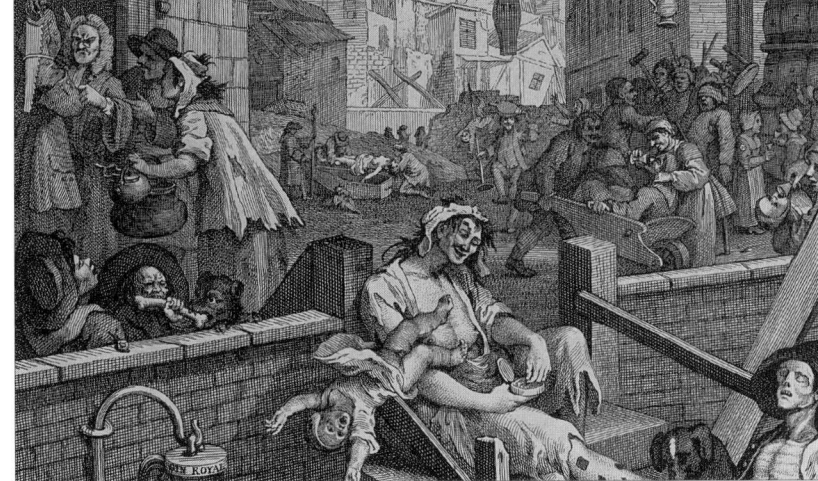

Bottom right: A drawing of a police constable and inspector apprehending a thief, shows the uniforms worn by police officers in the 1890s. (Wellcome Collection)

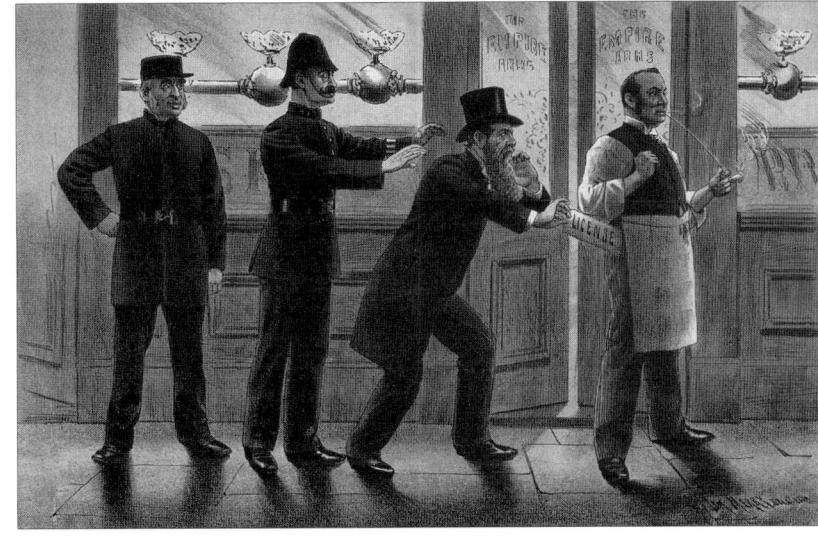

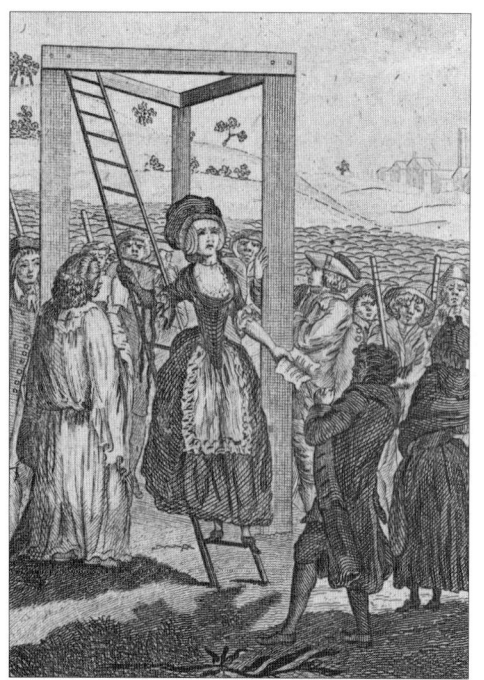

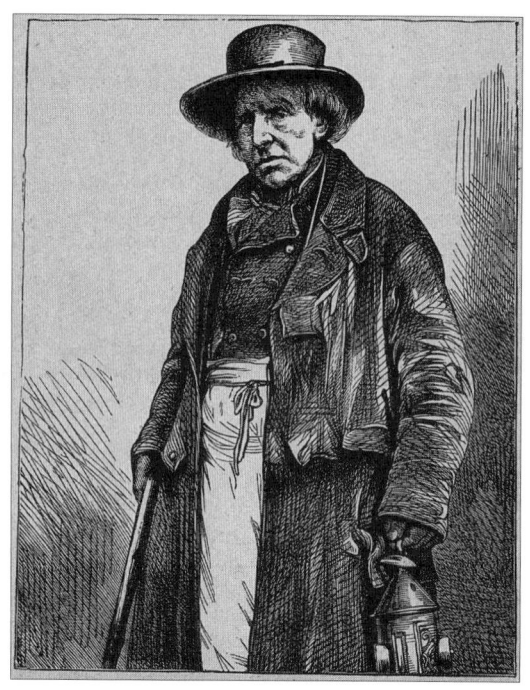

An etching from the 1795 Newgate calendar depicting the execution near Oxford of Miss Blandy in 1752 for the murder of her father by poisoning. (Wellcome Collection)

An engraving of the last London night watchman, William Anthony, 1880. (Wellcome Collection)

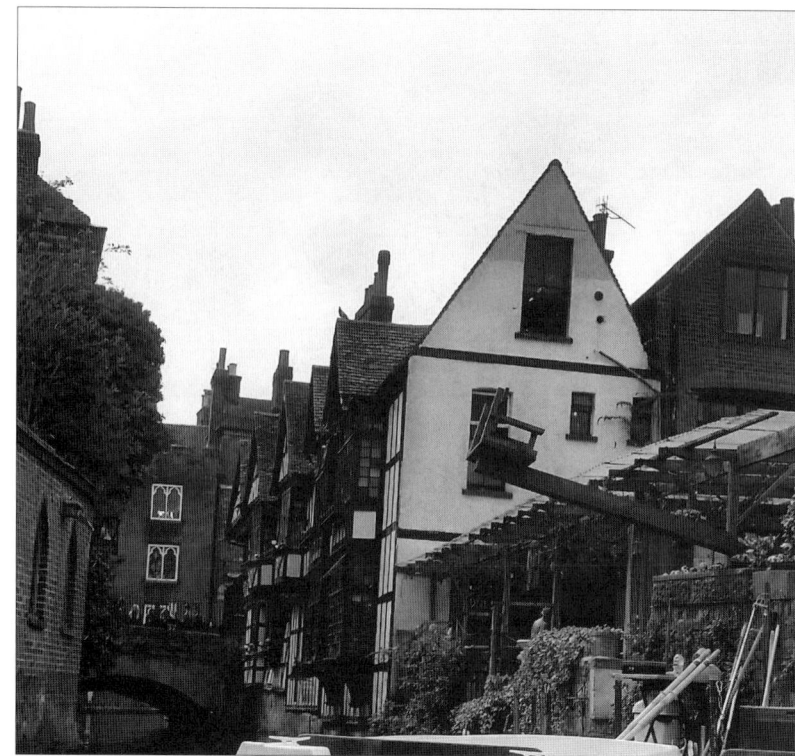

A medieval ducking stool hanging over the river Cam in Cambridge, England, taken in 2019. (Erin Fetterly)

As mentioned earlier, Mary was the last woman in Britain to be burned for the charge of petty treason, as society was beginning to shift away from harsh, tortuous punishments. The concept of killing a superior was thought to be an extreme attack against the stability of society, which led to the continued practice of burning women for this offence long after the last man suffered this fate in 1612.

The eighteenth century marked a period of growth and development for Britain and its people. Amid economic, scientific, social, and cultural changes, it's unsurprising that the justice system underwent transformations too. Women's violence surged and only began a slow but steady decline toward the end of the century. The rise of print culture brought an increased enjoyment and fascination with crime stories to the general public. While courts became more sympathetic towards infanticidal mothers, acknowledging the struggles that may have led them to commit such crimes, some were still heavily scrutinised, particularly in Scotland. Magistrates and juries were occasionally more reluctant to convict women, viewing them as weaker and in need of protection. However, female killers were treated similarly to men, if not worse. These judicial attributes coincided with the abolition of the burning of women, reflecting society's desire to move away from brutal punishments and torture. By the end of the century, Britain was steadily moving closer to industrialisation, impacting women and the criminal world through increasingly modernised legislation, structures, and systems, shaped by the particular values and opinions of Victorian society, which held many distinct views regarding women.

Chapter Five

THE NINETEENTH CENTURY

The nineteenth century was a time of development and industrialisation, bringing Victorian Britain to the brink of the modern world. New legislation, medicine, and attitudes emerged, influencing women within the criminal justice system. Although women remained secondary to men, their societal roles expanded as they took on more jobs, ultimately paving the way for the suffragette movement by the century's end. With the progression of modernity, a growing distaste for violence, particularly in the context of the death sentence for women, became evident. Contemporary commentary on the criminal justice system often highlights the court's reluctance to impose the death penalty on women. Perceptions of female crime in nineteenth century Britain served as direct reflections of the morals and values prevalent in society. Criminal women deviated from the traditional ideals of femininity admired throughout Victorian society, leading to their classification as 'fallen women'.

At the century's outset, the Old Bailey reported about twenty-two per cent of the offenders tried as female, constituting approximately twenty-five per cent of all indictments for killing. This percentage includes figures for infanticide, contributing to the higher count. When excluding infanticide and manslaughter charges, the percentage drops to about eight. The number of women brought to court as offenders significantly decreased compared to the previous century, and continued to decline throughout the 1800s. Nonetheless, female wrongdoers remained a prominent part of the criminal landscape, bringing with them scandal, intrigue, and wickedness.

The middle and working classes experienced expansion throughout the

1800s, with the working class becoming more predominant due to the millions of new jobs created by the Industrial Revolution. This growth in the working class was reflected in nineteenth century crime. In Scotland, spontaneous, public homicides were prevalent within the working class, often stemming from insults, questioned honour, and impulsive actions. Household items, fists, and feet were common weapons, reflecting the working class's expressive methods. Similar incidents occurred in these populations across British cities, with certain areas, particularly cities like London and Edinburgh, gaining notoriety for crime. Some crimes, especially theft, were tied to class inequalities, and these disparities were more pronounced in urban areas.

While a substantial number of accused murderesses hailed from the working class, the middle class also had its share of delinquent women. Women throughout history have committed murder for various reasons, such as escaping a horrendous marriage, seeking revenge, an abusive husband, engaging in a love affair, mental instability, defence of honour, or acting in self-defence. Middle class women, in particular, may have sought an escape, if only temporarily, from the strict regimes and expectations of Victorian society. Some attempted to break with their traditional roles, facing consequences that resulted from frivolous decisions born out of a desire for something different. Although not true for every middle-class murderess, some were stifled by their living conditions and lacked adequate means to express themselves. For some, these limitations led their desires to manifest in unexpected and sometimes disastrous ways, while others were pushed over the edge into unprecedented and unhealthy behaviour. Women from all classes garnered societal approval and status from their respectable and proper behaviour, as they lacked influence in other areas that would afford them similar approval. Additionally, women faced more public scrutiny than men did.

In Scotland, women accounted for about nine per cent of homicide indictments in the first half of the nineteenth century. Despite the lower percentage, Scottish women's crimes were just as brutal as those committed by men. This number might not include infanticide indictments, which would significantly increase the count. Similar to the early modern period, most women chose the home as the murder setting and were more likely to kill family members, close friends, and neighbours rather than engage in spontaneous, public brawls. Scottish women also displayed a preference for using physical violence more than English or Welsh women when committing murder. In Wales, the percentage of women brought before the courts was very small when compared to England and Scotland possibly due to the smaller population and of Welsh courts' and people's lenient attitudes toward female felons, which manifested in displays of notable mercy.

The study of anatomy experienced a surge during the Enlightenment and continued to advance during the Victorian period, attracting more students and doctors. This knowledge brought about discoveries concerning the body and forensic techniques that found their way into the criminal justice system, resulting in impactful advancements, especially in dealing with murder or infanticide. For instance, before a case could be classified as murder or infanticide, a doctor's testimony was required to determine that the victim died from inflicted wounds.

The print culture of the 1800s thrived with broadsides, newspapers, pamphlets, ballads, books, and more, spreading throughout the streets and towns of Britain. News, knowledge, and information were omnipresent, catering to a hunger for sensational and scandalous stories that fuelled public excitement or invited judgement, leaving readers grateful to be mere observers. Crime stories became a popular choice of entertainment and news as they satisfied the public's craving for the latest and most extraordinary narratives. Printers engaged in fierce competition, often overemphasising or embellishing facts, similarly to today's tabloids, to capture public attention. Researchers are urged to approach these sources with a discerning eye in order to obtain a more accurate depiction of events. Despite the popularity of various print forms, newspapers in particular became ingrained within society, becoming a regular component in the daily lives of most upper- and middle-class Britons.

Starting in late-eighteenth-century England, there was an increasing focus on recording detailed information about criminals, a trend that continued throughout the nineteenth century. By the century's end, copious amounts of comprehensive details on criminals from the previous 100-150 years were available. This surge in information collection was fuelled by the Enlightenment's pursuit of knowledge, learning, recording, and collecting. The state exhibited a growing interest in understanding criminal behaviour, initiating investigations into juvenile crime, and the link between crime and education. Statistics were also collected to monitor prisoner changes during imprisonment. The underlying goal was a sincere desire to comprehend criminals and the root causes of crime.

In Wales, a significant change to the legal system occurred with the abolishment of the Court of Great Sessions in 1830. Established after Wales was assimilated into the English criminal justice system during the sixteenth century, the court's removal in 1830 further integrated the Welsh legal system into the English assizes circuit, a move that wasn't met with enthusiasm by the Welsh population.

When discussing infanticide during the nineteenth century, records often included young children, prompting their inclusion in the broader discussion of infanticide rather than general murders. Sympathetic attitudes toward infanticidal mothers grew during this period, coinciding with an increased understanding and support for mental health issues contributing criminal acts, especially infanticide. While not reaching modern standards, this shift in perspective was influenced by the notion that women giving birth alone in pain-filled, panicked states would more than likely suffer mental distress. Many people pitied these women's circumstances, whether they were stuck in unfair situations or represented 'fallen women'. To avoid the death penalty, some mothers were charged with concealment of birth. This charge usually resulted in a lighter sentence, typically imprisonment ranging from months to years. Despite suspicions of infant murder, there was a growing reluctance to execute mothers, leading to the imposition of a lesser charge.

According to Old Bailey statistics, no woman charged with infanticide between 1800 and 1900 was executed for her crime, yet eighty-seven women faced accusations of infanticide. Most were found guilty of concealment of birth, and received prison sentences. This reflects a distinct treatment of infanticide or young child murder during the nineteenth century.

Regarding the cases of Ann Smith and Sarah Dixon in 1804 and 1805, both were charged with concealment of birth, but the the former received a one-year prison sentence, while the latter faced two years. The reason for the discrepancy is unclear. Both women's infants were born prematurely, and neither acted violently. In cases like these women played crucial roles in the courtroom, with individuals possessing medical knowledge often called upon to determine whether the child was born alive, potentially exonerating the mother.

Some women like Annie Cherry in 1887, were found guilty of killing their infants but were declared insane and not in control of their actions. Annie's case involved a long and stressful labour, with her behaviour markedly different afterward. Her testimony hinted at her lack of sanity, describing how she initially said that she had given the child to a gypsy woman, but later admitted to drowning it. She described how she placed both warm and cold water in a basin and proceeded to test the temperature for the child's safety, before putting the child into the water. She also said that she placed the child gently into the hole in the garden when burying it, again to not cause it harm. She was adjudged to be of unsound mind and imprisoned at Her Majesty's Pleasure.

Betty Amplet from Gloucester, executed in 1810 for the murder of her six-week-old infant child, provides another example. Betty killed her child by hitting her in the head and throwing her into a pond, where the infant briefly cried before passing. A person walking by heard the crying and found the child. Charged with premeditated wilful murder, which could be considered infanticide, Betty served as a cautionary tale, highlighting the shocking contrast between her outward appearance as a personable, respectable young woman and the alarming act she committed. Penitent and accepting of her fate, Betty awaited her execution.

The people of Victorian England expressed heightened concern over cases of infanticide and child murder. There was a surge in public interest, alarm, and disdain, making it a significant aspect of criminal culture that captured everyone's attention. London, in particular, witnessed a disturbing increase, with three bodies discovered in a single day in February 1861, and contributed to nearly half of the total child murders in England and Wales.

The infant death rate during Victorian England was utterly unacceptable, as reflected in statistics from coroners' inquests between 1861 and the first half of 1862. The findings revealed a staggering 1877 child deaths, encompassing cases of wilful murder, children found dead, and instances of suffocation. The prevalence of infanticide within society was exacerbated by increased attention and vocalisation through print media, emphasising the alarming rise in such incidents.

Victorian literature portrayed a shift in societal attitudes towards infanticide, acknowledging both the mother and child as victims. This rhetoric demonstrated a greater understanding of the challenges faced by mothers and the unimaginable circumstances that might lead to such tragic decisions.

Given the high number of infanticide cases, people, particularly those in healthcare professions, yearned for change. Criticism targeted the lack of support services for single mothers, social conditions, and legislation related to illegitimacy, such as the New Poor Law of 1834. This law imposed financial burdens on single mothers, compelling them to bear the cost of their child's upkeep or face the workhouse. It also stripped the mother of her ability to request financial support from the father for the child's maintenance, placing immense pressure on single mothers. Although this law was later amended, its detrimental effects persisted for a decade. These restrictions illustrate the financial limitations and burdens that unwed mothers would have faced, particularly if their pregnancy led to job loss. Married women also experienced pressure if they, along with their husbands, lacked the financial means to raise their child. Another significant factor that confronted these women, as mentioned earlier, was shame. The stigma surrounding illegitimacy persisted, and single mothers had to grapple with a tarnished reputation if their situation was revealed.

These challenges prompted the establishment of more children's charities throughout the century, such as the Homes of Hope in 1860. The Foundling Hospital, founded in 1739, became a refuge for abandoned infants, and the existing institutions struggled to meet the overwhelming demand. Inadequate social conditions and sanitation, particularly in impoverished areas, compounded the challenges faced by the poor and working classes. Additionally, poor citizens made up a large part of society, and this would have included many destitute mothers. The gradual reforms initiated during the beginning of the century, coupled with improved social systems, accessibility, and support, eventually contributed to a decline in infanticide rates as desperate mothers gained more viable options and assistance.

Scotland's infanticide problem resembled that of England, particularly concerning illegitimacy, which often served as the underlying motive for many cases. The 1800s witnessed changes in Scottish judicial attitudes and legislation towards infanticide, with increasing leniency observed. Although the death sentence was still handed out to some women throughout the century, courts exercised discretion, and only about thirteen per cent of accused women were sentenced to death. While this percentage is higher than in England or Wales, it signifies a shift toward more lenient approaches. In 1809, the Concealment of Birth Act was introduced in Scotland to replace the strict 1690 statute, presenting concealment of birth as an alternate charge to infanticide. This lesser charge carried a maximum penalty of two years in prison, a more palatable option compared to the death penalty. Some women could petition the court for a lesser sentence before their trial, and if granted, they might face banishment, transportation, whipping, or imprisonment.

In 1808, Barbara Malcolm became one of the last women in Scotland to be executed for child murder after she killed her eighteen-month-old daughter. While her case might not fit the definition of infanticide, it occurred due to circumstances similar to those infanticidal mothers find themselves in. Barbara's desperate situation, marked by the refusal of the child's father to help and her inability to work, garnered some public awareness, and highlighted the desperation she felt when committing her crime.

In Wales, attitudes towards infanticide differed from those in England and Scotland, displaying more understanding and leniency, especially in the early nineteenth century. In 1803, in Wales and England repealed the 1624 statute that assumed the guilt of an infanticidal mother until proven otherwise, deeming it outdated. Similar to Scotland, Wales favoured the charge of concealment of birth over infanticide and adjusted legislation to impose a maximum punishment of two years in prison. This aligned with the attitudes of most Welsh judges' who aimed to deter and punish while moving away from hanging women for this, or any offence. To exemplify this shift, only five women were hanged for murder or infanticide in Wales from 1730 to 1830.

One such case involved Mary Morgan, who was sentenced to death in 1805 for infanticide. Her sentence sparked confusion in some parts of Wales, revealing different attitudes within the country regarding women's crimes. The areas that were more lenient than others, contested that Mary did not deserve the death penalty. Another example highlighting the growing leniency throughout Wales was the acquittal of Maria Williams in 1813. When she sought assistance from her local parish to help raise her child and was denied, she resorted to throwing her four-month-old into a lead pit, resulting in its death. After fleeing to Cheshire, she admitted her actions upon arrest but was eventually acquitted. The court possibly recognised the dire situation she was in, and understood her desperation. While not excusing her actions, it may have elicited sympathy and guilt, sparing her from the noose.

The Capital Punishment Amendment Act of 1868 marked the end of public executions as societal disdain for violence increased. Subsequently, executions usually occurred within prisons. The Anatomy Act, effective in 1832, ceased the dissection of murderers' corpses after execution. This change is evident in cases of criminal women following this date, as those executed before continued to be dissected and anatomised. In the early decades of the century, women who pleaded pregnancy after conviction and were found to be pregnant received temporary reprieves, which occasionally turned permanent. After 1848 however, any reprieve granted to a pregnant woman found to be with child remained permanent after her child's birth. This plea became less common during the nineteenth century, with its last use at the Old Bailey in 1880. By 1840, Victorian society had shifted away from the brutality of previous centuries, using the death penalty only for men and women convicted of murder or high treason.

Imprisonment gained prominence as a punishment for various crimes, leading prisons across Britain to function more than ever before. This period saw prison development, despite issues such as overcrowding and unsanitary conditions. Throughout the century and into the twentieth century, ongoing reforms sought to improve prisons. The gendered approach to reforming the criminals within prison walls was evident, with women's prisons focusing on 'moral regeneration', as described by Zedner in her article *'Women, Crime, and Penal Responses: A Historical Account'* (1991). In contrast, male regimes emphasised discipline and deterrence. Imprisoned women faced a heightened stigma. They became social pariahs, which made it challenging to find employment or assistance, pushing them towards illegal activities for survival. This cycle often led them back to criminality and possibly imprisonment. Statistics from the nineteenth century indicate there were more female repeat offenders in prisons than male. The term 'penal servitude', denoting imprisonment with hard labour, replaced transportation by the middle of the century, as mandated by the 1853 and 1857 Penal Servitude Acts. Additionally, the punishment of whipping, though not often associated with murder, was abolished for women in 1817.

While nineteenth century juries marked a notable improvement in fairness, a woman's appearance, demeanour on the stand, and the circumstances surrounding her crime continued to influence them. If a woman indicted for murder appeared calm, feminine, and polite, she was likely to receive more sympathy, consideration, and respect than a woman who displayed anger, frustration, or rudeness.

As the century progressed, both the justice system and society became increasingly intrigued by purported biological reasons for women's deviance, an interest not extended to explanations for male crime. Mental insufficiency was often analysed as the cause of many women's behaviour, and this focus on women's mental health persisted and grew as the twentieth century began. While these theories may accurately link mental health to criminal acts, they wrongly perpetuate the stereotype of women as mentally weak, enslaved to their impulses and desires. Women who committed crimes while embodying unfeminine, or masculine qualities faced harsher treatment, being considered more unnatural or inhuman than those who adhered to feminine expectations. Mental illness was unfairly linked to so-called feminine attributes, often associated with women's reproductive biology, projecting them as weak and vulnerable.

The handling of insanity began to evolve in the nineteenth century. The 1800 Act for the Safe Custody of Insane Persons Charged with Offences empowered court officials to imprison anyone they deemed unable to differentiate between right and wrong, regardless of guilt. 1848, the M'Naughten Rules were established as the first 'test' for insanity, which introduced criteria to determine a defendant's sanity. These steps aimed to understand the role of mental health in criminal behaviour. However, some policies may have been overly controlling, lacking the knowledge and support to take care of those who truly needed it. If a woman was believed to be insane at the time of her crime, she was likely to be sentenced to imprisonment at Her Majesty's Pleasure. During the nineteenth century, hospitals for individuals with mental instabilities began to open, though the treatment, both physically and emotionally, remained primitive compared to modern medical and moral standards.

In Scotland, an analysis reveals that in cases of homicide, women were sentenced to hang more frequently than men. This could be attributed to women's higher likelihood of using poison, seen as a premeditated act with an automatic penalty of death. Another reason might be related to the discussed deviation from expected passive and weak traits in women, resulting in harsher treatment. Nevertheless, there was a shift over the eighteenth and nineteenth centuries, viewing women as more in need of protection than dangerous, aligning with increased leniency towards infanticidal mothers and a growing reluctance to impose the death penalty on women.

With the continued professionalisation of constables, sheriffs, thief catchers, and other roles related to crime regulation, the Metropolitan Police was established in 1829. This initiative brought about a formal and regulated service designed for safety and crime control in London and its surroundings, setting the stage for the development of cemented, professionalised systems throughout the country.

The punishment of women and the alterations to it were influenced by ideas about what was appropriate to subject women to both in public and private. Concerns about the children potentially left behind by these women, and the perceived ability of women to endure certain punishments also played a role. While these considerations benefitted many women who were spared certain penalties, they were rooted in Victorian ideas, stereotypical behaviours and expectations of women.

During the nineteenth century and into the twentieth century, serious crime became associated with masculinity, given the majority of offenders were men, and the attributes of masculinity aligned with these criminal acts. On the other hand, women were often linked to crimes of a more sexual nature like prostitution or infanticide. When a woman committed a serious offence typically attributed to men, she was viewed as particularly threatening and faced harsh punishment, unlike her counterparts who were punished more leniently for committing accepted feminine crimes.

As discussed earlier, there is an abundance of records on criminal women from the nineteenth century. The Old Bailey is filled with detailed court records and Ordinary Accounts, while numerous broadsides showcase scandalous crime stories throughout Britain. Newspapers were plentiful as go-to sources for crime news. Given this wealth of information, it is important to note that the numerous women being discussed here represent only a fraction of the nineteenth century murderesses across Britain.

The next four women under consideration received significant publicity during and after their trials, with books, articles, and essays dedicated to their crimes. These women are relatively well known, and their wicked stories have solidified their positions as some of the most devious Victorian murderesses.

At the top of the list is Mary Pearcey, a twenty-six-year-old woman who lived in London during the latter part of the 1800s. Also known as Eleanor Wheeler, she lived with a man named John Charles Pearcey. Despite not being married to him, she adopted his name during their three-year relationship. Their separation was prompted in part by Mary's growing fondness for a man named Frank Hogg. Starting in 1886, Mary and Frank began spending time together, although they allegedly did not consummate their relationship until after Frank's marriage to a woman named Phoebe in November 1888. Despite his marriage, Mary and Frank continued their relationship, and Phoebe, unaware of the affair, welcomed Mary into their home. Mary spent time at the Hoggs' house, visiting Phoebe, Frank's sister, and his mother.

On 24 October 1890, Frank returned home to find Phoebe and their young daughter missing. The next morning, they had not returned, prompting Frank to search for them at Phoebe's father's house. With no success, he returned home to find his family reading a newspaper article about a body being found. The police inspector arrived, and Frank sadly identified his wife's body. Subsequently, Mary was arrested on suspicion of murder. Further investigation revealed evidence against Mary, including a note inviting Phoebe to tea, and blood on Mary's clothes and kitchen surfaces. Mary perpetrated a vicious assault on Phoebe when she arrived for tea. She ruthlessly slashed her throat almost to the point of severance, stabbed her, delivered blows to her head, attacked her with a fire poker, and either suffocated the infant or abandoned her somewhere where she succumbed to the harsh cold. There were also eyewitness accounts of Mary pushing a pram down the street the evening of the murder, more than likely carrying Phoebe and the child. The child's body was discovered on 26 October, leading to Mary's arrest for the murders of both Phoebe and her daughter. She was found guilty and hanged on 23 December 1890.

Mary's story is brutal, and it takes an interesting twist as she is considered the sole female suspect in the Jack the Ripper murders. While lacking concrete evidence, several fascinating coincidences surround her. She resided in London during the same period as the murders, which abruptly ceased around the time of her hanging. Furthermore, her method of killing bore a striking resemblance to Jack the Ripper's. Additionally, the postage stamp on one of Jack the Ripper's letters, was much later analysed for DNA, which was found to belong to a woman. While in prison, Mary sent a letter to a Madrid newspaper with the cryptic message 'M.E.C.P. Last wish of M.E.W. Have not betrayed'. Some speculate M.E.C.P. could refer to four of Jack the Ripper's victims: Mary, Elizabeth, Catherine, and Polly. How intriguing to consider Jack the Ripper might have been a woman, as a woman covered in blood could move through the streets unnoticed, because it would be assumed she was a midwife, so nothing was amiss.

Our next tale is about the cruel story of Amelia Dyer, a woman arrested on 3 April 1896, in Reading, England, charged with the murder of Doris Marmon and Harry Simmons. These infants, whose mothers were unable to care for them, paid Amelia to foster them as her own. Their bodies, showing signs of strangulation, were discovered in a carpet bag at the bottom of the River Thames near Reading, the 5th and 6th bodies of children to be found in the same area in two weeks.

Amelia Dyer, born in Bristol in 1839 into a respected and well-off family, faced tragedies in her youth, losing two siblings and her mother, followed by her father's death during her teenage years. As an adult, she struggled with mental health, spending time in asylums. By 1869, widowed with a daughter, Amelia sought a means of financial support. Learning about the practice of parents paying women to care for their babies, she started her own business. However, instead of caring for the children, she would murder them shortly after taking them in, reporting their deaths as accidental or due to poor health. This disturbing practice, known as baby farming, was unfortunately not uncommon during the Victorian period. Amelia was not the only woman to participate in this money-making horror story. Many women, most of whom were single, were desperate to have someone take in their young child because they couldn't afford to feed and care for them or couldn't remain employed while caring for a child. These situations were very similar to the tragic circumstances infanticidal mothers found themselves in.

In Victorian England, the child mortality rate was alarmingly high so the deaths of the infants in Amelia's care didn't initially attract any attention. However, the extraordinary rate at which children under Mrs Dyer's care were perishing eventually caught the attention of her doctors. Subsequently, she received a six-month labour sentence for neglect. Undeterred, Mrs Dyer continued her abhorrent business and, in 1895, relocated to Reading. Fearing detection by authorities, she shifted to disposing of the bodies herself, instead of reporting the deaths to a doctor. This decision ultimately sealed her fate.

Amelia's fortunes took a turn in the spring of 1896 when a box discovered in the Thames, passing through Reading, revealed a distressing sight - an infant girl's lifeless body. The crucial clue lay in the stamped brown paper wrapping, bearing the label 'Midland Railway' dated 24 October 1895. The parcel also contained an address in Caversham that when investigated was associated to Mrs Dyer's married name, Mrs Thomas. Armed with this information, Detective Constable James Beattie investigated, learning from neighbours that Amelia had since moved to Kensington Road in Reading. Upon reaching her new residence, Beattie discovered newspaper articles featuring adoption ads, piles of baby clothing, and the identical fabric tape found wrapped around the baby's neck in the box. Although the exact identity of the deceased, more than likely Helena Fry, remained elusive due to decomposition, Amelia was taken into custody, but was granted a remand as authorities sought additional evidence.

The incriminating evidence surfaced through the discovery of six more infants in the Thames during dredging, with a carpet bag proving pivotal as it contained the lifeless bodies of two children – Harry Simmons and Doris Marmon. Given the recent occurrence of these murders, the bodies were still distinguishable. The female infant bore strangulation marks around her neck, identical to the tape found on Helena Fry. The boy's cause of death was determined to be strangulation, and it was presumed the girl had met a similar fate too. The parents of these children were traced, and the mother of the female child positively identified her. She had entrusted her infant to Amelia a few weeks previously for care and nursing. The boy's guardians were also located, revealing that he was given to Amelia around the same time as the infant girl. These revelations ultimately sealed Amelia's fate, leading to her indictment for the murder of both children, though the Old Bailey records only specify the trial for Doris Marmon, not Harry Simmons. Nevertheless, the Old Bailey proceedings extensively discussed both murders.

Prior to the final trial on 20 May 1896, numerous inquests and hearings into the murders, and the hard work of three local policemen, unveiled the extensive thirty-year practice of baby farming by Amelia Dyer. As they painstakingly connected the dots and amassed evidence, it became apparent that even before Amelia's case commenced, thirty to forty babies had been discovered in the Thames near London. During the case's progression, at least one more body was discovered near Reading. By the time of her final trial at the Old Bailey, an overwhelming amount of evidence implicated Mrs Dyer, shifting the primary question from her guilt to her sanity. Subjected to examinations by various doctors and psychology experts, it was eventually determined that her defence's plea of insanity lacked validity. Amelia Dyer was found guilty of the wilful murder of Doris Marmon and responsible for numerous others. She received a death sentence, and while in prison, she wrote a confession detailing her actions and asserting the lack of involvement of her family members in her deeds. Amelia Dyer was executed on 10 June 1896.

Authorities presume the number of babies Amelia may have murdered could be in the hundreds, considering her nearly thirty-year involvement in baby farming, during which hundreds of children passed through her house. The case of Amelia Dyer stands out as the most prolific of baby farming incidents throughout the Victorian period. However, this dark chapter led to a significant shift in British legislation regarding childcare and safety. Amendments to The Infant Life Protection Act of 1872 were made in 1896 to ensure the registration and supervision of individuals caring for children who were not their own. Subsequently, in 1908, the Children's Act was enacted, making it mandatory to register foster parents and granting additional authority to local police to ensure the welfare of foster children.

Catherine (Kate) Webster is another Victorian woman whose crime caused a significant public uproar. Born Catherine Lawler in County Wexford, Ireland, in 1849, not much is known about her early life. However, by the time of her most serious crime in 1879, she had already faced brief imprisonment for larceny several times, once before leaving Ireland. Upon arriving in England, she accumulated three more convictions, establishing herself as a familiar figure in the London criminal scene.

In 1879, Kate was introduced to a widow through a mutual acquaintance, a woman for whom she occasionally performed service work while substituting for her friend and landlady. Julia Thomas, the widow, was seeking a general servant, and Kate commenced working for her at her Richmond residence in January 1879. Mrs Thomas was known for her eccentricity and occasional irritable demeanour, which neighbours attested to. Kate, conversely, was intimidating and disliked being told what to do. Mrs Thomas, sensing Kate's formidable nature, tried to avoid upsetting her. Their working relationship continued until 3 March 1879. On that day, Kate claimed to have visited her young son and then to have had some drinks at a local alehouse before returning to Mrs Thomas' house. Upon arriving late, Mrs Thomas expressed displeasure, as she was eager to attend church but couldn't leave until Kate returned. A disagreement ensued, more than likely triggering Kate's later actions. The circumstances surrounding the murder of Mrs Thomas remains a subject of debate, with questions about whether it was premeditated or not. After Julia left for church, Kate continued to have a few more drinks.

Upon Julia's return, their argument escalated, and while the exact details of the altercation remain unclear, it is reasonable to assert that Kate assaulted Mrs Thomas, quickly rendering her incapacitated. Kate claimed to have pushed Mrs Thomas down the stairs, but Elliott O'Donnell, in his book *Trial of Kate Webster,* pointed out that a neighbour in the connecting house only heard a small thud. O'Donnell argued that if a woman was thrown down the stairs, there would have been a significant noise and a likely scream. Subsequently, with Mrs Thomas incapacitated but still alive, Kate swiftly placed her hands around Mrs Thomas' neck and strangled her. Though O'Donnell suggested the possibility that Mrs Thomas might not have been dead after this, but only stunned and faint, Kate proceeded to carry her to the kitchen, where she gruesomely began to dismember Julia into small pieces. Kate continued, boiling some of the dismembered parts while burning the entrails and bones. Shockingly, there's even a chance, supported by the testimony of a neighbouring woman, that a few days after the murder, Kate sold two jars of 'premium fat,' at the local alehouse, unwittingly rendered from Mrs Thomas.

Having packed three parcels with Mrs Thomas' remains, Kate disposed of a foot and some other small body parts, while enlisting a friend's son to help her dispose of the remaining box and bag. Kate hatched a plan to assume Mrs Thomas' identity, dress in her clothes and jewellery, sell off her furniture, and then return to Ireland. Over the following days some of the body parts she disposed of were discovered. When she encountered a curious neighbour who started asked questions around 18 March, Kate became spooked and immediately left for Ireland. Unfortunately for Kate, a letter of hers was found in one of Mrs Thomas' dresses, which she had given a friend of hers to sell, along with papers belonging to Mrs Thomas in another. As these discoveries unfolded, the friends who had assisted Kate with Mrs Thomas' belongings began to piece together the dreadful story.

Eventually, it was identified that Kate was posing as Mrs Thomas, and the real victim was identified as Julia Martha Thomas. Kate was apprehended in Ireland on 28 March. In the ensuing months, the story unfolded through witness testimonies and uncovered evidence. Despite Kate's attempts to implicate those who had assisted her after the murder, their innocence was eventually declared. On 30 June, Kate's trial concluded. Despite her declarations of innocence, composed demeanour, cleverness, and convincing speech, she was found guilty of the murder of Julia Martha Thomas and sentenced to be hanged. Throughout the trial and her time in prison, her composure, sternness, and assumed indifference were noted. Her attitude, perceived as coldness, persisted until the day before her execution when she admitted her guilt and denied the involvement of the people she had previously implicated. On 29 July 1879, she was executed at Wandsworth prison. Kate's crime stirred public interest due to her cruel and brutal temperament, along with her ability to deceive. The Richmond Murder became a topic of discussion across the country.

Mary Ann Cotton, is another infamous nineteenth century murderess, who gained notoriety for poisoning most of her family members with her arsenic lined teapot. The likely motives behind her crimes, collecting life insurance money and/or making room for a new lover by eliminating the old one, are debated. Mary Ann's story is a devious one; born in 1832 near Seaham Harbour, County Durham, she lost her father at the age of fourteen. After working as an under nurse for a nearby family, she apprenticed as a dressmaker upon her return home at age nineteen.

Mary Ann eventually married William Mowbray, and after moving away, they returned, claiming to have lost four children in the last five years. Over the next three years, three more of their young children died of what was diagnosed as gastric fever, although arsenic poisoning has similar symptoms. William died shortly after, and Mary Ann inherited all of the children's and William's life insurance money. She then married George Ward, but shortly after both he and Mary Ann's mother suddenly died.

Taking a job as a housekeeper to Mr James Robinson, Mary Ann married him in June 1867. Between June and December 1867, all five of Robinson's children, along with Mary Ann's daughter Elizabeth, died of supposed gastric fever. Robinson's sisters grew suspicious of Mary Ann and speculated that she had poisoned them. After parting ways with Robinson due to her spending habits and insistence on procuring life insurance, Mary Ann married Frederick Cotton. They moved to West Auckland with Frederick's two boys, Frederick Jr. and Charles Edward, and had a son named Robert. Living with them was a lodger named Joseph Nattrass.

Over the following year, everyone in the Cotton household, except Mary, succumbed to what appeared to be gastric fever. Some speculate Mary Ann's desire for Nattrass might have contributed to the death of Frederick Sr. A similar assertion suggests that her final lover named Quick-Manning could have been the cause of Nattrass' demise due to Mary Ann's desire for him. While there isn't ample evidence to support these claims, it is plausible that Mary Ann had other motives beyond financial gain for her multitude of murders.

The death of Charles Edward in July 1872 finally sparked the attention of local authorities, prompting a request for an autopsy to investigate any sign of foul play. After a medical analysis, arsenic was discovered in the boy's organs, along with definitive signs of arsenic poisoning. Mary Ann was arrested for the murder, triggering an investigation that unveiled a pattern of deaths possibly caused by poisoning in her past. Authorities focused on gathering more evidence, planning to exhume the bodies of Joseph Nattrass and the two other Cotton boys. Arsenic was found in Nattrass' body, providing additional, though not conclusive, evidence against Mary Ann.

Despite her imprisonment, Mary Ann's stay was extended because she was pregnant. She gave birth in prison and cared for her child for several weeks before the baby was placed with another family. Mary Ann's final trial took place in March 1873, when she was found guilty of the murder of Charles Edward Cotton. Although no specific evidence existed, she was also suspected of the murder of at least fifteen other family members. She was sentenced to death by hanging and spent her remaining weeks in Durham gaol. Described as cold, calm, and reserved, by the time of her execution, she seemed resigned to her fate. Despite continuously claiming her innocence, and never fully admitting guilt, she did suggest that she may have accidentally poisoned them. Authorities were sceptical of and confused by this statement, as she committed these murders over months and years, making it nearly impossible to have been accidental.

On the day of her execution, Mary Ann actively prayed, sobbed and exhibited signs of great distress. She was executed on 24 March 1873, leaving behind a tale of treachery and deviousness. Notably, her execution was intriguing as records indicate that the 'press' were allowed into the gaol to write about and witness the execution. This marked a new chapter in the world of print, news, and journalism, as about twenty people witnessed the execution and reported on it in a narrative tone for the public.

As previously mentioned, numerous cases of murders occurred

throughout nineteenth century Britain, involving a wide variety of victims, motives, and causes. The case of Mary Ann Cotton highlighted the significant attention given to poison as the chosen method of female killers during the 1800s. Poison became increasingly prevalent during this era due to its easy accessibility, administration, especially within the home, and the clandestine nature of the crime. However, the deceptive and secretive nature of poisoning, coupled with the stark betrayal of expected warm, motherly, and wifely duties, led both the public and the courts to despise this crime, resulting in harsh punishment for perpetrators. These traits, along, with the inability to protect oneself, instilled fear, anxiety, and intrigue. Consequently, when a poisoning incident occurred, it was sensationalised by the print media and public. A newspaper article from 1856 described the use of poison as the latest trend in crime. Despite its popularity, poison was not the exclusive method of murder employed by women in the nineteenth century.

Arsenic and laudanum emerged as two of the most frequently used substances for poisoning. Laudanum, initially used in medicine, could be lethal at certain concentrations, and arsenic, with various household applications including rat poisoning, was relatively easy to obtain. Other substances such as strychnine, chloroform, vitriol, and prussic acid were also relatively easily acquired. Public anxiety surrounding poison led to the Arsenic Act of 1851, which introduced new regulations on the purchase of the substance, to combat its nefarious use. The Act specified that arsenic could not be sold to anyone under the age of twenty-one, and required the customer to be personally known by the seller or have a mutual acquaintance who would vouch for them. Additionally, the seller had to record the reason for purchasing the arsenic, and the poison had to be coloured, often by using soot or indigo, to aid in identification.

Due to the fear among men regarding the rise in poisonings

orchestrated by women, a sexist amendment was briefly added to the arsenic bill, permitting the sale of arsenic only to adult men. This amendment did not endure, and by the time the Act was finalised, it only restricted the age of the purchaser, not their gender. The use of poison gradually declined by the end of the century, particularly due to advancements in medicine which made it easier to identify certain poisons during autopsies.

While poison was a prevalent weapon across Britain, the comparison between Scotland and England, reveals significant differences. From 1807–1859, almost fifty per cent of the female perpetrated homicides in England were caused by poison, while in Scotland, the figure was around twenty-six per cent. In 1831 Glasgow, Mary Byers was executed for poisoning John Martin alongside her husband, by overdosing him with laudanum and subsequently robbing him. Mary admitted her guilt, but her husband only confessed on the day of execution. Similarly, in Somerset, Sophia Edney, employed poison in her crime. On 5 March 1836, her husband, John Edney succumbed to an illness later determined, through post-mortem examination, to have been caused by arsenic in his food. Sophia, accused of murder as she was the one responsible for cooking, was found guilty and hanged on 14 April 1836.

Mary Mckinnon, a Scottish woman like Mary Byers, did not resort to poison for her crime. According to records, her act was not premeditated but rather a spur of the moment incident. In 1823, Mary was executed for the murder of William Howet, whom she allegedly stabbed with a sharp instrument, various reports mentioning a knife or a skewer). Mary vehemently maintained her innocence, never confessing to the crime for which she was hanged.

The altercation with William began inside Mary's brothel/public house, where William initiated a fight. Mary intervened between Howet and another woman to quell the disturbance. When he pulled her hair, Mary in self-defence, grabbed a knife and unintentionally stabbed him.

Despite the circumstances suggesting a possible manslaughter charge, Mary did not receive any leniency. Even as she awaited execution, Mary cut her hair to give to her friends. Her behaviour remained calm and resigned to her fate after both attempts for remission or mitigation were denied. Despite the uncertainties surrounding McKinnon's culpability, especially if her only intent was to stop a drunken brawl that could have endangered her business or others, she faced a harsh fate. Mary's punishment seemed influenced more by her profession and previous reputation, making her a victim of the gendered and class biases within the High Court of the Justiciary and society.

Mary Timney's 1862 execution stands out as the last public hanging of a woman in Scotland. She was indicted for killing Ann Hannah, a neighbour with whom Mary had a history of disagreements and dislike. Mary eventually confessed to taking a wooden mallet one morning and confronting Ann, which resulted in Ann's head being fatally bashed in. Evidence, including bloody clothes and the mallet found in Mary's house supported her guilt. Mary claimed no premeditation in her confession, attributing the crime to provocation, dismissal of complaints, and intimidation from Ann, her brother, and the local police constable. Her intent was to confront Ann, but not to kill. Mary's execution caused public uproar, particularly among women who expressed their disgust at the public execution of a woman. They were horrified by the mistreatment of Mary's daughter Susan, who had been pressured to provide evidence against her mother. This would have been most traumatising for a child.

Petitions, signed by at least 6,000 people were sent in an attempt to stay Mary's execution, but they were rejected by the Home Office and never reached Queen Victoria. Mary's execution became the last of its kind for women and prompted new legislation on female punishment. Instead of instilling a sense of stability and safety, as intended by the government, it had a demoralising effect on the public, eroding trust in the institution.

One advocate, persisting in campaigning for Mary's commutation of punishment even after her execution, contributed to the eventual end of the death sentence. Although it took another fifty years for this change to come about in Scotland, public execution was soon abolished.

As Wales was increasingly reluctant to impose the death penalty, especially for women, a unique case catches our attention. In 1801, Alice Clarke, who confessed to the premeditated killing of her young child, was sentenced to hang. Her execution was temporarily respited due to her pregnancy, but it was later carried out. Many women in similar situations didn't plead guilty, increasing their chance of acquittal. Alice Clarke, like Mary Morgan, was one of only five women hanged for murder or infanticide in Wales from 1730-1830.

ANN HEYTREY (C.1804–1820)

Ann Heytrey (c. 1804 - 1820) has a tragic and brutal story. Born in Sharlecote, Warwick, she was described as a stout girl with a plain and calm expression. Ann did not fit the expected image of a female criminal, illustrating the nineteenth century's specific idea and expectation regarding the appearance and behaviour of women who committed crimes. The debate over Ann's age adds a layer of complexity to her story, with one source listing her as twenty-three years old, while a broadside suggests she was only sixteen, potentially making her the youngest murderess examined in this book. Ann, being sixteen, would also support the immense intrigue that the trial and execution had on the people of Warwick.

On 29 August 1819, in the town of Ashow near Leamington, Ann Heytrey viciously killed her mistress, Mrs Dormer, by slashing her throat and stabbing her multiple times. The motive for the murder remains uncertain, with sources mentioning the devil commanding Ann or Ann expressing an unexplained urge to do it. Despite minor variations in the details of the news stories, the overall horrifying narrative remains consistent. On the evening of 29 August 1819, Ann, Mrs Dormer, Mr Dormer, their four children, and three gentlemen were all dining together at the Dormers' home. After dinner had concluded, everyone left, except for Ann and her mistress.

Ann and Mrs Dormer went outside to pick vegetables from the garden. Once back inside, while cutting the vegetables, Ann had a sudden thought or whisper, compelling her to murder her mistress. One account describes her running out, returning, and knocking Mrs Dormer out of her chair with her fist before stabbing her, while others simply state that she ran and knocked her mistress out of her chair. Mrs Dormer, fatally wounded, fought back, screaming at the attack and lying on the floor for almost a minute, while Ann stood above her, before staggering up and running up the stairs to her bedroom. Ann followed her up the stairs with a carving knife (though one source says it was a hatchet) and found her close to passing out. Ann went to her and began to cut and stab with the knife, which included slicing her throat. Described in the 1820 broadside *The Last Awful Moments And Dying Confession of Ann Aytry*, as 'from ear to ear'. Mrs Dormer tried to fight back until she couldn't. Only then, once she stopped moving, did Ann let her go, put the knife on the body to stage a suicide, and proceed back downstairs.

Upon the return of Mrs Dormer's children, they noticed blood on the floor, and Ann appeared agitated. They inquired about their mother's whereabouts, and initially, Ann claimed she had gone for a walk. However, upon further questioning, she stated that Mrs Dormer had gone into the garden. One of Mrs Dormer's daughters went upstairs, entering her mother's room, and let out a scream upon discovering her lifeless body on the floor. The others rushed to the scene and immediately questioned Ann about her involvement. Her response was a firm 'no' when asked if she had committed the act and 'no' when questioned about anyone else being in the house.

Suspecting dishonesty, the constables were summoned.

Ann was taken into custody as a suspicious character, and it was during this time that she confessed her guilt to J. Bellerby, constable of Kenilworth, and recounted the events of the evening in question. According to one report, once she had admitted her guilt, she seemed resigned to die, which contributed to her stoic demeanour during the trial. Indicted for wilful murder, Ann was transferred to Warwick gaol to await her trial at the Warwick assizes a few months later. During her imprisonment, she was repeatedly asked why she committed the crime, but her response remained consistent – she didn't know. One report suggested that the only discernible cause might have been her denied attendance at a wake she had requested to go to. The veracity of this claim and whether it truly motivated the murder remained uncertain, as Ann steadfastly stuck to her explanation.

Interestingly, during her trial, she apparently pleaded not guilty, despite confessing to the constable. Throughout the proceedings, she remained relatively stoic, though occasional agitation and fidgeting with her shawl were noted. After witnesses presented their evidence, and Ann's confession to the constable was recounted, the court asked if she had anything to say in her defence, to which she remained silent. Found guilty of both murder and petty treason, she was immediately sentenced to hang and be drawn upon a hurdle to the place of execution. By the early nineteenth century, burning for petty treason had been abolished and replaced with hanging.

While awaiting execution, Ann penned letters to Mrs Dormer's daughters, Mr Dormer, and her own mother. Each letter expressed deep remorse for her actions. In the letter to Miss Dormer, Ann conveyed profound sorrow for the harm inflicted on the family, sought forgiveness, and hoped that God would provide solace. She urged others not to heed voices urging harmful acts. The letter to Mr Dormer echoed these sentiments, emphasising Ann's lack of animosity towards Mrs Dormer and expressing regret for the pain inflicted on the family. She wished them happiness and divine forgiveness. Her letter to her mother expressed repentance, sought forgiveness, and hoped for reconciliation in the afterlife. Ann's letters were profoundly remorseful, reflecting her belief in divine forgiveness for her sins.

At her execution on 19 April 1820, Ann was attired in all black and transported on a hurdle to the execution site outside Warwick gaol. She remained remorseful and accepting. When questioned again about the motive for her act, she reiterated that she didn't know why and suggested the devil might have prompted her. Addressing the crowd, she shared a brief account of the events, urging them not to follow her example. Describing herself as an unhappy wretch, she expressed love for her mistress, said a prayer, and was hanged in front of numerous spectators who had come to witness the end of this widely discussed crime. Her body was handed over to local surgeons for dissection, and her letters were passed along.

While much of Ann's s tale was conveyed to the constable of Kenilworth by Ann herself, it is challenging to ascertain if any details align with the final speech she delivered about the murder just before her execution. Two reports about Ann's criminal acts mentioned a rumour circulating before the incident, that suggested she had committed infanticide. One report dismissed these rumours as fabricated, while another, in a dismissive tone about Ann's faith, claimed she killed her mistress, who had once spared her from prosecution for a prior crime. If this is a reference to that rumour, the preceding report had already debunked its inaccuracy months earlier, during her trial and execution. This addition to the report appears to be included merely as additional fodder against Ann.

As possibly the youngest murderess in this book, Ann's story remains unfortunate and upsetting, with the motives driving her to commit such a crime remaining a mystery.

MARGARET SHUTTLEWORTH (–1821)

The intriguing tale of Margaret Shuttleworth (nee Tindal) is a curious and rather gloomy one. Margaret Tindal was actually born in Gothenburg, Sweden, to Scottish parents who owned a tavern called the Scots Inn. Her father, Alexander, had been part of the British military service before deserting and fleeing to Scotland with his wife Janet. He had also played a role in some illegal smuggling initiatives in Scotland, which he continued once they moved to Sweden. Margaret, and her father shared a fondness for excessive drinking, and he died young while they were in Sweden. Her parents had six children, though three died abroad, and in 1791, Janet returned to Montrose, Scotland, with her children, when young Margaret was just five years old.

Margaret's education was limited as her mother earned modest wages, and had children to care for; so she was sent off at an early age to be a children's nursery maid. Unfortunately, Margaret experienced a tragic accident in this job when a child she was looking after fell from a great height and died a few days later. This event undoubtedly left an impact on young Margaret. After the accident, she worked in a local tavern as a servant and was described as attentive, always clean, and although not extravagant, she was always well groomed and tidy. After working at another inn, Margaret met Henry Shuttleworth, an educated English corporal of marines from Birmingham, and they were soon wed. They moved to Portsmouth and then Taunton, where they were respected, and Margaret was known as a pleasant neighbour with a proper demeanour.

Eventually the couple returned to Montrose, just north of Dundee, where Henry became a grocer and spirit dealer. They took over a neighbour's tavern, and initially Margaret, averse to drinking, dismissed servants who frequently indulged in the habit. However, she later succumbed to drinking herself, attributing it to changes in Henry's demeanour and their unsuccessful tavern. Their marriage, once relatively happy when Margaret was sober, deteriorated into a tumultuous relationship marked by anger, arguments, and occasional violence. Due to these factors, Henry was uncomfortable and unwilling to welcome many visitors. Her behaviour disturbed their home life, and there were speculations that, fuelled by a found letter, Henry contemplated leaving Margaret for his family in England before his death. This may have been the motive for Margaret in her drunken state to kill Henry, but the letter was excluded from evidence, and its authenticity unproven.

The tragic turn in Margaret and Henry's relationship reached its climax on the night of Friday 27 April, or early in the morning on Saturday, 28 April 1821, when Henry was fatally struck multiple times on the head with a fire poker. The exact events of that night remain unknown, as there were no witnesses. That evening, Margaret, heavily intoxicated, had a heated exchange with Henry. Angered, she even punched through the kitchen window, prompting Henry to ask their servant, Catharine, to put her to bed. Catharine complied, placing Margaret's in her ground floor room, while Henry slept on the second floor due to their ongoing quarrels. Catharine reported seeing Henry chatting with a neighbour before leaving for the night.

Margaret, recalled waking up around 4am to get water, and discovering Henry's lifeless body at the bottom of the stairs near her door; she had accidentally tripped over him. Assuming he fell, she immediately went to find Catharine, looking in the kitchen and then upstairs. When she couldn't find her, Margaret ran to the closest neighbour for help. She summoned her mother, and sister, who advised her to fetch the local doctor. Catharine returned after hearing about the incident, and Margaret, seemingly unaffected, called out to her for support. Throughout the trial, Margaret's emotional detachment was emphasised, though it was noted that she was frequently intoxicated in the days leading up to her arrest. The absence of tears, however, doesn't necessarily imply guilt, as people express emotions differently, and Margaret may have hidden hers, or drowned hers with alcohol.

Margaret was taken into custody on Sunday, but, as was mentioned, appeared indifferent. One reason for this may have been her confidence in her innocence, believing the court would come to the same conclusion. She was transferred to Forfar jail and later to Perth jail to await her trial. During her confinement, she continued to drink, selling some of her goods to obtain spirits. Her trial took place on 19 September 1821, where the details of the investigation were discussed. Some aspects of the case, particularly concerning the murder weapon, are slightly mismatched. A fire poker, which was crucial evidence against Margaret, was discovered at the scene with blood and hair on it, but witnesses disagreed on the hair's colour, adding complexity to the case. Another witness said that when he saw the poker it was clean. This is very interesting and confusing, especially when it was the key piece of evidence against Margaret.

Margaret's hands were found to have blood on them, and a spot of blood was present on her apron. She explained that when she tripped over Henry, she bent down and felt around him, including his head, resulting in her getting covered in his blood. The doctor who came to investigate said that Margaret had seemed upset and shaken. The doctors, after the autopsy, confirmed that the injuries to Henry's head could not have resulted from a fall down the stairs but from three or four blows to the head by a strong object, supporting the theory of the poker as the murder weapon. Another witness reported hearing Margaret threaten Henry with the poker in her drunken state before she went to bed. It was also revealed in court that Henry had been drinking that night too and was unsteady on his feet.

The court suggested Margaret was likely guilty because she was alone in the fully locked house the night before, and in the morning when she found her husband. In Margaret's defence, her counsel raised several points, questioning why she would stay at home until Sunday, only to be arrested if she had committed the crime. He also highlighted the contradiction of her being so intoxicated that she couldn't undress herself for bed, yet supposedly wielded a murder weapon. He hypothesised that Henry had been drinking that night and may have engaged in a quarrel with someone. This individual might have intended to kill him but refrained from robbing him upon hearing the barking of their terrier.

The jury, however, reached a unanimous decision of guilt on 20 September 1821, asserting that 'murder, more especially by the wife upon her husband, is similarly forbidden by the laws of God and man'. This statement reflects a gendered bias, suggesting that a wife killing her husband was especially heinous, highlighting the unequal treatment of women in the courtroom still present in the nineteenth century. Margaret was then ordered to be taken back to the tolbooth (jail) of Perth to await her execution that was supposed to take place on 1 November 1821 in Montrose.

During her time awaiting her execution, she could no longer access the liquor she desired, but interestingly, she appeared content and accepting of her fate, though while maintaining her innocence. Around 200 townspeople petitioned the government twice for a pardon, and Margaret also wrote a petition. The first petition succeeded, granting her a one-month reprieve, but her guilt was later reaffirmed. Another execution date was set for 7 December 1821.

Despite engaging in religious devotions and maintaining composure during her confinement, a subsequent petition for pardon, signed by influential individuals, failed to secure her release. It also stated that the town resisted a public execution, especially that of a woman, which was a situation people wanted to be treated delicately. The crowd outside the jail expressed discontent at the verdict, shouting 'Shame!', when the news reached them. Margaret, upon hearing the result, remained calm, expecting the outcome. The night before her execution, she was visited by her sister and mother. She displayed great composure about her impending fate and willingly participated in recommended religious proceedings.

The day of her execution, Margaret continued to exhibit acceptance and composure. She wore all black with a white apron, presenting herself as very well kept and clean. As she stood on the platform, she joined in the prayer. After the rope was fastened around her neck, she addressed the large audience of around 4,000 spectators, primarily female. Margaret expressed her innocence but cautioned them about the sins of drunkenness and Sabbath-breaking, actions that had allegedly led her to this point. Her final words expressed her love for her husband and her life, her insistence on innocence, and a prayer. Her body was sent to Edinburgh for dissection, and the inhabitants who had left town in opposition of the execution, slowly returned.

Margaret's guilt is questionable as no conclusive evidence was provided, a standard required today, and she maintained her innocence until the end. Despite the absence of clear proof, she was hanged for the alleged murder of her husband. Similar to Mary Mckinnon, Margaret's sentence might have been influenced by factors beyond inconclusive evidence. Margaret's intoxication on the night of the murder and her frequent under-the-influence state, combined with her vocal and assertive nature, may have swayed the court and jury against her, as these traits were considered improper, unfeminine, and unnatural for a woman. Such biases were prevalent in courts across Britain, not just Scotland.

MARY ANN BURDOCK (C.1797–1835)

Mary Ann Burdock, aged between thirty and thirty-five, resided in Bristol as the mistress of a lodging house with a man named Mr Wade, with whom she lived as his common law wife. Born near the town of Ross, Herefordshire, she grew up in Kentchurch. At the age of nineteen, she moved to Bristol to work in service and secured a job with a poulterer. However, she was dismissed due to allegations of stealing and improper conduct. Subsequently, she married a man named Agar, a tailor, who supposedly left her. She then had a son and daughter with a man named Thomas. After Thomas, she met Mr Wade, a tailor who also owned a lodging house on Trinity Street. Mary Ann assisted in running the lodging house, and despite financial struggles, Mr Wade aimed to open a new shop for his trade.

Our story takes us to October 1833, when a relatively wealthy sixty-year-old woman from London, Mrs Clara Ann Smith, boarded with Mr and Mrs Wade (Burdock). A widow, Mrs Smith had previously boarded with them for several days. Upon her return, she stayed with them for a few weeks. Known for her wealth, she possessed around £2,000 in cash and numerous trinkets and clothes, Mrs Smith was rarely clean and spent extended periods in bed, feeling unwell and requiring care. During Mrs Smith's stay, Mary Ann hired two servant girls. The first, Charlotte, assisted Mrs Smith for several weeks, and after she left, Mary Ann hired a fifteen-year-old girl named Mary Ann Allen. Miss Allen was unwittingly present when Mrs Smith suddenly died two days later.

Five days before the unfortunate incident, Mrs Burdock enlisted Mr Evans, an occasional boarder, to procure arsenic from the local druggist, citing a rat problem. However, there had been no known rat problem in the lodging house. Mr Evans obtained the arsenic with the assistance of two witnesses, as required by the new law, and gave it to Mrs Burdock.

On the evening of 26 October 1833, Mrs Smith, already feeling unwell, had complained about a sore mouth and throat. Mrs Burdock went to her room where Miss. Allen was looking after her and offered her some gruel. Mrs Smith initially declined but was persuaded by Mrs Burdock. After a short period, Mary Ann returned with the gruel in a bowl. The details of the following minutes vary between three different versions of the story. According to Mrs Burdock's version, she and Mr

Wade had put some arsenic into Mrs Smith's milk the previous day, but it wasn't enough to cause immediate harm. Therefore, on the 26th, Mr Wade added more arsenic to her gruel, which Mary Ann then brought to Mrs Smith's room. At the point of stirring, Miss Allen supposedly walked in and questioned Mary Ann, who dismissed the query and proceeded to feed Mrs Smith the gruel.

Mrs Burdock's long-standing servant, Miss Evans presented a different version of events. According to her, Mrs Burdock came downstairs and asked for some milk whey for Mrs Smith, which she prepared and sent away with Mrs Burdock. Mrs Burdock quickly returned, stating it was too sour, and requested more, which Miss Evans prepared and sent up. Miss Evans went to bed shortly after and was only awakened when informed that Mrs Smith had died. The final version of events comes from Miss Mary Ann Allen, the girl in charge of assisting Mrs Smith. After asking Mrs Smith if she wanted some and persuading her, Mrs Burdock disappeared for several minutes. Upon her return, she went into her bedroom, and Miss Allen followed. Miss Allen observed Mrs Burdock take out a small packet and add yellow granules into the gruel. When questioned, Mrs Burdock claimed it was just something to help Mrs Smith's stomach, but urged Miss Allen not to inform Mrs Smith that something had been added to her gruel, fearing she wouldn't drink it if she thought it was poisoned. Mrs Burdock stirred the yellow granules into the gruel and proceeded to take it to Mrs Smith, who drank half of it before deciding that she'd had enough. Mrs Burdock took the bowl away.

While these three versions share some similarities, they also contradict each other. It is difficult to determine the truth, but Miss. Allen's version provides the most detailed account. Regardless of which version is more accurate, Mrs Burdock played a role in poisoning Mrs Smith in each one, although in her version she shares the blame with Mr Wade.

Five minutes after consuming the gruel, Mrs Smith began to feel sick, writhing and moaning in discomfort. When asked if she was okay, Mrs

Smith told Mrs Burdock to leave her alone. Miss Allen noticed Mrs Burdock was smiling as she turned to leave. As her anguish continued, Miss Allen, concerned, suggested calling a doctor. Mrs Burdock refused, not wanting to draw attention to the poisoned woman, stating truthfully that Mrs Smith had a fear of doctors. They sat at Mrs Smith's bedside for several hours, and when she stopped stirring, Miss. Allen, assuming she was asleep, went to check and discovered she was indeed dead. Mrs Burdock went over and confirmed that she was dead. Mrs Burdock proceeded to go through Mrs Smith's belongings, making comments about stealing and that she may have been an excessive drinker. They cleaned up her body and sought assistance from Miss Evans. After laying out Mrs Smith's body, they went downstairs for tea, and were joined by Mr Wade.

The next day, Mrs Burdock made preparations to bury Mrs Smith, and on 28 October, she was laid to rest in St. Augustine's Churchyard in Bristol in a simple oak coffin with a small service. Following Mrs Smith's death, things began to go suspiciously went well for Mr and Mrs Wade. They appeared to acquire a substantial amount of money, buying new furniture, depositing at least £500 into the bank in May of 1834, and assisting in reviving Mr Wade's shop. Over the next fourteen months, Mary Ann continued to prosper financially, Mr Wade passed, leaving Mary Ann with his shop and Mary Ann remarried a Mr Burdock who was also in the clothes trade.

Cut to December 1834; there are a few different reports about what happened. One account states that some friends of Mrs Smith came looking for her in Bristol because they hadn't heard from her for several months. After asking around, they were horrified to learn that she had died, and worse still, that it had been fourteen months ago. Another report suggests that her nephew heard she had passed and went to check on her possessions, knowing that she had many. It is possible that both of these scenarios occurred. However, when questioning the whereabouts of Mrs Smith's substantial property, they were all told by Mrs Burdock that she had none. This made them very suspicious, as they knew how well-off Mrs Smith had been. Consequently, the situation was brought to the attention of the authorities, who decided that exhuming Mrs Smith's body and searching for signs of foul play would be the best action. This exhumation took place on 26 December 1834.

Once exhumed, Mrs Smith's body underwent rigorous testing by medical professionals. Upon examination, they observed a copious amount of a thick, yellow substance around her stomach. The doctors attributed this to arsenic poisoning, and after four separate tests, their conclusion was confirmed. With this evidence, the investigation intensified, leading to the arrest of Mrs Burdock for the murder of Mrs Smith by arsenic poisoning. The trial took place from 10 to 12 April 1835, during which most of the previous facts were presented to the jury. Mrs Burdock pleaded not guilty and the Recorder, the chief legal officer of the court, noted that he was intrigued and baffled at the unusual gap between the victim's death and the trial. On 13 April 1835, the jury delivered a guilty verdict, and Mrs Burdock was sentenced to hang. Throughout the proceedings, Mary Ann maintained a relatively firm and closed off expression, displaying little sign of fear, nerves, or anger, except for a brief moment during the reading of the verdict.

As she awaited her execution, Mrs Burdock appeared apathetic, though angered by the outcome, and barely acknowledged the religious preaching provided to her. Later revelations indicated that during her confinement, she admitted her guilt while also blaming Mr Wade, to a female attendant. On the day of her execution, 15 April 1835, she displayed little nervousness, maintaining a firm and steadfast demeanour. Dressed in black, she participated in religious preaching in the chapel before heading to the gallows. During the preaching, the reverend commented that when women deviate from their traditional virtues, it often leads to criminal acts. This statement reflects societal attitudes toward criminal women, a sentiment prevalent throughout the early modern period that persisted into the nineteenth century.

She was led to the place of execution where thousands of spectators had gathered. Underneath the scaffold, she recited more prayers with the reverend. Climbing the stairs of the scaffold, she continued to pray, expressing her concern for her children and requesting that her love be sent to her husband and friends. Once the rope was attached, she almost immediately signalled for the drop. Afterward, her body was buried within the gaol property, as the dissection law was now abolished, and the spectators slowly dispersed. Some of this information is taken from broadsides printed throughout the investigation. As previously pointed out, some facts may be skewed or exaggerated for selling purposes. However, by reading the trial records and comparing all of the broadsides, a coherent story emerges. It remains unclear what led Mary Ann to commit her dreadful deed. Was it cruelty, greed, or a simple, profound desire to lift her family out of financial struggle? Perhaps, it was a combination of all these factors that unfortunately transformed her from a respected mistress to a convicted murderess.

MARGARET JENKINS (1854–)

The crime of Margaret Jenkins is a brutal one, capable of sending shivers down anyone's back and making the squeamish squirm. Although her offence was heinous, her punishment differed significantly due to her mental instability, setting her case apart from many of the other women examined. Her story, along with Margaret Shuttleworth's, illustrates how certain nineteenth century cases elicited incredible support and sympathy from the public. Margaret was born in 1854 in Wales, near Pontypridd, and grew up in the same area. Unfortunately, she lost both her parents at a young age. As she matured, she met David Jenkins, whom she happily married. They became a respected, content couple, relocating to Treherbert, Wales, around 1886. The couple had many friends and neighbours, and despite the loss of four children, they were left with seven in May 1894.

Mrs Jenkins had been suffering from inexplicable spells for several years, affecting her behaviour during those periods. It is challenging to define this health issue in modern terms due to the limited understanding of mental health in nineteenth century Britain, which only encompassed general knowledge of popular disorders such as depression, mania, melancholia, and hysteria. Before the birth of her last child, Margaret had one of these spells, and, according to a friend, had not been the same since.

On the morning of 18 May 1894, the Jenkins children left for their daily activities, leaving infant Elizabeth Jane, just six weeks old, with Margaret. Mr Jenkins, a collier (miner) who had recently returned to work after a period of unemployment, was sleeping upstairs. The family had been struggling financially surviving on only bread and water for several weeks. Exacting a burden on everyone, Mrs Jenkins carried the pressure, perhaps more than anyone else. While everyone was away or asleep, something came over Mrs Jenkins; she took her husband's axe, placed her infant child on the salting block in the pantry, and struck her several times, eventually severing her head.

Afterward, a despondent and vacant Margaret woke Mr Jenkins and instructed him to get up. When he asked about the child's whereabouts, and received no reply, he asked again. Margaret coldly mentioned the infant was in the pantry and that she had 'finished it'. Horrified, Mr Jenkins went to the pantry, where he witnessed the lifeless infant lying on the salt block. Unable to bear more, he retreated in shock, then called his thirteen-year-old son, David, to assess the scene. David emerged distressed, stating that the baby's head had been severed. Mr Jenkins informed the boy that Margaret had killed the child.

The local police were summoned, and constable Tom Bryan(t) swiftly arrived at the house, accompanied by his colleague. Upon entering, he found Mr and Mrs Jenkins sitting at the kitchen table. After hearing about the incident, he went to the pantry and was distraught at the scene. The child lay on the salting block with several cuts, including a severed finger, and one hanging on by only skin, while the poor child's head was on the floor (or on the salting block, as some sources contradict), clearly detached from the body. When he emerged, he asked a few more questions and arrested Mrs Jenkins for the wilful murder of her infant girl. In a dazed state, Mrs Jenkins admitted to the crime she had committed, with an axe.

She was taken to Treherbert police station to await the coroner's inquest. Described as 'pitiable' by someone at the police station, she was withdrawn and kept moaning. When asked if she understood what was happening, she replied that she knew what she did. As news of the incident began to spread, crowds gathered inside the house to support Mr Jenkins and his children. The coroner's inquest took place on Monday, 21 May, at Pontypridd police court, where Margaret was charged with wilful murder. On their way into the court, crowds gathered around to see the prisoner. Many people, particularly women, showed visible signs of sympathy and distress at the sight of Margaret. Witnesses were heard, and the jury delivered a guilty verdict, but requested that her sanity be questioned and considered.

The coroner inquired about the prevalence of women succumbing to puerperal mania if depressed shortly after giving birth, to which the doctor replied yes, but that she was probably past the instance of puerperal mania. He suggested it was perhaps lactation mania brought on by feeding, which had been known to lead to anger and violence towards loved ones. Despite this testimony and multiple pieces of evidence from witnesses, the coroner denied the request for an insanity rider and charged her with wilful murder. The evidence supporting her mental health difficulties was immense. A friend noticed Margaret acting peculiar days before the incident, describing her as feeling giddy with pain in her head and expressing a desire to die, and feeling like everything was turning. She told one of her neighbours the morning of the incident that she wished she would die that day. These exchanges, coupled with her far and recent past of mental health struggles and a doctor's testimony, clearly indicated that she was struggling and was likely not in control of her actions.

After the proceedings, the way down to the charge room below the court was lined with crying women displaying great sympathy toward Margaret and her situation, including her sister, who was visibly distraught. These instances of public support illustrate the changing attitudes of people surrounding mental health, crime, and women that transpired over the nineteenth century.

She was sent to Cardiff gaol to await a local court trial the following Wednesday. It was noted that while in prison, she experienced deep depression. On Wednesday, 23 May, Margaret stood trial in Cardiff for the murder of her infant daughter. After hearing the evidence, the jury again returned a verdict of guilty but insisted on a plea of insanity. It was postulated that Margaret was suffering from melancholia when she committed the murder. She was set to appear at the next assizes with a plea of insanity. Before this occurred, she was seen by medical professionals for a mental health assessment. The Swansea (also referred to as the Glamorgan) Assizes took place on 27 June 1894. At the trial, the medical witnesses concluded that she was insane based on their examinations and, therefore, not in control of herself. The magistrate concluded that with this verdict, there was no need for a trial, and she was deemed insane and sentenced to be held in prison at Her Majesty's Pleasure.

The case of Margaret Jenkins illustrates some of the changes the 1800s brought to the criminal justice system, including a greater understanding throughout the courts and the public of mental illness, and a growing sympathy for overwhelmed, unstable, and incapable mothers. What became of Margaret Jenkins after her imprisonment is unclear, but as mentioned previously, the state of prisons in the nineteenth century was abysmal, prompting a significant overhaul. Hopefully, Margaret was in a satisfactory prison where she could be comfortable; or maybe she was in an asylum, which was no better than the prisons. There were a few pieces of legislation regarding mental health instituted during the following century that would have been beneficial for Margaret had they been available during her trial. Whatever the outcome, Margaret and her daughter were victims of her mental health, and it made Margaret commit an unspeakable crime. Luckily for Margaret, her deficiencies were recognized, and her life was spared, though what kind of life she had in confinement could be debated. If Margaret were alive today, hopefully she would have received the help she required much sooner, and this tragedy might have been prevented.

The overall attitude of nineteenth century Britain towards criminal women was two-fold. First, there was a definite and visible growth in sympathy and leniency within society and the courts, as people gained a wider perspective on what might have led these women to act in these ways. This included a minimal, but developing understanding of mental health and how it might cause someone to commit acts they normally would not. The second general characteristic is that despite this growing leniency, if a woman committed a crime (especially in relation to homicide) and departed from the traditional and expected Victorian roles of women, femininity, and motherhood, they would be punished and used as examples for other women to stay away from the criminal world. This is a very broad overview of women's crime in the nineteenth century, and these two themes are by no means the only aspects of women's crime during the 1800s. As we inch closer to modernity, one will observe that there is still a need for major developments and shifts in understanding, before reaching today's standards, which as we all know, are still less than perfect.

Chapter six

THE TWENTIETH CENTURY, TO 1960

The twentieth century brought with it a new era for women. New opportunities, a growing respect for female opinion, and a start towards the equality of men and women. There were more women than ever in the science and medical fields; the suffragette movement was gaining momentum and succeeded in giving women the much-awaited right to vote. Women were beginning to hold minor roles within government and criminal justice institutions, and there was a gradual move away from the view of women as only housewives and mothers. This century also brought changes and developments to Britain's criminal justice system, many of which directly related to the women caught within it. For the purposes of this book, this chapter will only discuss women and crime up until 1960, shortly after the last woman was judicially hanged in Britain. It serves as an ideal transitional era, situated between historical attitudes and legislation from previous centuries that remained in effect, and modern ideologies and systems that were beginning to take shape. There is definitely an overlap between pre- and post-1960s ideologies throughout the twentieth century, but progressive 1960 poses the perfect stopping point for this historic overview.

Over the centuries, the prevalence of violence and murder in society has significantly diminished, with the twentieth century making a notable shift where such acts were no longer expected or accepted in daily life. Moreover, at the beginning of the twentieth century, the number of women standing trial for crimes in British courts reached an all-time low, accounting for only nine per cent of defendants tried at the Old Bailey. However, there were intermittent spikes in female crime rates during the first half of the twentieth century, particularly during the First and Second World Wars when women assumed more male centred roles, which were more inclined to lead to crime.

An unfortunate influence during the early twentieth century was the eugenics movement, buoyed by the emerging field of psychiatry. Eugenics, is an ideology that was embraced by the middle and upper classes, that aimed to control societal wellbeing by preventing individuals with perceived criminal tendencies, mental insufficiencies, or biological inadequacies from reproducing. This movement had a profound impact on various segments of society, including women within the criminal justice system. Women, who were often considered the primary bearers of mental health issues, were disproportionately targeted by this movement, which falsely assumed that criminal women were led astray due to biological issues. It was also assumed that those from the poorer classes who were dubbed 'degenerate women', were inherently promiscuous and extremely fertile, which made them dangerous.

A prevailing notion in 1914 perpetuated the idea that all criminal women were driven by sexual mania, regarding them to have a 'disease' rooted in their sexuality. This aligned with the longstanding belief system that deviant women were more likely to commit crimes related to sexuality and that most sexual tendencies were still morally questioned. The growing tenet that mental deficiencies were the cause of criminal tendencies was gaining traction. Including the notion that mental instability and female crime made sense because it corresponded directly with the perception that criminal women were inherently flawed due to their diversion from expected female behaviour and qualities.

There were many criminals whose actions were influenced by some form of mental illness, but instead of seeking to aid them and others in similar situations, the eugenics movement aimed to eradicate them, asserting this as the root cause of delinquency and degeneracy. Today, most people recognise that these beliefs were skewed in many respects, with eugenics primarily serving as a means for privileged individuals in society to exert control over those they believed less worthy. Unfortunately, certain forms of eugenics persist even now, illustrating that we still have a considerable way to proceed toward achieving an equitable society.

The Mental Deficiency Act of 1913 marked a ground-breaking legislative development, where mentally deficient individuals were categorised as either idiots, imbeciles, feeble-minded or moral defectives, and subsequently provided with supervised care. This significantly impacted the criminal sphere, especially for women, who were often declared mentally deficient, leading to a shift away from punitive measures. In 1913, approximately 30,000 women were imprisoned in Britain; following the Act's implementation, the number dropped to 11,000 by 1925 and further to 2,000 by 1960. The act underwent amendments in 1927 and was eventually repealed by the 1959 Mental Health Act, integrating psychiatric hospitals under the same legislation as other medical institutions. This change aimed to offer better medical care for psychiatric patients, including women placed in these facilities, instead of prisons. The shift in terminology from 'deficiency' to 'health' reflected a more positive and open-minded approach to mental health concepts.

Murder methods in the first half of the twentieth century varied, but often involved household tools like pokers, bricks, and knives. Poison use decreased but was still occasionally documented. This aligns with the notion that women typically committed homicides inside or near their homes, utilizing readily available objects. Infanticide methods commonly included either suffocation or blunt force trauma to the head. Occasionally, more violent acts such as throat cutting or stabbing occurred, or children were left, exposed to the elements.

The publishing of Old Bailey court proceedings ceased in April of 1913 due to changes in legislation and funding. Despite this, the Old Bailey record, spanning 300 years, remains a valuable resource filled with detailed accounts of criminals, criminal records, and court proceedings. While various detailed court and trial records from the first half of the twentieth century are accessible in British archives, finding records from the eighteenth and nineteenth centuries is often more straightforward due to the focus of historic digitisation efforts on older documents. The digitisation of archived documents has exploded over the past decade and provides millions of digital pictures, documents, and records for people around the world to access and study.

The early twentieth century marked the era of newspapers. Stemming from their popularity in the nineteenth century, newspapers became the primary source for news, and the main medium to broadcast the latest crime news and gossip. They included photographs which offered the average citizen a more intimate glimpse into the crime being reported, and evoked a stronger emotional response, whether negative or positive, about the information presented. Although Broadsides had gradually faded from popularity, newspapers continued to hold their ground, eventually collaborating with radio broadcasts until the latter half of the century, when television and other forms of media took over.

One of the most noteworthy changes in infanticide legislation during the twentieth century was the passing of the 1922 Infanticide Act. Following this, the charge of infanticide no longer carried the death penalty and was replaced with a maximum sentence of two years in prison. It also established the understanding that a mother could experience some form of mental dysfunction up to a year after the birth of her child. These changes clearly illustrated the new forward-thinking belief in the mother as a victim alongside the infant. Despite the low execution rate for infanticide over the previous century, this development in the justice system aligned with society's desire to move away from the violence and depravity of the death sentence. Consequently, prison, became the standard punishment for the majority of crimes. Subsequently, England and Wales introduced the 1938

Infanticide Act, demonstrating growing leniency and understanding of mental health's potential impact on mothers. The Act specified that if a mother killed her child under one year old, due to mental instability caused by her pregnancy, childbirth, or lactation, she could be charged with infanticide instead of murder, which greatly lessened the sentence carried by a murder charge, which was life in prison. This Act closely resembled the 1923 legislation, but was more specific about the mental struggles mothers might face.

While infanticide unfortunately persisted in Britain at the turn of the century, it was not the epidemic that was witnessed during the Victorian period. The Old Bailey accounts for twenty-two women being brought before the courts for infanticide between 1900 and 1913. Although the numbers after this period aren't as clear, it is safe to assume the number of incidents and convictions was decreasing. By the twentieth century, concealing the act of infanticide would have been much more challenging, which led to the assumption that the majority of infanticide cases would not have gone unnoticed and would be recorded in judiciary documents.

Child welfare emerged as a growing concern in the early twentieth century, with various institutions and organisations established to support illegitimate or needy children. While these places symbolised improvements from previous centuries, unmarried mothers still faced significant stigma, which impacted their reputation, social standing, and mental wellbeing. By the end of the discussed time period around 1950-1960, one of the most impactful developments for women's sexual health was introduced – the contraceptive pill. This innovation provided women more freedom and control over their sexual health, which resulted in fewer unexpected pregnancies, fewer illegitimate children, fewer cases of infanticide, and less women being incarcerated for such crimes.

In January of 1903, Louisa Beaumont was convicted of manslaughter after secretly giving birth to a female child. She had made no preparations for the birth, assaulted the infant, and left it in the yard. Although the child recovered from exposure, she succumbed to head injuries inflicted by a blunt instrument. There were also injuries to her ribs, but the cause of death was the fatal head wound. Louisa was sentenced to five years of imprisonment with penal servitude.

In 1904 and 1905, Mildred Cole and Clara Bridges were both indicted at the Old Bailey for murdering their newborns. Mildred tied a tight string around her child's neck, which resulted in a manslaughter conviction and a six-month hard labour sentence. The autopsy revealed that the baby had been born alive and had died from the string being tied around its tiny neck. Clara was indicted for stabbing her infant with a pair of scissors and hitting it over the head. She was deemed not responsible for her actions due to her mental state and when she was examined she was in deep shock about what she had done and threatened suicide. She was charged with concealment of birth as she had kept her pregnancy a secret, but not murder.

Eleanor Martha Browning, in 1913, sliced her infant's throat due to puerperal insanity. Initially, she felt fine and healthy, but approximately three weeks after giving birth, she complained she was depressed and that her milk had ceased, rendering her unable to nourish the baby. The next morning, she was found on the stair landing covered in blood, and the infant was found on the kitchen floor with her throat cut. She was declared insane by one practitioner, and it was corroborated by another at Holloway Prison. She was declared guilty but insane at the time of the murder and not responsible for her actions. She was sentenced to be imprisoned at His Majesty's Pleasure. It is unclear if she was placed into a medical facility or asylum, or if she was kept in prison and monitored by doctors. These sentences were different because one woman experienced temporary insanity, but was mentally stable during questioning, where the other woman experienced long term mental health difficulties.

In Scotland, Elizabeth Lawrie was charged with murdering her son by throwing him into a clay pit filled with water. She told her brother that she had tied a piece of shawl around his neck and threw him in'. The body of the infant was discovered by some workmen, and Elizabeth was indicted. Her trial occurred on 9 May 1911 at the Glasgow High Court of the Justiciary, where she faced charges of murder by suffocation and pleaded guilty. However, her charge was later reduced to culpable homicide, resulting in an eighteen-month prison sentence. Without thorough medical examination, it remains challenging to determine whether the infant died from suffocation due to the shawl around his neck or drowning in the water. The court leaned towards the charge of suffocation, possibly influenced by her statement and the potential evidence available.

The twentieth century brought new scientific and medical developments, and approaches, including in the field of psychiatry. With greater understanding and advancement came changes in the way female criminals were examined and understood. These new ideas weren't necessarily always correct or fair in regard to gender or class, but they represented progress towards a deeper understanding of the human mind. Women offenders were viewed as mentally stifled, not inherently malicious. Their deviance was biologically linked, innate within a woman. It was a concept that diminished them as indequate members of society, but it was recognised as something beyond their control. Some of these women grappled with poor mental health, but it shouldn't have been assumed that criminal women were automatically mentally deficient. This perpetuated the belief that women were weak and unstable, both mentally and physically, stemming from the stereotypes of the early modern and Victorian periods. The courts began to prescribe specialised treatment for offenders declared mentally ill, moving away from the blanket approach of incarceration for all. While this was positive, there was a lack of proper treatments and understanding of the myriad mental health issues they encountered. Most cases were still perceived as insanity, despite the likelihood of various illnesses being present. Some treatments were primitive and often rather brutal, and the treatment centres and asylums they were placed in were less than adequate, with individuals often experiencing mistreatment.

Momentous changes to legislation regarding capital punishment occurred during the first half of the twentieth century, and permanently altered the criminal justice system. One of the most impactful developments was the 1957 Homicide Act introduced in England and Wales. It brought about many modifications to the laws of murder, the first being that if someone commits murder while in the process of some other offence, they will not be charged with murder but with manslaughter, provided a there was no malice aforethought. To be charged with murder, premeditation had to be proven. The act also introduced a new provision concerning 'diminished responsibility' when a murder occurred, allowing for a reduced charge if defendant a was either coerced or not in control of themselves. This provision extended itself to cases involving insanity and the lack of control or understanding of one's reactions. This aspect of the law will be directly relevant to a case discussed later on. Another controversial section of the new legislation discussed lighter sentencing when provocation was present.

Holloway Prison holds significant historical importance in the context of women's crime. Constructed in 1852, it transitioned into a female-only prison in 1903. Originally, it accommodated men, women, and children over the age of eight. However, when Newgate prison closed in 1902, and a new policy stipulated the separation of male and female prisoners, Holloway transformed into an exclusively female facility. It even had provisions for keeping babies with their mothers until they turned one year old. Most inmates served relatively light sentences, and all the prisoners were engaged in gender assigned work, such as cooking, cleaning, and sewing. During the early twentieth century, Holloway housed numerous suffragettes as the women's rights movement was quickly growing. After the First World War there were significant efforts to reform the prison, improve its conditions, and provide necessary care and services. However, conditions deteriorated after the Second World War. Around 1960, a desire for change led to the demolition and rebuilding of Holloway over the following twenty-five years. Conditions fluctuated until the prison's closure in 2016, leaving an indelible mark on the history of women's crime in nineteenth and twentieth century Britain. Another integral institution in the history of women and crime is Newgate. Closing its doors in 1902, Newgate was demolished to make way for the new Central Criminal Court, known as Old Bailey, which opened in 1907, and is the building we see today.

The first murderess to face the gallows in the twentieth century was Louise Masset, and her execution, like others to come, fuelled the public's growing disapproval. In October 1899, she maliciously murdered her three-and-a-half-year-old son, Manfred. Louise, a single French governess, who fell pregnant, sent her young son to a foster family of sorts, to keep her job. Although she visited him weekly and was considered a good and loving mother by her friends, things took a sombre turn when she met a young Frenchman named Lucas, with whom she became romantically involved.

In early October, Louise informed the foster family (the Gentle's) that she was retrieving Manfred to take him to his father in France. A few days later she showed up and collected her son. They headed to Dalston Junction Station, and tragically, young Manfred was never seen alive again. His lifeless body was discovered later that evening in the woman's bathroom, wrapped only in a shawl. The autopsy determined strangulation as the cause of death along with a large gash in his head, inflicted by a brick found next to his body. Louise was already en route to London Bridge Station, planning to meet Lucas in Brighton, when

Manfred's body was found, and when the newspaper report about the murder was released, she hurried back to London. She went to her friend and reported that she was wanted for murder but maintained that she was innocent.

Despite her claims, Louise was arrested and stood trial. Throughout the proceedings, she insisted on her innocence, weaving a story about sending Manfred off with two women from Chelsea whom she had met earlier. They were supposed to house him and provide him with an education. However, no one could corroborate this story. Despite the lack of a clear motive, Louise was found guilty of murder in December, and sentenced to hang on 9 January 1900. The absence of a motive raised questions among those protesting the punishment, while others on the opposing side questioned how she knew the murdered child in the newspapers was her son if she didn't commit the crime. Speculation arose about motives related to the child's father, something in Louise's past, or possibly tied to her desire to be with Lucas, creating a contested mystery.

One newspaper headline vividly illustrates the shock at the verdict and disdain at the thought of the new year and millennium beginning with such an event. One paper even remarks that it was the first hanging at Newgate since the execution of Amelia Dyer in 1897. The negative reactions to the sentence show how infrequent executions had become and how people felt about the punishment. Petitions went out, signed by fellow French citizens and governesses, but they were not successful. Despite the dislike of capital punishment, many people were still horrified by this case and how she could do something like that. They were so appalled that, at her execution, once the black flag was raised, symbolising its completion, the thousands who had gathered next to Newgate cheered. The mixture of responses illustrates how complex and questionable the justice system was, even in the 1900s. Louise was the first, and one of the last women of the twentieth century to be hanged.

The last hanging of a woman in Wales occurred in August 1907, preceding England by several years. Rhoda Willis, also known as Leslie James, (her alias), was a baby farmer. Similarly, to Amelia Dyer from the previous chapter, she advertised baby adoptions in newspapers and charged fees for taking in infants. Although not as prolific as Amelia Dyer, Rhoda took a dark turn that ultimately led her to the gallows, causing shock, disgust, and disdain among Welsh citizens.

The first baby she took in was initially cared for, but she abruptly left it on a Salvation Army doorstep after a few months, along with a note instructing them to care for the baby. This infant was exposed to the harsh, early spring weather and, upon discovery, tragically died a few weeks later. The second child, whose death she was responsible for, led to her arrest. In April 1907, Rhoda adopted a newborn baby from a family in Monmouthshire and received a handsome payment for taking the child in. Regrettably, the infant did not survive the journey home. During the train ride, Rhoda suffocated the poor infant and concealed her in a parcel. Upon returning, Rhoda placed the parcel in her room and continued with her routine. She struggled with a severe drinking problem and one night, she returned home very drunk and subsequently fell out of bed the next morning. Her landlady, coming to her aid, noticed the box on the floor. Upon opening it, she discovered the infant's lifeless body. Horrified, she immediately called the police and Rhoda was arrested.

She was found guilty and sentenced to be hanged. The verdict caused an uproar, especially since the death penalty for a woman was rare in Wales and despised by the public. A petition circulated, advocating for a reduction of sentence to manslaughter and imprisonment, but it was unsuccessful. Rhoda was hanged on 17 August 1907, seemingly resigned to her fate and filled with remorse. In addition to being the last woman to be hanged in Wales, she was also the first and last woman to be hanged at Cardiff prison. It is interesting to mention that about a year before this horrid event, Rhoda was hit by a bicycle and suffered a head injury. She spent a few weeks in an infirmary, and it wasn't until after this incident that she had her first encounter with the law when she stole something. Could her head injury have altered her decision-making process or contributed to her inclination toward crime? It is challenging to know, but it definitely should have been considered in her trial and sentencing. The public's disgust at Rhoda's fate and their sheer uproar sent a clear message that the death penalty would no longer be tolerated, a sentiment that was starting to be shared in Scotland and England as well.

In 1934, Aberdeen, Scotland, was rocked with a shocking murder case that had the entire town on its feet, watching. It was the murder of an eight-year-old girl named Helen Priestley, who was sent out by her mother on an errand on 20 April and never returned. An all-night search party was sent out to look for her, but she wasn't found until her body turned up in a sack in the lobby of the tenement where she and her parents lived. The suspects for the murder were their neighbours, Mr Alexander Donald and Mrs Jeannie Donald, who were said to have strangled young Helen, and stabbed and cut her with a knife. Jeannie never clicked with Helen's mother, but besides a dislike for them, no clear motive is given. A neighbour heard a scream around 2pm on 20 April and that was all.

Mrs and Mr Donald were arrested in their home and taken to the local police station as a crowd of at least 2,000 gathered around their building, waiting to see the accused and cheered and booed as they were taken to the station. Jeannie was described as looking thin, pale, and haggard, while Donald was described as slim. It is interesting how more attention was paid to the woman's appearance than to the man's. This biased gender reaction highlights the troubling notion that her appearance held greater significance in her case, than her husban's did in his. Regrettably, this bias was a persistent element in the treatment of female criminals throughout the preceding centuries.

They were charged with murder and sent to prison to await their trial on 16 July, with both pleading not guilty upon arrest, and Jeannie stating that she didn't even see Helen that day. Before their trial, however, Mr Donald was acquitted; his charges were dropped, and he was released on 11 June. The articles about the case are unclear as to why he was acquitted, while Jeannie was still slated to stand trial in July. At her trial, Jeannie continued to plead not guilty. To her utter dismay, her nine-year-old daughter Jeannie was brought to provide testimony. She spoke intelligently and clearly, though one can imagine the event was probably scarring for such a young girl. This part of the trial, coupled with Jeannie's distraught reaction to her daughter's attendance, seemed to touch many of the women present in the courtroom. Various pieces of evidence were given, which pointed to Mrs Donald as the perpetrator. After deliberation, on 23 July the jury, which finally included five women, found Jeannie guilty, and she was sentenced to death. This was a rare and shocking sentence that made Jeannie faint when she heard it. She was sent back to prison to await her execution on 13 August.

Unlike many of the women in this chapter and others, Jeannie's sentence was reprieved. It was reduced to life imprisonment and was reduced even further when she was released ten years later in July 1944. Jeannie continued to live out her life and passed away in 1976.

The ideal way to conclude this overview of murderous women throughout British history is by exploring the stories of two historically significant figures: Susan Newell, was the last woman hanged in Scotland, and Ruth Ellis, was the last woman hanged in all of Great Britain. These women stand as poignant markers in the annals of British criminal history.

Susan Newell (c.1893–1923)

Susan Newell, formally Macalister, earned notoriety as the central figure in the 'Go-Car(t) Tragedy', 'Go-Car(t) Murder' or 'Coatbridge

Murder' as dubbed by the newspapers. This murder captivated Scotland, especially considering the absence of hangings in Glasgow for seventy years. Susan holds the distinction of being the first and last woman executed at Duke Street prison, despite community efforts to commute her sentence. Duke Street prison in Glasgow, initially established in 1798, transitioned into a women's prison in 1882, operating as such until its closure in 1955. Susan lived in the Coatbridge area, just outside Glasgow, with her second husband, John Newell, a twenty-nine-year-old subway worker, and her six- to eight-year-old daughter, Janet McLeod. There is debate about Susan's exact age, but she was approximately twenty-eight to twenty-nine when the incident occurred. The incident in question unfolded on 20 June 1923, resulting in the ruthless murder of thirteen-year-old schoolboy John Johnston(e).

Apparently, Susan was in a state of anxiety and frustration due to financial constraints and frequent loud arguments with Mr Newell, which jeopardised their housing situation. This was the setting inside the Newell house when young John came calling. He had finished school for the day and was assisting a friend delivering newspapers. He was admitted inside and was not seen alive again. The details of what transpired inside the house which led to the murder remain unknown, witnessed only by the murderess. Once young John was inside however, neighbours heard a loud commotion and three thumps. Janet, Susan's young daughter, later disclosed that upon returning home that day, she interrupted her mother wrapping up the boy's body in a red carpet or bedsheet.

Susan's landlady and her friends observed her making two trips to and from the house, and by morning, Susan had left with Janet to dispose of the body. Using a wooden cart as transportation, she enlisted her daughter's help to sit on the concealed body as Susan pushed it all several miles towards Duke Street, on the other side of town. A lorry driver offered assistance, to transport them all, while unaware of the cart's macabre cargo. Upon reaching their destination, the cart slipped slightly, revealing John's foot and head. Although unnoticed by the driver, an onlooker named Helen Elliot alerted the authorities. Robert Foote and James Campbell investigated, witnessing Susan, who had just discarded the boy's body, attempting to evade discovery by climbing over a garden wall. They apprehended her, and in her nervous state, Susan hastily admitted to having the boy's body in her cart, claiming that her husband had committed the crime in anger, and she was merely disposing of the evidence; a false narrative she repeated in court. She was arrested and a call was made for her husband, who later surrendered himself to the police station at Haddington.

Susan and her husband faced charges for the murder. According to the post-mortem examination, poor John suffered a severe blow to the head with a blunt instrument, possibly a poker. Subsequently, he was strangled so brutally that his spinal cord was severed at his neck. The examination also showed burn marks and singed hair on the left side of his neck and head, but the cause of death was determined to be asphyxiation and spinal cord damage. Both husband and wife pleaded not guilty to the murder charge, with John providing an alibi supported by his family, claiming he wasn't at home that day or night due to attending a funeral with his family. During the trial from 18-19 September 1923, Susan appeared cool, unbothered, and slightly vacant. Despite attempts to plead insanity, she was declared perfectly sane by experts, who concluded that she committed the murder in an upset state.

John was acquitted, but the jury found Susan guilty of murder. Despite the changing attitude towards capital punishment, she was sentenced to hang. However, the jury recommended mercy; a contributing factor in the petition that was sent to the Secretary of Scotland, seeking leniency for Susan. Unfortunately, the petition was unsuccessful, and Susan was executed on 10 October 1923, at Duke Street Prison, becoming the last woman in Scotland and one of the last in Britain to be hanged. The community held a grand funeral in support of the boy and his family.

Susan's execution evoked significant community upset and she was even described as brave by several newspapers. This illustrates how anti execution people were becoming; despite her atrocious crime, the people showed sympathy towards a murderess. Susan's case underscored that hanging women was no longer acceptable in Scotland. Her last words were 'do not put that thing on me!' as the white execution cap was placed on her head, adding colour to an otherwise dreadful occasion.

RUTH ELLIS (1926–1955)

The final woman to be featured in this historical overview is Ruth Ellis (nee Neilson), the last woman judicially hanged in Britain. Born in Rhys, Wales in 1926, as the fourth of six children, Ruth and her family moved to Basingstoke after her musician father lost his job. Despite financial struggles, Ruth was determined not to live in poverty. Described as an ambitious young woman, she focused on perfecting her charm, looks, positivity and zest for opportunity.

When she was eighteen, she fell in love with a Canadian serviceman who was overseas during the war. She wanted to marry him but unfortunately, as she found out she was pregnant, she discovered he had a wife and two children back home. Poor Ruth was devastated, and because of this incident, she felt betrayed and lost her faith in men, love, and human relationships. She said that she felt emotionally cold afterward, and that her future relationships with men were different because of it. She gave birth to her son in 1944 and to provide for them both, Ruth worked a variety of jobs around London. She worked in a factory, was a waitress and a shop worker at Woolworths. However, these jobs didn't pay nearly as much as the more risqué opportunities she pursued in some of London's more elusive bars and clubs. She worked as a model for a camera club and by 1946 was serving as a hostess and call girl at a few clubs and brothels run by a well-known vice boss. Although these jobs were a little racy and slightly dangerous, Ruth was making it on her own and earning a substantial income for her and her son, though she was still searching for financial stability.

This is where George comes in. In November 1950, she married a man named George Johnston Ellis, a divorced dentist who had a slight problem with alcohol. Their brief marriage was filled with arguments over money, and they had separated by the time their daughter, Georgina was born in October 1951. A few years later she met David Moffatt Drummon Blakely, at one of the disreputable establishments she managed in Knightsbridge. He was a racing car enthusiast who was relatively well known among the public. Unfortunately, this was one of the two men who would control and change her life. They became lovers, though they both had other relationships, and David struggled with his indulgent drinking and possessiveness over Ruth. Possibly to distance herself from David (though she was infatuated with him), she attained another lover named Desmond Edward Cussen. This was the second man who would drastically and devastatingly change her life. He was an ex-serviceman who now sold tobacco, and like David, was an avid racing fan.

Over time Cussen watched as Ruth and Blakely fought, and he offered to marry Ruth to get her away from him. She declined the offer as she was head over heels for Blakely regardless of their arguing. Over the next few years, Ruth lived back and forth with both men. In the spring of 1955, she was living with Blakely in Kensington. This infatuation she harboured intensified the pain when Blakely began distancing himself, seemingly attempting to end their relationship around Easter 1955. Blakely went away for the Easter holiday to a friend's place in Hampstead, leaving a devastated and angry Ruth in Kensington.

This knowledge sent Ruth spiralling, and with the encouragement of Cussen, and the jealousy and hurt fuelled by Blakely, she made a horrible decision. On 10 April 1955, after consuming too much alcohol (Pernod apparently) and taking several tranquillisers, she took the .38 revolver that Cussen had given her and taught her how to use, and headed to Hamsptead. In Ruth's statement to the authorities, she mentioned taking a taxi to Hampstead, but other sources claim that Cussen actually drove her, which greatly adds to his already high culpability.

As Ruth arrived at the Magdala public house where Blakely was buying more drinks for his gathering, she spotted him coming out. Although she was some distance away, she claimed that he looked up, saw her, and looked away again. It was at this moment that she pulled the gun out of her purse and fired four shots at him. When the police arrived, Blakely was on the ground, and Ruth, in a confused state of shock, admitted to shooting him. She expressed her confusion and willingly accepted her arrest, saying 'thank you'. This interaction alone should have indicated that she was not in the right frame of mind when she committed the murder.

Ruth was arrested and held until her trial. She pleaded not guilty, intending to argue provocation on Blakely's part. She refused to plead insanity and insisted that it was not premeditated. Although she admitted feeling the urge to kill him, it remains uncertain whether she would have taken that step or felt that way if she hadn't been influenced by Cussen or highly intoxicated. During her trial, Ruth never included Cussen in her testimonies. Maybe she was trying to protect him, but she doesn't mention his crucial involvement until the day before her execution. By this time, it was too late, as Cussen had fled and could not be located to answer for his role in the murder. This situation is regrettable because his involvement might have potentially spared her from the gallows, as it could have been considered provocation or persuasion, diminishing her responsibility in the matter. However, as mentioned earlier, Ruth inexplicably refrained from implicating him until it was too late.

At her trial, a psychiatrist speaking in her defence advocated for a charge of manslaughter. However, the reasoning he used was inaccurate and sexist, reflecting lingering early modern and Victorian views of women as the weaker sex, both physically and mentally. He argued that when dealing with infidelity, women became more hysterical than men, losing their mental faculties and resorting to more primitive decision making. He claimed she was weak minded at the time, and too focused on what had happened to her. She was unable to think clearly, and exhibited 'emotional immaturity'. After deliberation, the judge found no evidence to support the verdict of manslaughter. The jury, despite societal revulsion for capital punishment, shockingly sentenced her to hang. However, this would be the last time such an execution occurred.

The verdict sparked enormous public outcry, as execution was becoming viewed as a brutal, outdated, and unnecessary by most of society. Ruth's life and situation garnered significant attention due to her well-kept appearance, blonde hair, edgy lifestyle, and association with the racy areas of Kensington and Mayfair. She was exactly the type of criminal that would fuel public interest. There were petitions sent out that gathered thousands of signatures, including one with thirty-five signatures from the London County Council. Despite the immensity of the protest, no leniency was shown to Ruth, and she was executed on 13 July 1955. Described as courageous, poised, and calm during her execution, she admitted that she would rather be hanged for a crime she committed than live an uneventful, destitute life. At her execution, at least a thousand people gathered outside Holloway prison, with some attempting to break down the barriers to talk and pray with Ruth. People were disturbed and revolted at the verdict she received, and wanted to show their disagreement and sympathy. Teachers at a school near Holloway prison reported that some of their young students were deeply distressed by the event because they witnessed the crowds and the spectacle. The children were profoundly affected by that day, and the teachers remarked that if the disgust of society wasn't enough to stop this process, the effect on children should be considered.

People all over the world were disturbed and devastated over Ruth's sentence. It makes sense that her execution changed British legislation and was the last of its kind. Ruth's execution quickly enacted the law of 'diminished responsibility' in the Homicide Act of 1957, which is the exact piece of legislation that could have saved her. It applied directly to her situation with Cussen and possibly with Blakely; it was not fair that she was held entirely responsible for her actions. Ruth's execution advanced the abolishment of the death penalty for murder in Britain, a change realised in 1965 for England, Scotland, and Wales, and in 1973 for Northern Ireland. Unfortunately, capital punishment remained in place in Britain for certain crimes like treason until 1998. Thanks to Ruth, no woman in Britain has to endure a tragic death like hers ever again.

The first half of the twentieth century set the stage for our modern criminal legislation and women's equality in Britain and beyond. Female participation in crime was at an all-time low, yet despite this, several women managed to gather crowds and make headlines for their devious conduct.

The notion that women's criminal behaviour stemmed from biological inadequacies and, consequently, mental deficiencies, became the prevailing belief of both the criminal and medical worlds. There was a budding overall interest in mental health and its role in crime, with women receiving the brunt of the attention. Their descent from social norms and feminine attributes were often blamed on failing mental health. This did have a positive effect in creating an interest in mental health and slowly fostering a general understanding of sufferers and their connection to criminal acts. On the other hand there were also some extreme ideas: sexist misnomers that portrayed women as unstable, weak, not in control, and secondary to men in physical, emotional, and mental health.

Prisons began to be supplemented with institutions and asylums for criminals announced unfit for prison, representing a step toward better, tailored care and attention for people struggling with mental health issues. However, these alternatives wouldn't come into full fruition for several decades. While they offered better options for offenders than traditional prison, they still lacked the care and systems needed by the patients.

Since the 1960s, female crime in Britain has persisted but remained consistent with the low numbers of the first half of the twentieth century, though there have still been instances of notorious women making headlines. While there are still aspects of the Western World's criminal justice system that require adaptation and change, significant progress has been made over the past 700 years, contributing to a more equitable experience for both men and women. Today, we can appreciate and be grateful that the systems and legislation from previous centuries are no longer in place. The twentieth century marked a period of understanding and growing equality. As women assumed more roles within society and advocated for egalitarianism, the criminal justice system began to view them as more than subordinate women, dastardly dames or lowly housewives, but as people.

CONCLUSION

The history of women and crime in Britain is a complex topic, sparking numerous debates on their treatment within the criminal justice system compared to men. While criminal women were treated with slightly more leniency during indictments, sentencing, and punishments, female murderesses were an exception. This changed with the growing desire to move away from violent punishments, particularly the death penalty, an idea that began to gain prominence in the late eighteenth century. However, the impact wasn't fully realised until the twentieth century. This evolving philosophy led to increased leniency within the courts and new legislation, particularly evident in infanticide cases and the reduced number of women sentenced to capital punishment.

Since the later medieval era, if a woman was convicted, the punishments were severe and they were treated very similarly to men, if not worse at times. Throughout history, when women were found guilty of murder, they were treated as pariahs – unnatural, wicked beasts who defied the expected behaviours and traits of women and punished harshly. Murder itself came with a death sentence, not to mention petty treason – a female dominated crime that carried the sentence of being burnt at the stake. Women were consistently seen as inferior to men, which was reflected in various aspects of the criminal justice system. The charge of petty treason for one, the use of the scold's bridle if women talked back to their husbands, the original inability to plead benefit of the clergy, the New Poor Law that restricted the ability of a single woman to ask their child's father to help pay for their upbringing, and the assumption that all criminal women were mentally weak at a biological level, to list a few. This does not mean that men weren't punished severely and often gruesomely. It emphasises, however, that women weren't treated as equals.

It's mentioned above that women were thought of as unnatural and wicked; sometimes rightfully so. Some of these murderous women were horrendously cruel, brutal, and malicious, not because they lacked the accepted traits for women at that time, but due to the vile action they committed. Yes, infanticidal mothers did the unthinkable and went against the ingrained responsibility of being a mother, but most were faced with unimaginable situations that most people today couldn't conceive of. Others were suffering from mental health issues that they didn't know how to cope with.

From 1674–1913 the Old Bailey recorded 1192 cases where women were brought before the court for murder, including manslaughter and infanticide: 554 of these women were deemed guilty. One hundred and ninety-nine women committed murder, fourteen committed petty treason and 163 committed infanticide. This is only representative of London, and its surrounding area but provides a sense of the scale of female homicide over those 300 years. In late medieval England, the homicide rate for men and women was twenty deaths for every 100,000 people. By the late twentieth century it was only one for every 100,000. This illustrates how much our society has changed over the past 700 years and how violence is no longer an everyday aspect of life.

The span of 700 years provides a profound insight into the relationship between women and crime, particularly in regards to women who have committed homicide. While women were more inclined to commit murder within the confines of their homes and against family members, murderesses displayed no discrimination when it came to victims, weapons or settings. They took the lives of husbands, in-laws, children, infants, newborns, masters and mistresses, employers, friends, mothers, and fathers. Their methods were diverse, involving strangulation, slicing, stomping, stabbing, kicking, punching, poisoning, shooting, burning, drowning, and bashing. The array of weapons used included, bricks, guns, knives, scissors, their hands and feet, fire pokers, floors, boiling pots, fire, windows, tankards, tape, arsenic, laudanum, axes, and hatchets. The variety in their actions and choices highlights the complexity of their motives and circumstances.

Whether Sarah, Mary, Elizabeth, Margaret, Mary Ann, Alice, Agnes, Susan, Ruth, Rachael, Bessie, Emma, Anna, Kate, Jeannie, Joan, Ann(e) or any other British murderess, they were all different. They all had their own story and their own unfortunate circumstances that led them to murder. They all fall under the category of 'Women Who Kill', but do they really? For many, some form of punishment was just, as they exemplified wicked wrongdoers. However, for others, they were victims of the gendered biases and judicial policies of their times, and it cost them dearly. Seven hundred years of women against the criminal justice system. Seven hundred years of British murderesses. Each with a tantalising tale.

Bibliography

'A briefe discourse of two most cruell and bloudie murthers, committed bothe
in Worcestershire, and bothe happening vnhappily in the yeare 1583. The first
declaring, how one unnaturally murdered his neighbour, and afterward buried
him in his seller. The other sheweth, how a woman unlawfully following the
deuillish lusts of the flesh with her seruant, caused him very cruelly to kill her owne
husband'. London: Roger Warde, 1583. In Early English Books Online. (accessed 17
May 2023).

'A Correct Account of the Trial and Proceedings in the case of Mary A. Burdock,
for felony and murder at the Bristol Assizes, April 10th, 1835', [Broadside].
Bristol: John Davies, 1835. British Library, 74/1880.c.20.(367).

'A full … account of the execution of Mrs Margaret Tyndalor Shuttleworth, etc.,
1821'. British Library, 1851.c.19.(43.).

'A full and particular Account of the Life, Trial, and Behaviour of John Quin and
Mary Bailey, Executed for the Murder of Cornelius Bailey, the Husband of Mary
Bailey at Portsmouth, 1784', [Broadside]. British Library, cup21 g33/19.

'A full and particular Account of all the Prisoners which took their trials at the
Castle of York on Tuesday the 23d of July, 1765, with the Punishment inflicted
upon them for their several offence', [Broadside]. 1765. British Library, cup21
g33/53.

'A Full and true account of a most barbarous and bloody murther, committed by
Esther Ives, with the assistance of John Noyse a cooper; on the body of William
Ives, her husband, at Rumsey in Hampshire, on the fifth day of February
1686. Together with the miraculous and wonderful discovery of the murther
and murtherers. As also an account of their tryals at the last assizes, holden at
Winchester, where being found guilty of the said murther, they received sentence
of death, viz. John Noyse to be hang'd, and Esther Ives to be burnt. With their
manner of behaviour and execution, according to the said sentence'. London: P.
Brooksby, 1687. In Early English Books Online [online database]. (accessed 17
November 2022).

'A hellish murder committed by a French midwife on the body of her husband, Jan.
27, 1687'. London: Randal Taylor, 1688. In Early English Books Online [online
database]. (accessed 21 May 2023.

'A MOTHER ACCUSED OF CHILD MURDER'. Morning Post, June 28, 1894, p.
7. link.gale.com/apps/doc/R3214439137/GDCS (accessed 8 July 2023).

'A remarkable account of the penitent carriage and behaviour of the whip-makers
wife, both before and since her confinement in Newgate. To which is added,
The relation how strangely her house was troubled and disturbed that night her
maid Mary Cox died. Attested by a person then present. As also added several
remarkable passages relating to her murthering the said maid: with an account of

her decent burial. Publish'd to prevent false reports. Licensed according to order', [Broadside]. London: Richard Janeway, 1689'. British Library, 85/Cup.645.e.1.(4).

'A true and particular account of the three most horrid murders, that have lately been committed in the county of York, with the trials of the murderers, at the York assizes; viz. Ann Haywood ... John Wilkinson ... Benjamin Oldroyd ... With their condemnation, execution, &c'. London: T. Evans, ca. 1811. British Library, 1609/5905.(3.)

'A true copy of the paper, delivered the night before her execution, by S. Malcolm to the Rev. Mr Piddington [and published by him]'. London: Piddington, 1732. British Library, 518.f.71.

'A true translation of a paper written in French, delivered by Margaret Martell to the under-sheriff at the time and place of her execution, at Suffolk-street end, July 16, 1697, for the barbarous murther of Elizabeth Pullen, wife of Paul Pullen, Esq'. London: E. Mallet, 1697. In Early English Books Online [online database]. (accessed 20 April 2023).

'A warning for bad wives: or The manner of the burning of Sarah Elston Who was burnt to death a stake on Kennington. Common neer Southwark, on Wednesday the 24th of April 1678. For murdering her husband Thomas Elston, the 25th of September last. and likewise the execution and confession of John Masters, and Gabriel Dean his man; who were executed for robbing on the highway. Together with their behaviour, last vvords, and confession at the place of execution. With allowance. Ro. L'Estrange'. London: D.M., 1678. In Early English Books Online [online database]. (accessed on 17 May 2023).

Aberdeen Child Murder Charge, Husband And Wife Before Sheriff, Crowd Gathers Outside Court. *Dundee Courier*, April 27, 1934, p. 7. https://www.britishnewspaperarchive.co.uk (accessed 27 July 2023).

Aberdeen Child Murder Charge, Woman to be Tried in Edinburgh. *Dundee Courier,* June 30, 1934, p. 10. https://www.britishnewspaperarchive.co.uk (accessed 27 July 2023).

'Aberdeen Scenes. Crowds See Arrest Of Couple. Helen Priestley Murder. Court Hearing In Camera'. *Ballymena Weekly Telegraph*, May 5, 1934, p. 5, British Newspaper Archive (accessed 27 July 2023).

'Alleged Wholesale Poisoning'. *Times*, October 7, 1872, p. 10, Gale (accessed July 13, 2023).

Amussen, Susan Dwyer. 'Punishment, Discipline, and Power: The Social Meanings of Violence in Early Modern England.' *Journal of British Studies* 34, no. 1 (1995): 1–34.

'An Account of the Last Dying Words and Execution of Mrs Shuttleworth. For the Murder of her Husband, on Friday the 7th of December inst. 1821, at Montross, near Edinburgh', Montross Review, 1821', [broadside]. *The Word on the Street*, National Library of Scotland [database], APS.3.96.15, (accessed 12 April 2023).

Appleton, Arthur. *Mary Ann Cotton: her story and trial*. London, Michael Joseph, 1973, British Library, X.200/8456.

Arnot, Meg and Usborne, Cornelie. *Gender and Crime in Modern Europe*. London, UCL Press, 1999.

August, Andrew. 'A Horrible Looking Woman: Female Violence in Late-Victorian East London.' *Journal of British Studies* 54, no. 4 (2015): 844–868.

Baldwin, Jayne. *Mary Timney – The Road to the Gallows*. Stranraer, Scotland, Clayhole Publishing, 2013, British Library, YK.2014.a.19524.

Balfour, J. *A Memorial of the Conversion of I. Livingston, Lady Waristoun. With an Account of her carriage at her Execution, July 1600*. edited by C.K. Sharpe, Edinburgh, 1828, British Library, 1373.g.24.

Ballinger, Anette. 'A Crime of Almost Unspeakable Cruelty and Wickedness: Gender, Agency and Murder in Scotland – The Case of Jeannie Donald.' *Social & Legal Studies* 28, no. 4 (2018): 429–449.

Barker, Hannah and Chalus, Elaine (eds.). *Women's History: Britain, 1700-1850, An Introduction*. London, Routledge, 2005.

Bayley, K.E. (ed.). *Two Thirteenth-century Assize Rolls for the County of Durham*, vol. 127, 1916. British Library, Ac.8045/65.

Beattie, J.M. *Crime and the courts in England 1660-1800*. Oxford, Princeton N.J., Clarendon Press, 1986.

Beattie, J. M. 'The Criminality of Women in Eighteenth-Century England.' Journal *of Social History* 8, no. 4 (1975): 80–116.

Behlmer, George K. 'Deadly Motherhood: Infanticide and Medical Opinion in Mid-Victorian England.' *Journal of the History of Medicine and Allied Sciences* 34, no. 4 (1979): 403–427.

Bennett, Rachel, E. *Capital Punishment And The Criminal Corpse In Scotland, 1740–1834*. Palgrave Macmillan, 2018.

'Betty Amplet, Who was Executed at Glocester, on Monday, the 13th of August 1810, for the Willful Murder, of her Female Bastard Child', [broadside]. Bristol, Bonner, 1810, British Library, 1880.c.20.(327.).

Billingham, Josephine Elaine. *Piteous Performances: Representations and Contexts of Infanticide in Tudor and Stuart Literature of Stage and Street*. PhD diss., University College London, 2015.

Blumberg, Arnold. 'Drawn and Quartered.' *Medieval Warfare* 5, no. 2 (2015): 49–52.

Bolton, Brenda and Stuard, Susan Mosher. *Women in medieval society*. Philadelphia, University of Pennsylvania Press, 1976.

Brigden, James. *That Takes Guts: 7 Gory Execution Methods From Tudor England. Sky History*, 2023, History (accessed 20 May 2023).

Brown, Yvonne Galloway and Ferguson, Rona (eds.). *Twisted Sisters: Women, Crime and Deviance in Scotland Since 1400*. East Lothian, Tuckwell Press, 2002.

Buckley, Angela. *Amelia Dyer and the baby farm murders*. Reading, Manor Vale Associates, 2016, British Library, YK.2017.a.3577.

Butler, Sara M. 'More than Mothers: Juries of Matrons and Pleas of the Belly in Medieval England.' *Law and History Review* 37, no. 2 (2019): 353–396.

Butler, Sara M. *The language of abusive marital violence in later medieval England.* Leiden, Boston, Brill, 2007.

Calendar of Assize Records: Surrey indictments James I. HMSO, 1982, British Library, GP-RP I (2c).

Callahan, Kathy. 'Women Who Kill: An Analysis of Cases in Late Eighteenth-and Early Nineteenth-Century London.' *Journal of Social History* 46, no. 4 (2013): 1013–1038.

'Case Against John Newell And Susan Newell (1923), Glasgow'. *MyGlasgow*, University of Glasgow, 2023, Glasgow (accessed 11 November 2022).

'Chopping Her Child's Head Off'. *Huddersfield Chronicle*, 21 May 1894, p. 3, link-gale-com.ezproxy.lib.bbk.ac.uk (accessed 3 August 2023).

Clark, Sandra. 'Deeds Against Nature: Women And Crime In Street Literature Of Early Modern England.' *SEDERI*, no. 12 (2002): 9–30.

'Coatbridge Crime. Women Charged with Murder. Husband Surrenders To Police'. *Aberdeen Press and Journal*, June 23, 1923, p. 7, British Newspaper Archive (accessed 21 July 2023).

Cockburn, J.S. (ed.). *Crime in England, 1500-1800.* Methuen, 1977.

'CONFESSION OF MARY ANN BURDOCK'. 28 April 1835, p. 4. https://go-gale-com.ezproxy.lib.bbk.ac.uk (accessed 7 July 2023).

Conley, Carolyn A. *Debauched, Desperate, Deranged: Women Who Killed, London 1674–1913.* Oxford, Oxford University Press, 2020.

'CONSCIENCE MONEY – The Chancellor of the.' *Times*, 15 August 1907, p. 3, Gale (accessed July 25, 2023). 15 August 1907, p. 3. https://go-gale-com.ezproxy.lib.bbk.ac.uk (accessed 25 July 2023).

'COURT OF KING'S BENCH'. *Freeman's Journal*, 26 April 1820, Gale (accessed July 2, 2023).

'Crowds Demand To See Mrs Ellis, Police Reinforcements Outside Prison'. *The Times*, 13 July 1955, p. 8, https://go-gale-com.ezproxy.lib.bbk.ac.uk (accessed 23 July 2023)

'CUMBERLAND LENT ASSIZES.' *Lancaster Gazette*, 10 March 1821, Gale (accessed 2 July 2023).

D'Cruze, Shani and Jackson, Louise A. (eds.). *Women, Crime and Justice in England since 1660.* Basingstoke, Palgrave Macmillan, 2009.

'Dalston Railway Murder. Prisoner Before The Magistrates'. *Hull Daily News*, 4 November 1899, p. 10, British Newspaper Archive (accessed 12 July 2023).

Davies, R. R. *The Survival Of The Bloodfeud In Medieval Wales.* Wiley 54, no. 182 (1969): 338–357.

'Death Sentence On Woman Accused Of Slaying Child, Collapse, 'Unspeakable Cruelty' – The Judge'. *Sheffield Independent*, 24 July 1934, p. 1, British Newspaper Archive (accessed 27 July 2023).

'Death Sentence On Woman, Murder Of Racing Driver'. *The Times*, 22 June 1955, p. 6, https://go-gale-com.ezproxy.lib.bbk.ac.uk (accessed 23 July 2023)

Devereaux, Simon. 'The Abolition of the Burning of Women in England Reconsidered.' *Crime, History & Societies* 9, no. 2 (2005): 1–27.

Dolan, Frances E. *Dangerous familiars: representations of domestic crime in England, 1500–1700*. Ithaca, Cornell University Press, 1994.

Dolan, Frances E. 'Home-Rebels and House-Traitors: Murderous Wives in Murderous Wives in Early Modern England.' *Yale Journal of Law & the Humanities* 4, no. 1 (1992): 1–32.

Donnachie, Ian. *Malcolm, Sarah. Oxford Dictionary of National Biography*, 2004. https://www.oxforddnb.com (accessed 20 April 2023).

Douglas, Heather, and Simon Bronitt. *Phillips' Brief: Patriarchal Terrorism and Burning at the Stake: The Petty Treason of Elizabeth Herring 1773. Criminal Law Journal* 39 (2015): 272–275.

'Dreadful news from Southwark, or, A true account of the most horrid murder committed by Margaret Osgood, on her husband Walter Osgood a hat-maker, on Saturday the 31th [sic] of July 1680 whom she most barbarously murdered, by cleaving his head whilst he was asleep, cuting [sic] off his ears, and wounding him in several other places in an inhumane manner: together with her examination and confession of the whole fact before the justice of the peace, and commitment of her to prison till tryal'. London: s.n., 1680. Early English Books Online [online database]. (accessed 17 November 2022).

Durston, Gregory. *Victims and Viragos: Metropolitan Women, Crime and the Eighteenth-Century Justice System*. Suffolk: Arima Publishing, 2007.

Durston, Gregory. *Wicked Ladies: Provincial Women, Crime and the Eighteenth-Century English Justice System*. Newcastle upon Tyne: Cambridge Scholars Publishing, 2013.

'Echoes of Holloway Prison'. Islington Council, 2023. https://www.islington.gov.uk (accessed 27 July 2023).

Elton, G.R. 'Introduction: Crime and the Historian.' In J.S. Cockburn (ed.), *Crime in England, 1500–1800*, Methuen, 1977, pp. 1–14.

Emsley, Clive, Tim Hitchcock, and Robert Shoemaker. *Crime and Justice and Punishment. Old Bailey Proceedings Online*, 2018. https://www.oldbaileyonline.org (accessed 15 June 2023).

Emsley, Clive, Tim Hitchcock, and Robert Shoemaker. *Gender in the Proceedings. Old Bailey Proceedings Online*, 2018. https://www.oldbaileyonline.org (accessed 15 October 2022).

Emsley, Clive, Tim Hitchcock, and Robert Shoemaker. *Historical Background – History of The Old Bailey Courthouse. Old Bailey Proceedings Online*, 2018. https://www.oldbaileyonline.org (accessed 1 June 2023).

Emsley, Clive, Tim Hitchcock, and Robert Shoemaker. *About The Proceedings. Old Bailey Proceedings Online*, 2018. https://www.oldbaileyonline.org (accessed 27 July 2023).

Ewan, Elizabeth. 'Disorderly Damsels? Women and Interpersonal Violence in Pre-

Reformation Scotland.' *The Scottish Historical Review* 89, no. 228 (2010): 153–171.

Ewan, Elizabeth. 'Impatient Griseldas: Women and the Perpetration of Violence in Sixteenth-Century Glasgow.' *Florilegium* 28 (2011): 149–168.

'Execution At Cardiff, Baby Farmer, Condemned at Swansea, Pays the Extreme Penalty. The Crime for Which Rhoda Willis Suffered Death. Her Sad Life Story and Last Days'. *Herald of Wales*, August 17, 1907, p. 11. https://www.britishnewspaperarchive.co.uk (accessed 22 July 2023).

'Execution of Ann Heytrey, For the Murder of Her Mistress'. *Liverpool Mercury*, April 28, 1820, p. 358. link.gale.com/apps/doc/BC3203930417/GDCS?u=birkb&sid=bookmark-GDCS (accessed 2 July 2023).

'Execution of Mary Ann Cotton'. *Lloyd's Illustrated Newspaper*, March 30, 1873, p. 4. https://go-gale-com.ezproxy.lib.bbk.ac.uk (accessed 13 July 2023).

'Execution of Mary MacKinnon, Glasgow, Mayne and Co, 1823', [broadside]. *The Word on the Street*, National Library of Scotland [database], L.C.Fol.73(049), (accessed 21 April 2023).

'FATAL FIGHT AT ABERDARE'. *Western Mail*, May 23, 1894, p. 7, link-gale-com.ezproxy.lib.bbk.ac.uk (accessed 3 August 2023).

Feeley, Malcolm, and Deborah Little. 'The Vanishing Female: The Decline of Women in the Criminal Process, 1687-1912.' *Law and Society Review* 25, no. 4 (1991): 719–757.

Fisher, Pam. 'Getting Away With Murder? The Suppression Of Coroners' Inquests In Early Victorian England And Wales.' *Local Population Studies* 78 (2007): 4762.

Garay, Kathleen E. 'Women and Crime in Later Medieval England: 1388–1409.' *Florilegium* 1 (1979): 87–109.

Gaskill, Malcolm. *Crime and Mentalities in Early Modern England*. Cambridge: Cambridge University Press, 2000.

Geltner, G. 'No-Woman's Land? On Female Crime and Incarceration, Past, Present, and Future.' *Justice Policy Journal* 7, no. 2 (2010).

'Genuine and Authentic Account Of The Life, Trial, and Execution of Elizabeth Brownrigg'. London: R. Richards, 1767, Wellcome Collection, ESTC T12476.

'Ghastly Trek. Details of Glasgow Horror, The 'Washing' in the Go-Car. How the Crime was Discovered'. *Edinburgh Evening News*, 22 June 1923, p. 7, https://www.britishnewspaperarchive.co.uk (accessed 21 July 2023).

'Girl's Body In Sack, Man and Wife Charged With Murder'. *Western Mail*, 27 April 1934, p. 12, https://www.britishnewspaperarchive.co.uk (accessed 27 July 2023).

'GLAMORGAN ASSIZES'. *Western Mail*, 28 June 1894, p. 7, link.gale.com/apps/doc/BA3205230852/GDCS (accessed 8 July 2023).

'Glasgow High Court Indictments. A Paisley Case'. *Paisley Daily Express*, 2 May 1911, p. 2, https://www.britishnewspaperarchive.co.uk (accessed 12 July 2023).

'Go-Car Murder. Petition For Reprieve'. *The Scotsman*, 29 September 1923, p. 8, https://www.britishnewspaperarchive.co.uk (accessed 21 July 2023).

Goodare, Julian. 'The Scottish Witchcraft Act.' *Church History* 74, no. 1 (2005): 39–67.

'Governess's Crime, Recovered By A Retirement'. *Leeds Mercury*, 25 September, 1907, p. 7, https://www.britishnewspaperarchive.co.uk (accessed 17 July 2023).

Gowing, Laura. *Ingenious Trade: Women and Work in Seventeenth-Century London*. Cambridge: Cambridge University Press, 2021.

Gowing, Laura. 'Secret Births and Infanticide in Seventeenth-Century England.' *Past & Present* no. 156 (1997): 87–115.

Grant, Alexander. 'Murder Will Out: Kingship, Kinship and Killing in Medieval Scotland. In Kings, Lords and Men in Scotland and Britain, 1300–1625.' *Essays in Honour of Jenny Wormald*, edited by S. Boardman and J. Goodare, 193–226. Edinburgh: Edinburgh University Press, 2014.

Green, Thomas A. 'The Jury and the English Law of Homicide.' *Michigan Law Review* 74 (1976): 413–499.

Griffith, Richard. Dealing with incidents of feticide and infanticide in England and Wales. *British Journal of Midwifery* 23, no. 5 (2015): https://www.britishjournalofmidwifery.com (accessed 26 July 2023).

Griffiths, Arthur. *The Chronicles of Newgate* vol. 1. London: Chapman and Hall, 1884.

Grimes, Leslie. *Deeds Against Nature: Gender And Disorder In Print, 1590–1700*. MA diss., Georgia State University, 2019.

Gross, Charles (ed.). *Select Cases from the Coroners' Rolls, A.D. 1265-1413: with a brief account of the history of the office of coroner*, vol. 9. London: B. Quaritch, 1896, British Library, Ac.2176.

Hanawalt, Barbara A. *Crime and Conflict in English Communities, 1300–1348*. Cambridge: Harvard University Press, 1979.

Hanawalt, Barbara A. 'The Female Felon in Fourteenth-Century England.' *Viator* 5 (1974): 254–269.

Hanawalt, Barbara A. 'Violent Death in Fourteenth and early Fifteenth century England.' *Comparative Studies in Society and History* 18, no. 3 (1976): 297–320.

Hartlen, Chelsea D. M. *Managing Criminal Women in Scotland: An Assessment of the Scarcity of Female Offenders in the Records of the High Court of Justiciary, 1524-1542*. MA diss., Halifax, Dalhousie University, 2014, https://dalspace.library.dal.ca (accessed 29 April 2023).

Hartman, Mary S. 'Murder for Respectability: The Case of Madeleine Smith.' *Victorian Studies* 16, no. 4 (1973): 381–400.

'Helen Priestley Case. Alexander Donald Released Yesterday. Order Of Crown'. *Aberdeen Press and Journal*, 12 June 1934, p. 7, https://www.britishnewspaperarchive.co.uk (accessed 27 July 2023).

Helfield, Randa. 'Poisonous Plots: Women Sensation Novelists And Murderesses Of The Victorian Period.' *Victorian Review* 21, no. 2 (1995): 161–188.

Higginbotham, Ann R. 'Sin of the Age: Infanticide and Illegitimacy in Victorian London.' *Victorian Studies* 32, no. 3 (1989): 319–337.

'High Court In Glasgow'. *Strathearn Herald*, 24 June 1911, p. 8, https://www.

britishnewspaperarchive.co.uk (accessed 12 July 2023).

'High Court in Glasgow'. *The Scotsman*, 20 June 1911, p. 5, https://www. britishnewspaperarchive.co.uk (accessed 12 July 2023).

Hindley, Charles (ed.). *The Roxburghe Ballads*, vol. 2. London: Reeves and Turner, 1874.

Hopkins, A. (ed.). *Selected Rolls Of The Chester City Courts, Late Thirteenth and Early Fourteenth Centuries*, vol 2, series 3. Manchester: The Chetham Society, 1950.

Horler-Underwood, Catherine E. *Aspects of female Criminality in Wales, c. 1730-1830: Evidence from the Court of Great Sessions.* PhD diss., Cardiff University, 2014.

Howard, A.J. (ed.). *Medieval gaol delivery rolls for the county of Devon.* Middlesex, 1986, British Library, YC.1987.b.6013.

Howard, Elizabeth Anne. *Women and Crime In Sixteenth-Century Wales.* PhD diss., Cardiff University, 2020.

Howard, Sharon. *Crime, Communities And Authority In Early Modern Wales: Denbighshire, 1660-1730*, PhD diss., Aberystwyth, University of Wales, 2003.

Hultquist, Aleksondra. Matriarchs, 'Murderesses, and Coquettes: Investigations in Long-Eighteenth-Century Femininities.' *The Eighteenth Century* 53, no. 1 (2012): 119–124.

Hunnisett, R.F. (ed.). *Bedfordshire Coroners' Rolls*, Streatley, Beds, 1961, British Library, Ac.8018.

Hunnisett, R. F. (ed.). *Calendar of Nottinghamshire coroners' inquests, 1485–1558.* Nottingham, Derry & Sons, 1969, British Library, Ac.8097/2.

Hunnisett, R. F. (ed.). *Sussex Coroners' Inquests 1485-1558*, vol. 74. Lewes, Sussex Record Society, 1985, British Library, 8553.180000.

Hunnisett, R.F. (ed.). *Sussex coroners' inquests 1558–1603.* Kew, PRO Publications, c1996, British Library, YC.1998.b.609.

Hunnisett, R.F. 'The Medieval Coroners' Rolls.' *The American Journal of Legal History* 3, no. 3 (1959): 205–221.

Hurl-Eamon, Jennine. 'Female Criminality in the British Courts from the Middle Ages to the Nineteenth Century.' *Journal of Women's History* 21, no. 3 (2009): 161–169.

Ireland, Richard W. *Land of White Gloves?: A History of Crime and Punishment in Wales.* Oxon; New York, Routledge, 2015.

Isobel, McLean. *Justiciary Court Records.* National Archives Scotland, 1750–1815, JC26/243.

Jackson, Mark (ed.). *Infanticide: Historical Perspectives on Child Murder and Concealment, 1550-2000.* Hants, Ashgate, 2002.

Jenkin, Anna Clare. *Perceptions of the Murderess in London and Paris, 1674–1789*, PhD diss., University of Sheffield, 2015.

Jenkins, Dafydd and Owen, Morfydd E. *The Welsh Law of Women: Studies Presented to Professor Daniel A. Binchy on his Eightieth Birthday, 3 June 1980.* Cardiff, University of Wales Press, 1980.

Johnson, Lizabeth. 'Married Women, Crime and the Courts in Late Medieval Wales.' In *Married Women and the Law in Premodern Northwest Europe*. edited by Beattie Cordelia and Stevens Matthew Frank, 71–90.

Kane, Stuart A. *Wives with Knives: Early Modern Murder Ballads and the Transgressive Commodity. Criticism* 38, no. 2 (1996): 219–237.

Kent, Susan Kingsley. *Gender and Power in Britain, 1640–1990*, London, Routledge, 1999.

Kermode, Jenny and Walker, Garthine (eds.). *Women, Crime and the Courts in Early Modern England*. London, Routledge, 1994.

Kesselring, K.J. *Making Murder Public: Homicide in Early Modern England, 1480-1680*. Oxford, Oxford University Press, 2019.

Kesselring, K. J. '"Murder's Crimson Badge": Homicide in the Age of Shakespeare.' In *The Oxford Handbook of the Age of Shakespeare*. edited by Malcom Smuts, 543–558. Oxford, Oxford University Press, 2016, pp. 543–558

Kilday, Anne-Marie. *Women and Violent Crime in Enlightenment Scotland*. Rochester, The Boydell Press for The Royal Historical Society, 2007.

Kimball, Elizabeth G. (ed.). *A Cambridgeshire Gaol Delivery Roll 1332-1334*, vol. 4. Cambridge, Cambridge Antiquarian Records Society, 1978, British Library, P.801/1445(4).

King, Peter. 'Making Crime News: Newspapers, Violent Crime and the Selective Reporting of Old Bailey Trials in the late Eighteenth Century.' *Crime, History & Societies* 13, no. 1 (2009): 91–116.

Knapp, Andrew and Baldwin, William. *The Newgate Calendar; Comprising Interesting Memoirs of the Most Notorious Characters Who Have Been Convicted of Outrages on the Laws of England Since the Commencement of the Eighteenth Century; With Occasional Anecdotes and Observations, Speeches, Confessions, and Last Exclamations of Sufferers*, vol. 1. London, J Robins and co., 1824.

Knelman, Judith. 'The Amendment Of The Arsenic Bill.' *Victorian Review* 17, no. 2 (1991): 1–10.

Knox, W. W. J. and Thomas, L. 'Homicide in Eighteenth-Century Scotland: Numbers and Theories.' *The Scottish Historical Review* 94, no. 238, Part 1 (2015): 48–73.

Knox, W. W. J. and Thomas, L. 'Homicide in Eighteenth-Century Scotland: Numbers and Theories.' *The Scottish Historical Review* 98, no. 247, Part 2 (2019): 214–240.

Kyd, Thomas. *The Trueth of the Most Wicked and Secret Murthering of Iohn Brewen, Goldsmith of London: Committed by His Owne Wife, Through the Prouocation of One Iohn Parker Whom She Loued: For Which Fact She Was Burned, and He Hanged in Smithfield, on Wednesday, the 28 of Iune, 1592, Two Yeares After the Murther Was Committed*. London, T. Orwin, 1592, in *Early English Books Online* [online database], (accessed 1 May 2023).

Lacey, Nicola. 'Women, crime and character in the 20th century.' *Journal of the*

British Academy, vol. 6, 2018, pp. 131–167

Landau, Norma. 'Gauging crime in late eighteenth-century London.' *Social History*, vol. 35, no. 4, 2010, pp. 396–417

'Last woman hanged for murder in Great Britain'. *History.com*, 13 August 2020, https://www.history.com (accessed on 8 December 2022).

Lawler, Catherine. *Trial of Kate Webster*. ed. by Elliott O'Donnell, Edinburgh; London, W. Hodge & Co, 1925, British Library, 6496.d.1/13.

Leuschner, Kristin Jeanne. *Creating the 'Known True Story': Sixteenth- and Seventeenth-Century Murder and Witchcraft Pamphlets and Plays*. PhD diss., UCLA, 1992

'LLOFRUDDIAETH YN MHONTYPRIDD', *Y Werin Dydd Sadwrn*, 26 May, 1894, p. 3, https://newspapers.library.wales (accessed 20 April 2023).

Loengard, Janet Senderowitz. 'Legal History and the Medieval Englishwomen: A Fragmented View.' *Law and History Review*, vol. 4, no. 1, 1986, pp. 161–178

'LONDON, APRIL 18', *Jackson's Oxford Journal [1809]*, 22 April 1820, link.gale.com/apps/doc /Y3202653517/GDCS (accessed 2 July 2023).

'Louise Masset Executed Today. Crowd Cheer Outside Newgate. Confession Of The Crime', *Portsmouth Evening News*, 9 January 1900, p. 3, https://www.britishnewspaperar chive.co.uk.

'Louise Masset To Die? The Opening of the New Century will be Stained by the Hanging of a Woman! The Agony of Her Position has Turned the Wretched Woman's Hair White'. *Illustrated Police Budget*, 30 December 1899, p. 11, https://www.britishnewspaperarchi ve.co.uk (accessed 17 July 2023).

'M'naghten rule'. Cornell Law School Legal Information Institute, 2020, https://www.law.cornell.edu (accessed 10 July 2023).

Macfarlane, Alan. *The history of infanticide in England*. 2002, http://www.alanmacfarlane.com (accessed 27 April 2023).

MacMillan, Ken and Glass Melissa. 'Murder and Mutilation in Early-Stuart England: A Case Study in Crime Reporting.' *Journal of the Canadian Historical Association*, vol. 27, no. 2, 2016, pp. 63–91

Magrath, Jane. '(mis)reading the bloody body: the case of Sarah Malcolm.' *Women's Writing*, vol. 11, no. 2, 2007, pp. 223–236

Mangham, Andrew, '"Murdered at the Breast": Maternal Violence and the Self-Made Man in Popular Victorian Culture. *Critical Survey*, vol. 16, no. 1, 2004, pp. 20–34

Marsh, Christopher. 'Best-Selling Ballads and the Female Voices of Thomas Deloney.' *Huntington Library Quarterly*, vol. 82, no. 1, 2019, 127–154.

Marshburn, Joseph H. *Blood and knavery; a collection of English Renaissance pamphlets and ballads of crime and sin*. Rutherford, Fairleigh Dickinson University Press, 1973.

Martin, Randall. *Women, Murder, and Equity in Early Modern England*. New York, Routledge, 2008.

McKenzie, Andrea. '"His Barbarous Usages", Her "Evil Tongue".' *The American Journal of Legal History*, vol. 57, no. 3, 2017, pp. 354–384.

McKenzie, Andrea. 'The Prosecutorial Passions, An Emotional History of Petty Treason and Parricide in England, 1674-1790.' In David Lemmings and Allyson N. May (eds.), *Criminal Justice During the Long Eighteenth Century: Theatre, Representation and Emotion*, Taylor & Francis Group, 2018, pp. 41–61.

McMahon, Vanessa. *Murder in Shakespeare's England*. London, New York: Hambledon and London, 2004.

'Miscellaneous Articles.' *Aberdeen Journal*, 21 June 1820, link.gale.com/apps/doc/BA3205624584/GDCS (accessed 2 July 2023).

'Model Charged With Murder, Alleged Statement On Shooting'. *The Times*, 21 June 1955, p. 6, https://go-gale-com.ezproxy.lib.bbk.ac.uk (accessed 23 July 2023).

Moore, James. *The 5 Most Gruesome Tudor Punishments and Torture Methods. History Hit*, 2021, https://www.historyhit.com (accessed 20 May 2023).

Mosalski, Ruth. *The Horrible Story of the Last Woman to be Hanged in Wales. Wales Online*, 2017, https://www.walesonline.co.uk (accessed 12 July 2023).

'Mrs Newell Found Guilty in Go-Cart Murder Trial. Hears Death Sentence Unmoved. Husband Establishes His Alibi'. *Dundee Courier*, 20 September 1923, p. 5, https://www.britishnewspaperarchive.co.uk (accessed 21 July 2023).

'Mrs Newell Hears Her Fate. Faints On Being Informed That Reprieve Has Been Refused. Weeping and Wailing for Her Daughter'. *Dundee Courier*, 9 October 1923, p. 5, https://www.britishnewspaperarchive.co.uk (accessed 21 July 2023).

'Mrs Newell Pays Penalty For Go-Cart Murder. First Woman Executed in Glasgow For 70 Years. Like a Brave Woman She Died'. *Dundee Evening Telegraph*, 10 October 1923, p. 1, https://www.britishnewspaperarchive.co.uk (accessed 21 July 2023).

'Murder Appeal Withdrawn'. *Liverpool Echo*, 6 August 1934, p. 5, https://www.britishnewspaperarchive.co.uk (accessed 27 July 2023).

'MURDER AT TREHERBERT'. *Western Mail*, 19 May 1894, p. 6, link.gale.com/apps/doc/BA3205229254/GDCS (accessed 8 July 2023).

'Murder Of Little Boy. Former Kilsyth Resident'. *Kirkintilloch Gazette*, 29 June 1923, https://www.britishnewspaperarchive.co.uk (accessed 21 July 2023).

'MURDER OF MRS. DORMER. Further particulars. On Monday we mentioned the death of Mrs Dormer, aged about 50'. *Times*, 8 September 1819, p. 3, link.gale.com/apps/doc/CS51397928/GDCS (accessed 2 July 2023).

Murder upon Murder, Committed by Thomas Sherwood, alias, Countrey Tom: and Elizabeth Evans, alias, Canbrye Besse. [broadside]. London: T. Langley, 1635, http://ballads.bodleian.ox.ac.uk (accessed 19 May 2023).

Murther upon Murther: Or A True and Faithful Relation, Of Six Horrid and Bloody Cruelties, And Barbarous and Unheard of Murthers, And Tragical Villanies, Lately Committed in Several Counties of England. London: W.D., 1684 in Early English Books Online [online database], (accessed 21 May 2023).

'News'. *London Chronicle*, 14 August 1787–16 August 1787, p. 157, link.gale.com/apps/doc/Z2000587215/GDCS (accessed 27 April 2023).

'News'. *Weekly Journal or British Gazetteer*, 15 September 1716, p. 518, https://go-gale-com.ezproxy.lib.bbk.ac.uk (accessed 26 September 2022).

'News In Brief'. *The Times*, 9 July 1955, p. 3, https://go-gale-com.ezproxy.lib.bbk.ac.uk (accessed 23 July 2023).

Palk, Deirdre. *Gender, Crime and Judicial Discretion, 1780-1830*. Woodbridge, Suffolk, 2006.

Palk, Deidre and Shoemaker, Robert. *Sarah Malcolm 1710-1733. London Lives*, 2018, https://www.londonlives.org (accessed 15 April 2023).

Phipps, Teresa. *Medieval Women and Urban Justice: Commerce, Crime and Community in England, 1300-1500*. Manchester: Manchester University Press, 2020.

Picard, Liza. 'Crime and Punishment in Elizabethan England.' *Discovering Literature: Shakespeare & Renaissance*. British Library, 2016. https://www.bl.uk (accessed 19 May 2023).

Price, Cheryl Blake. 'Poison, Sensation, and Secrets in "The Lifted Veil".' *Victorian Review*, vol. 36, no. 1, 2010, pp. 203–216.

Rabin, Dana. 'It Will Be Expected by You All, to Hear Something from Me' Emotion, Performance, and Child Murder in Britain in the Eighteenth Century.' in *Criminal Justice During the Long Eighteenth Century: Theatre, Representation and Emotion*, edited by David Lemmings and Allyson N. May, Taylor & Francis Group, 2018, pp. 21–40.

Read, Sara. *Maids, Wives, Widows, Exploring Early Modern Women's Lives 1540–1740*. South Yorkshire: Pen and Sword Books Ltd, 2015.

Release Of Mrs Donald. *Aberdeen Press and Journal*, 25 July 1944, p. 4. https://www.britishnewspaperarchive.co.uk (accessed 26 July 2023).

'Released From Prison, Man Who Was Accused of Girl's Murder – Crown Order'. *Daily Mirror*, 12 June 1934, p. 9. https://www.britishnewspaperarchive.co.uk (accessed 27 July 2023).

Rodziewicz, Janka. 'Women and the Hue and Cry in Late Fourteenth-Century Great Yarmouth.' in *Women, Agency and the Law, 1300-1700*. edited by Kane Bronach and Fiona Williamson, London: Pickering and Chatto, 2013, pp. 87–97.

Roth, Randolph. 'Homicide in Early Modern England 1549-1800: The Need for a Quantitative Synthesis.' *Crime, History & Societies*, vol. 5, no. 2, 2001, pp. 33–67.

Salter, H.E. *Records of mediaeval Oxford. Coroners' inquests, the walls of Oxford, etc.* Oxford: The Oxford Chronicle Company, Ltd, 1912.

Samaha, Joel B. 'Hanging for Felony: The Rule Of Law In Elizabethan Colchester.' *The Historical Journal*, vol. 21, no. 4, 1978, pp. 763–782.

Samaha, Joel B. 'The Recognizance in Elizabethan Law Enforcement.' *The American Journal of Legal History*, vol. 25, no. 3, 1981, pp. 189–204.

Sandidge, Marilyn. 'Changing Contexts of Infanticide in Medieval English Texts.' in *Childhood in the Middle Ages and the Renaissance: The Results of a Paradigm Shift in the History of Mentality.* edited by A. Classen, Berlin, Boston: De Gruyter, 2017, pp. 291–306.

Sayles, G.O. (ed.). *Select cases in the Court of King's Bench Under Richard II, Henry IV and Henry V*, vol. 88. London: B. Quaritch, 1971, British Library, Ac.2176. [v.88].

'Scene At Sack Murder Trial, Mother And Daughter, Accused Woman's Sobs in Dock'. *Halifax Evening Courier*, 18 July 1934, p. 3. https://www.britishnewspaperarchive.co.uk (accessed 27 July 2023).

'Serious Charge Against A Woman'. *The Scotsman*, 24 March 1911, p. 8. https://www.britishnewspaperarchive.co.uk (accessed 12 July 2023).

Sharpe, J.A. 'Domestic Homicide in Early Modern England.' *The Historical Journal*, vol. 24, no. 1, 1981, pp. 29–48.

Sharpe, J.A. 'The History Of Crime In England c. 1300-1914: A Review of Recent Publications.' *The British Journal of Criminology*, vol. 28, no. 2, 1988, pp. 124–137.

Sharpe, Reginald, R. (rd.) (ed.). *Calendar of Coroners' Rolls of the City of London , A.D. 1300–1378*. London: Richard Clay & Sons, 1913, British Library, 010349.dd.37.

Shoemaker, Robert B. 'Print and the Female Voice: Representations of Women's Crime in London, 1690-1735.' *Gender & History*, vol. 22, no. 1, 2010, pp. 75–91.

Shoemaker, Robert B. 'Sympathy for the Criminal: The Criminal Celebrity in Eighteenth-Century London.' *Crime, History & Societies*, vol. 24, no. 1, 2020, pp. 5–28.

Shoemaker, Robert B. and Ward, Richard. 'Understanding The Criminal: Record-Keeping, Statistics And The Early History Of Criminology in England.' *British Journal of Criminology*, vol. 57, 2017, 1442–1461.

Shore, Heather. '"The Reckoning": disorderly women, informing constables and the Westminster justices, 1727–33. *Social History*, vol. 34, no. 4, 2009, pp. 409–427.

Spence, Laura. *Women Who Murder in Early Modern England*. MA diss., University of Warwick, 2010.

"Stratford-On-Housatonic', and News from Many Countries'. *The Illustrated London News*, 23 July 1955, p. 147. https://go-gale-com.ezproxy.lib.bbk.ac.uk (accessed 23 July 2023).

'SUMMARY OF NEWS'. *Western Mail*, 22 May 1894, p. 5. https://go-gale-com.ezproxy.lib.bbk.ac.uk (accessed 3 August 2023).

Symonds, Deborah A. *Notorious Murders, Black Lanterns, & Moveable Goods, The Transformation of Edinburgh's Underworld in the Early Nineteenth Century.* University of Akron Press, 2006.

Tarlow, S., and Battell, Lowman E. *Harnessing the Power of the Criminal Corpse.* Cham: Palgrave Macmillan, 2018.

Teachers Comment On Execution, School Near Prison 'In A Ferment'. *The Times*, 14 July 1955, p. 5. https://go-gale-com.ezproxy.lib.bbk.ac.uk (accessed 23 July 2023).

'The Alleged Wholesale Poisoning Cases'. *Times*, 21 October 1872, p. 11. https://go-gale-com.ezproxy.lib.bbk.ac.uk (accessed 13 July 2023).

'The Apprehending and Taking of Mrs Burdock (Late) Wade Of Trinity Street, On the Suspicion Of The Murder Of Mrs Clara Smith, With the examination of the Body, which was taken from the Grave on Wednesday Friday, Dec. 26 1834'. Bristol: J. Bonner, 1834. British Library, 1880.c.20.(366).

'The araignement & burning of Margaret Ferne-seede for the murther of her late husband Anthony Ferne-seede, found deade in Peckham Field neere Lambeth, hauing once before attempted to poyson him with broth, being executed in S. Georges-field the last of Februarie'. London: E. Allde, 1608. Early English Books Online [online database]. (Accessed 5 May 2023).

'THE AUCKLAND MURDERS'. *Morning Post*, 3 October 1872, p. 7. https://go-gale-com.ezproxy.lib.bbk.ac.uk (accessed 13 July 2023).

'THE CONDEMNED CRIMINAL MARY ANN COTTON'. *Blackburn Standard*, 19 March 1873, p. 3. https://go-gale-com.ezproxy.lib.bbk.ac.uk.

'THE CONDEMNED CRIMINAL MARY ANN COTTON'. *Dundee Courier*, 17 March 1873, p. 3. http://link-gale-com.ezproxy.lib.bbk.ac.uk (accessed 13 July 2023).

'The Crime Of Louise Masset. The Story Of A Poor Child'. *New Zealand Herald*, 3 February 1900, p. 2. https://paperspast.natlib.govt.nz (accessed 22 July 2023).

'The Go-Car Murder. Death Sentence Carried Out At Glasgow'. *The Scotsman*, 11 October 1923, p. 5. https://www.britishnewspaperarchive.co.uk (accessed 21 July 2023).

'The Go-Car Tragedy. Accused Before Sheriff At Glasgow.' *The Scotsman*, 10 September 1923, p. 5. https://www.britishnewspaperarchive.co.uk (accessed 21 July 2023).

'The Last Awful Moments And Dying Confession of Ann Aytry' [broadside]. Bristol, H. Bonner, 1820, British Library, 1880.c.20.(341).

'The last dying speeches and confessions of the three notorious malefactors who were executed at Tyburn on the 4th of this instant March 1681 giving an account of the several crimes for which they suffered which are as followeth, John Sadler for whipping a girl to death at Ratcliff, Roger Maiden for eight felonies and burglaries, Elizabeth Brown, alias White-head, for robbing the Two Cocks on London-Bridge and endeavoring to cut the maid's throat: with their penitential confessions as well in prison as at the place of execution'. London, Printed for T.B., in Early English Books Online [online database]. (accessed 20 May 2023).

'The Last Speech And Confession Of Anne Fogget, Burnt for the Murder of her Husband Abraham Fogget Who was Executed at York September 10 1716', [broadside]. Edinburgh, Margaret Reid, 1716, The Word on the Street, National Library of Scotland [database], Ry.III.c.36(025). (accessed 1 Dec 2022).

'The last speech and confession of Sarah Elestone at the place of execution who was burned for killing her husband, April 24. 1678. With her deportment in prison since her condemnation. With allowance. Elestone, Sarah, d. 1678'. London, T.D., 1678, in Early English Books Online [database]. (accessed 17 May 2023).

'The Life, Confession and Execution of Mrs Burdock who was executed at the New Drop, Bristol Gaol, for the murder of Mrs Clara Ann Smith, etc.', [broadside]. Bristol, J. Bonner, 1835, British Library, 1880.c.20.(368).

'The Mental Deficiency Act 1913'. *Meanwood Park Hospital*, 2023, http://www. meanwoodpark.co.uk (accessed 26 July 2023).

'The Mental Health Act 1959'. *The Health Foundation*, 2023, https://navigator.health. org.uk (accessed 26 July 2023).

'The Proceedings at the assizes in Southwark, for the county of Surrey begun on Thursday the 21th of March, and not ended till Tuesday the 26 of the same month, 1678: being an account of the trial of the woman for murdering her husband, with exact proof that came in against her, and her confession and pleas at the bar: upon which she was found guilty, and condemned to be burnt to ashes: as likewise, the trials and condemnation of two notorious high-way-men: of a woman for murdering her bastard-child: and of a man for another murder: together with a full relation of all other remarkable passages there, and the number how many are to die, with their several facts: how many burnt in the hand, and how many to be transported, and to be whipped. England and Wales. Assizes (Southwark)'. London, D.M., 1678, in Early English Books Online [database] (accessed 17 May 2023).

'The Proceedings of the Old Bailey, London's Central Criminal Court 1674–1913', [website]. https://www.oldbaileyonline.org.

'THE PROVINCES'. *Standard*, 21 May 1894, p. 3. link-gale-com.ezproxy.lib.bbk. ac.uk (accessed 3 Aug. 2023).

'THE RICHMOND MURDER'. *York Herald*, 2 Aug 1879, p. 3, British Library Newspapers, http://link-gale-com.ezproxy.lib.bbk.ac.uk.

'THE SUSPECTED WHOLESALE POISONING AT WEST AUCKLAND'. *York Herald*, 21 September 1872, p. 10, link-gale-com.ezproxy.lib.bbk.ac.uk (accessed 13 July 2023).

'THE TREHEI BE [ill] MURDER'. *Western Mail*, 22 May 1894, p. 6. https://go-gale-com.ezproxy.lib.bbk.ac.uk (accessed 8 July 2023).

'THE TREHERBERT TRAGEDY'. *Western Mail*, 24 May 1894, p. 7. link-gale-com.ezproxy.lib.bbk.ac.uk (accessed 3 August 2023).

'The Trial & Execution of Mrs Edney, At Ilchester, For the Wilful Murder of her Husband', [broadside]. Bristol, Bonner, 1836, British Library, 1880.c.20.(393.)

'The Trial of Margaret Tindal, alias Shuttleworth, for the murder of her husband, Henry Shuttleworth... on the 19th day of September, 1821'. Montrose, 1821, Internet Archive [database], https://archive.org (accessed 12 April 2023).

'The True narrative of the confession and execution of the prisoners at Kingstone-upon-Thames, on Wednesday the 16th of this instant March, 1681 viz. Margaret Osgood burnt for killing her husband, Mary Trot for several fellonies, William Abbot, Abel Hamersly, Thomas Savioury [brace] for robing on the high-way'. Edward Turner, William Wyer, John Brads.

'The true relation of the tryals at the sessions of oyer and terminer, held for the city of London, county of Middlesex, and goale delivery of Newgate; which began in the Old-Bailey the 17th of this instant January, and ended the 18th of the same. As particularly of Elizabeth Wigenton for whipping a girl to death at Ratcliffe. And John Peetly, for shooting a gentleman in Queen-street. Also the account of the proceedings with one John Bully a Popish priest. The number of the condemned, burnt in the hand, and to be whipped, with many other material tryals'. London, s.n., 1681, in Early English Books Online [online database]. (Accessed May 20, 2023).

'THE WEST AUCKLAND POISONING CASE'. *Morning Post*, 6 March 1873, p. 7. link-gale-com.ezproxy.lib.bbk.ac.uk (accessed 13 July 2023).

'The West Auckland Poisoning Case'. *Times*, 15 October 1872, p. 3, The Times Digital Archive, link-gale-com.ezproxy.lib.bbk.ac.uk (accessed 13 July 2023).

'The Whifflet Murder. Husband And Wife Formally Charged, Appearance At Local Courts'. *Coatbridge Leader*, 30 June 1923, https://www.britishnewspaperarchive.co.uk (accessed 21 July 2023).

'The Whipster of Woodstreet, or, A true account of the barbarous and horrid murther commited on the body of Mary Cox, late servant in Woodstreet, London'. London, W. Thackery, J. Millet and Alex Milbourn, 168 [broadside]. in Early English Books Online [online database]. (accessed 24 April 2023).

Travitsky, Betty S. '"A Pittilesse Mother?": Report of A Seventeenth-Century English Filicide.' *Mosaic: An Interdisciplinary Critical Journal*, vol. 27, no. 4, 1994, pp. 55–79.

'Trial of Mary Ann Burdock for the Wilful Murder of Mrs Clara Ann Smith, etc.'. Bristol, W.H. Somerton, 1835, British Library, 06496.a.5.(1.).

Turner, Wendy J. 'Mental Health and Homicide in Medieval English Trials.' *Open Library of Humanities*, vol. 4, no. 2, 2018, pp. 1–32.

van der Heijden, Manon. 'Future Research on Women and Crime.' *Crime History & Societies*, vol. 21, no. 2, 2017, pp. 123–133.

Walker, Garthine. *Crime, Gender and Social Order in Early Modern England*, Cambridge, Cambridge University Press, 2003.

Wallace, Leonard. *History of The Society of High Constables of Edinburgh. Edinburgh High Constables*, 2019, https://www.edinburghhighconstables.org.uk (accessed 31 July 2023).

'WARWICK ASSIZES'. *Glasgow Herald*, 1 May 1820, link.gale.com/ apps/doc/ BB3203426482/GDCS (accessed 2 July 2023).

Watson, Katherine D. 'Women, violent crime and criminal justice in Georgian Wales.' *Continuity and Change*, vol. 28, no. 2, 2013, pp. 245–272.

Welch, Heather L. *'Unnatural and Cruel Beasts in Women's Shapes': The Female Body in Early Modern England*. PhD diss., *Georgia State University*, 2020, https://scholarworks.gsu.edu (accessed 30 April 2023).

Westman, Barbara Hanawalt. 'The Peasant Family and Crime in Fourteenth-Century England.' *Journal of British Studies*, vol. 13, no. 2, 1974, pp. 1–18.

'Whifflet Murder Trial. Charge Against Man Withdrawn. Woman Condemned To Die. Foul Crime Capped By Plot To Hang Husband'. *Coatbridge Leader*, 22 September 1923, https://www.britishnewspaperarchive.co.uk (accessed 21 July 2023).

Williams, J. E. Hall, Read, J. C. 'The Homicide Act, 1957.' *The Modern Law Review*, vol. 20, no. 4, 1957, pp. 381–386.

Wingrave, John. *A Narrative of the many horrid cruelties inflicted by Elizabeth Brownrigg upon the body of Mary Clifford. Together with an account of the sufferings of Mary Mitchell and Mary Jones.* London, 1767, British Library, 613.f.23.(5.).

'Woman Hanged At Cardiff'. *The Weekly Mail*, 17 August 1907, p. 3. https://newspapers.library.wales (accessed 12 July 2023).

Wrightson, Keith. 'Infanticide In Earlier Seventeenth-Century England.' *Local Population Studies* vol. 15, 1975.

Zedner, Lucia. *Women, Crime, and Custody in Victorian England*. Oxford: Clarendon Press, 1991.

Zedner, Lucia. 'Women, Crime, and Penal Responses: A Historical Account.' *Crime and Justice* 14 (1991): 307–362.

Databases/Websites

National Library of Scotland
National Records of Scotland
National Archives
London Lives
Early English Books Online
National Library of Wales
British Library
Old Bailey
Oxford Dictionary of National Biography
Oxford English Dictionary
History.com
Essex Archives Online
History Hit
National Emergency Services Museum
Birkbeck, University of London Library
Oxford Referencing, Library Guides at Victoria University
British Newspaper Archive
History.com
Internet Archive
British History Online
GenGuide
US National Library of Medicine

INDEX